CLIVE BARKER

MANCHESTER
1824
Manchester University Press

Clive Barker

Dark imaginer

Edited by Sorcha Ní Fhlainn

Manchester University Press

Published by Manchester University Press
Altrincham Street, Manchester M1 7JA
www.manchesteruniversitypress.co.uk

British Library Cataloguing-in-Publication Data is available

ISBN 978 0 7190 9692 1 hardback
ISBN 978 1 5261 3569 8 paperback

First published by Manchester University Press in hardback 2017

This edition first published 2018

Contents

Figures

List of figures

Notes on contributors

Mark Richard Adams completed his doctorate entitled 'Unpacking the Industrial, Cultural and Historical Contexts of Doctor Who's Fan-Producers' at Brunel University. His research interests include fan cultures, television history, horror films, and queer theory. Recent publications include a chapter on masochism in *Screening Twilight: Critical Approaches to a Cinematic Phenomenon* (IB Tauris, 2014), and an examination of visual excess in the film *Valentine* for *Style and Form in the Hollywood Slasher Film* (Palgrave, 2015).

Xavier Aldana Reyes is Senior Lecturer in English Literature and Film at Manchester Metropolitan University and a founding member of the Manchester Centre for Gothic Studies. He is the author of various books, including *Spanish Gothic* (2017), *Horror: A Literary History* (editor, 2016), *Horror Film and Affect* (2016), *Digital Horror* (co-editor, 2015) and *Body Gothic* (2014). He is the editor of the Horror Studies book series run by the University of Wales Press.

Brigid Cherry is a researcher focusing on horror, cult media, and fan cultures. Her work on Clive Barker's film and fiction was completed during a Research Fellowship in Screen Media at St Mary's University, Twickenham, UK. She has previously written on the feminine aesthetic in *Hellraiser* and *Candyman*. She has also published work on research into *Doctor Who* fandom, Gothic television, Twilight and Supernatural fan fiction, and steampunk, and has written a book on fan handicrafting *Cult Media, Fandom and Textiles: Handicrafting as Fan Art* (Bloomsbury, 2017).

Kevin Corstorphine is Lecturer in English at the University of Hull, UK, where he teaches on American Literature and the Gothic. His research interests are in horror, the Gothic and fantasy fiction, with a focus on the representation of space and place. He has published on authors including Bram Stoker, Ambrose Bierce, H.P. Lovecraft, Robert Bloch, and Stephen King. He is currently working on haunted house stories and the intersections between fiction, 'real-life' narratives, and myth.

Daragh Downes is a Teaching Fellow in the School of English and in the Department of Germanic Studies at Trinity College Dublin. His chief research interests in English are Romanticism plus Charles Dickens and his milieu. He is co-editor (with Trish Ferguson) of *Victorian Fiction beyond the Canon* (Palgrave Macmillan, 2016).

Gareth James is an independent scholar researching industrial film and television history and marketing. He received his PhD from the University of Exeter for a thesis on the history of Home Box Office (HBO). He has also published on the branding strategies of BBC America, HBO and the Western, and American independent cinema. His other research interests include marketing theory and practice, the New Hollywood, and film and television exhibition.

Darryl Jones is Professor of English and Dean of the Faculty of Arts, Humanities, and Social Sciences at Trinity College Dublin, and a Fellow of the College. He is author/editor of 11 books, most recently an edition of Arthur Conan Doyle's *Gothic Tales* (Oxford University Press, 2016). He is currently working on H.G. Wells.

Sorcha Ní Fhlainn is Senior Lecturer in Film Studies and American Literature, and a founding member of the Manchester Centre for Gothic Studies at Manchester Metropolitan University. She is the author/editor of numerous publications, with a particular focus on vampires, the Gothic, Hollywood cinema, and popular culture, including *The Worlds of Back to the Future: Critical Essays on the Films* (McFarland, 2010) and *Our Monstrous (S)Kin: Blurring the Boundaries Between Monsters and Humanity* (The Inter-Disciplinary Press, 2010), and journal articles with *Adaptation* (Oxford University Press, 2015) and *Horror Studies* (Intellect, 2017). She is Reviews Editor for *Gothic Studies*, the journal of the International Gothic Association (Manchester University Press). Forthcoming publications include the monograph *Postmodern Vampires: Film, Fiction, and Popular Culture* (with Palgrave, 2018).

Harvey O'Brien teaches Film Studies at University College Dublin. He is the author of *Action Movies: The Cinema of Striking Back* (Columbia University Press, 2012), *The Real Ireland: The Evolution of Ireland in Documentary Film* (Manchester University Press, 2004), and co-editor of *Keeping it Real: Irish Film and Television* (Wallflower, 2004). He has contributed to journals including *Historical Journal of Film, Radio, and Television, Neo-Victorian Studies, Monsters and the Monstrous, Éire-Ireland,* and *Cineaste.* He is a member of the Board of Directors of the Irish Film Institute, former editor of the journal *Film and Film Culture,* and a former Associate Director of the Boston Irish Film Festival. He is a frequent media contributor and has writing and editorial credits on film and television work including *Seoda* (TG4) and *The Dying of the Light* (Flynn).

Bernard Perron is a Full Professor of Film and Game Studies at the University of Montreal. He has, among others, co-edited *The Routledge Companion to Video Games Studies* (Routledge, 2014) and *Z pour Zombies* (Les Presses de l'Université de Montréal, 2015). He has edited *Horror Video Games: Essays on the Fusion of Fear and Play* (McFarland, 2009) and also written *Silent Hill: The Terror Engine* (University of Michigan Press, 2012). His research and writing concentrate on video games and the horror genre.

Tony M. Vinci is Assistant Professor of English at Ohio University-Chillicothe, where he teaches Literature, Humanities, and Creative Writing. He is co-editor of *Culture, Identities, and Technology in the Star Wars Films* (McFarland, 2007) and has published articles in *The Journal of Popular Culture, Science Fiction Film and Television, The Faulkner Journal, The Journal of the Midwest Modern Language Association*, and numerous collections of literary scholarship and cultural criticism. His research interests include twentieth-century American literature and culture, ethics, trauma studies, critical animality studies, post-humanism, and speculative fiction and film.

Edward Timothy Wallington has a Master of Arts Degree in English from Florida International University, a second Master of Arts Degree in Linguistics for English Language Teaching from Lancaster University, a Diploma in Teaching English Overseas (ESOL) from Manchester University, and a Bachelor of Arts Degree in English from Leeds University. His research focuses on gothic literature and film.

Acknowledgements

This book, inspired by copious late nights enthralled by Clive Barker's numerous books, has been many years in the making, and made possible only with the generous support of many kind people. I would like to thank colleagues at Manchester University Press, who have been supportive throughout the book's Barkerian gestation, and to Matthew Frost, for his wit and wisdom when it was needed most.

This collection (and the conference at Trinity College Dublin in July 2011, which informed its inception) grew out of a desire to see new material on Barker beyond his early and seminal publications. Thank you, in particular, to Professor Darryl Jones, who supported me throughout the development and realisation of my Barker projects, and to the School of English at Trinity College, Dublin, for nurturing my dark dreams and scholarly life. Special thanks to Deborah Christie, Alwyn Lyes, Harvey O'Brien, Hannah Priest, Sarah Cleary, Maria Parsons, Dara Downey, Bernice M. Murphy, Elizabeth McCarthy, Diane Sadler, Ed King, Russell Cherrington, Sam Henderson, Phil and Sarah Stokes, William Hughes, Richard Caputo, Michael O'Rourke, and Jacob Huntley, all of whom helped and contributed their own special talents along the way.

Thank you to my supportive colleagues and friends at the Department of English at Manchester Metropolitan University, including Berthold Schoene, Jess Edwards, Sonja Lawrenson, and my fellow goths, Linnie Blake, Dale Townshend, and Xavier Aldana Reyes at the Manchester Centre for Gothic Studies. Together, we weave dark wonders!

I am indebted to the contributors of this book – Mark Adams, Xavier Aldana Reyes, Brigid Cherry, Kevin Corstorphine, Daragh Downes, Gareth James, Darryl Jones, Harvey O'Brien, Bernard Perron, Tony Vinci and Edward Timothy Wallington – for their inspiring chapters which, both individually and collectively, enrich Barker studies.

For all of their kindness and generosity (including the image reproductions in this book and the suitably demonic cover), thank you to Mark Miller and the whole team at Seraphim Inc., whose support and help has been invaluable; heartfelt thanks to the wonderful Johnny Raymond, and to the maestro, Clive Barker. I am deeply grateful for all of your support to realise this book, and for your continued generosity.

Finally, to my ever-patient and wonderful family – my mother Léin and late dad Micheál, my brother Eoghan and his lovely partner Dimitra, and to my husband and soul mate John Gilleese (and our cat, Mao) – I dedicate this book to all of you. May you all find your own special Barkerian doorway.

Introduction

1   Clive Barker, 'Cenobite', 1986.

'To darken the day and brighten the night': Clive Barker, dark imaginer

Sorcha Ní Fhlainn

In one of his more in-depth television interviews, while promoting his newly published novel *Weaveworld* in 1987, Clive Barker was introduced by host John Nicolson as having such a remarkable impact on the horror genre that, some believed, 'it could only be the product of a diseased mind'.[1] Rather than directly insult Barker on television, the description actually amused the author, a gleeful grin spreading across his youthful, handsome face. The television show, BBC's *Open to Question*, was far removed from the more typical book promotion television shows or talk show slots during which hosts gently prod and chat with the author to showcase their new novel. The thirty-minute interview quickly proceeded to take the form of a confrontational interrogation, with Barker positioned to offer a defence for the 'indefensible' horror genre. Topics were dominated by audience-led comments and queries which evidenced the cultural residue of moral panic, following on from the video nasty crisis that had gripped the UK in the early 1980s. There was a particular emphasis on the potential for copycat killings inspired by his work, or the potential viral spread of violence which, at any moment, threatened to burst forth from the screen simply because of Barker's appearance on the show. What was visible to the viewer was the fear Barker's work was capable of conjuring. His visions and creations were perceived as dangerous, subversive and, if left unchecked by moral codes and censorship, verged upon the obscene. One audience member aligned his material with the Moors murderers Myra Hindley and Ian Brady, while another, misunderstanding a joke, accused Barker of attending autopsies for perverse fun (rather than for research as Barker stated). Further queries included a genuine questioning of whether Barker possessed a 'warped' mind, followed by accusations that he was merely out for cheap thrills, and that he and his fellow filmmakers (including David Cronenberg and Wes Craven) were responsible for the desensitisation of viewers (a thinly veiled code for moral corruption) as a result of their sick and twisted creations in print or laid bare on screen. It was a hysterical response by many in the studio audience who had simply not read his books or watched his films (arguably, they may have been primed to ask such loaded questions) but it made for good television. Despite these concerns about the limits of violence on screen and its potential to infect and destroy the minds of innocent viewers – descriptions that echoed hysterical reactionary headlines from tabloid newspapers in the early 1980s, or Frederic Wertham's warning of the corruptive power of comic books in his 1954 book *Seduction of the Innocent* – Barker's articulate responses to these concerns were disarmingly charming, intellectual, and thoughtful. Rather than simply dismiss these concerns as nonsense, which one might expect, Barker did outline and expand upon his own drive to write metaphors for the human experience, and his exploration of it through fantasy. This line of questioning led to a more important and interesting revelation: what truly interests Barker is not simply the blood and guts of literature and cinema but rather the rearrangement and transformation of the human body, leading to a transcendence of the human condition. Clive Barker is all about the liberating possibilities of transfiguration.

This book is a necessary scholarly intervention. Since the late 1990s, with rare exception, critics and scholars have neglected Barker's works. This may seem strange to contemplate at first, as Barker has been an influential and bankable author since the mid-1980s; thirty years later his novels still debut on the *New York Times* best-seller lists, and his cultural influence and impact in the genre are widely regarded in the horror community; fans, scholars, and artists in the field continually point to Barker's career as a polymath as being far-reaching and significant. Despite these accolades, scholarly engagement with his work beyond the hugely successful *Books of Blood* and the *Hellraiser* series has been strangely stagnant. His numerous works in fiction, film, and art have come to occupy a unique identifier of his particular artistic vision; his diverse talents mark him among an enviable cohort of highly influential authors and filmmakers. Yet, the very nature of Barker's visions of horror, his ability to transcend genres (from horror to dark fantasy, from children's literature to poetry) and artistic forms (filmmaking, plays, sketches and painting, sculpture, photography) has, contradictorily, actually contributed to this strange scholarly omission. While fiction has remained Barker's primary creative outlet, he refuses to restrict himself to any one form for long without experimenting with another. The *Books of Abarat* series (2002–), for example, is published with glossy prints of paintings by Barker, which detail the fantastical world and its creatures, taking years to produce; all of these paintings are created to accompany an ongoing imaginative saga of a young girl's quest in a mythical realm where time is spread across a phantasmagorical archipelago. This makes Barker a rare trans-disciplinary figure for scholarly inquiry – a polymath in a continuous state of creating and imagining new worlds, creatures, and stories, and finding new ways to tell them. This book is, then, an invitation, to re-evaluate Barker's works by exceptional scholars who dare to peer beneath the fold of his challenging, exhilarating, and confrontational creations.

Clive Barker is a self-described imaginer. Born in Liverpool in 1952, he grew up feeding his imagination through sketching and creating monsters. Flashes of his childhood are revealed in his fiction filtered through descriptive memories of his boyhood in Liverpool, traced in the opening chapters of his novel *Weaveworld* (1987), in which his protagonist Cal Mooney discovers a magical carpet which conceals a doorway to another world. Barker, in an interview with his biographer Douglas Winter, revealed that he gained a reputation for being a dreamer at a young age: 'I was always an imaginative child, and my imagination had considerable range – from the very fanciful, light material to rather darker stuff … I had imaginary friends, and I liked monsters and drew monsters'.[2] His parents indulged his desires to create shows and theatrical performances too: his father Len Barker, a talented carpenter, built him a stage for puppet shows and helped young Clive paint backdrops to stage his backyard productions for the neighbourhood kids (with multiple shows each day). Barker never lost his taste for the monsters; they would later birth a significant career beginning in 1980s London, before migrating to the dream palace of Hollywood. Initially a student of Philosophy, Barker switched to a degree in English literature, graduating with honours from the University of Liverpool in 1974; he found academic study rather tedious, and, upon completion, quickly moved on to more personally fulfilling artistic pursuits and work in the theatre, which eventually led him to London. There, alongside many talented and creative friends, including Doug Bradley (who would become renowned as the Cenobite 'Pinhead' from *Hellraiser*) and Peter Atkins (novelist and screenwriter – *Wishmaster* franchise, *Hellbound: Hellraiser II*), this artistic motley crew of actors and writers collectively created The Dog Company, a fringe acting troupe wholly dedicated to producing avant-garde theatre and new forms of serious stage artistry. Their achievements included critical praise at the 1981 Edinburgh Fringe Festival for the 1980 Barker play *The History of the Devil*, with Doug Bradley cast as his infernal majesty.

Thoroughly dedicated to writing and directing increasingly demanding and ambitious plays for The Dog Company, Barker began to write short stories by night – at first, this was for interest and to amuse friends. In the process of these writing sessions, Barker soon found himself creatively unbound (by censorship and by scope) and entertained the possibility of potentially publishing some of these stories; within a few years, these night-time tales would become the six-volume *Books of Blood* which launched his career as a serious author of horror fiction. The success generated by the incredible word of mouth about the collection, each volume ripe with increasing visceral promise, was beyond Barker's expectations. The *Books of Blood* would prove to have considerable critical weight too, garnering traction both in the UK and the United States. Barker's star was on the ascent, complete with the now infamous endorsement by Stephen King as 'the future of horror' which would adorn Barker's publicity material and novels for decades to come.[3] Sphere published the six volumes of

Books of Blood, during which time they began carefully crafting Barker's next project, his debut novel, *The Damnation Game* (1985). The novel was not an immediate hit but soon it would prove to critics and fans alike that Barker was no one-hit wonder. *The Damnation Game* remains a firm favourite with many Barker readers because of its taut prose, bleak nihilism, and invigorating exploration of a modern Faustian bargain. The novel, for all of its horrific violence and gore, is a melancholy nightmare of emptiness in 1980s London, and garnered a nomination for the World Fantasy Award for Best Novel in 1986.

His creative reputation in horror circles quickly bled across into filmmaking; remarkably, within three years of his first successful publication, he was directing his first feature film and creating a nightmarish vision that would achieve cult acclaim and leave a bloody imprint in 1980s British cinema. Barker vehemently disliked the screen adaptations *Underworld* (1985) and *Rawhead Rex* (1986), finding his stories completely compromised by the filmmaking process. In order to bring his own unfiltered, extreme ideas successfully to the screen, Barker would have to be intimately involved with the process himself, and, thanks to the success of *Books of Blood* and *The Damnation Game*, his growing reputation bestowed a modest but intriguing bankability for New World Pictures. Based on his 1986 novella *The Hellbound Heart* – first published as part of Dark Harvest's third *Night Visions* anthology and edited by George R.R. Martin, and later published by HarperCollins as a stand-alone novella in the wake of its successful film adaptation – *Hellraiser* would prove to be the definitive reference point which would crystalise Barker in popular culture. Doug Bradley's 'Pinhead' became an iconic horror figure in late 1980s horror cinema, particularly due to the film's successful afterlife in the video rental market and its striking video-box cover of Pinhead holding the Lament Configuration.[4] A sequel was quickly planned (released within fifteen months) and scripted by Barker's long-time friend and fellow Dog Company member Peter Atkins, with Barker remaining on as executive producer, passing the directorial mantle to newcomer Tony Randel. *Hellbound: Hellraiser II* (1988) suffered from an enormous and unforeseen budget cut due to the financial shock of Black Monday in October 1987, when stock markets and currencies plummeted. A whole sequence exploring the inner world of Hell had to be abandoned as a result. This unforeseen budget issue certainly compromised some of the more ambitious elements of the film, but despite these difficulties, *Hellbound: Hellraiser II* is, on the whole, still considered the best of the *Hellraiser* sequels in the fan community. Some film critics were less generous in their appraisal – Roger Ebert of the *Chicago Sun-Times* famously loathed the films, describing *Hellbound: Hellraiser II* as 'simply a series of ugly and bloody episodes strung together one after another like a demo tape by a perverted special-effects man',[5] while his review of Barker's generally more critically favoured *Hellraiser* concludes on a particularly invidious note: 'Maybe Stephen King was thinking of a different Clive Barker.'[6] For critics like Ebert, Barker's visions of sticky fleshy nightmares firmly supported the notion that he possessed a depraved vision, and that his films were simply the product of a particular schlocky gore aesthetic with little critical value, in an era known for the horror genre's commercial saturation. BBC's resident film critic Barry Norman equally disliked *Hellraiser* but, when directly questioned by Barker about his unfavourable review while shooting BBC's *Film 1988* on the set of *Hellbound: Hellraiser II*, he quietly admitted he really did not like the horror genre. Doug Bradley fondly recalls Norman appearing evidently uneasy when he encountered Bradley in full Pinhead make-up and costume in the back corridors at Pinewood studios in early 1988; Norman's genuine distaste for the aesthetics of 1980s horror and gore was quite palpable to the actor.[7] Despite the scathing critical derision of these divisive films – according to Hollywood trade paper *Variety*, *Hellbound* is 'a maggotty carnival of mayhem, mutation and dismemberment, awash in blood and recommended only for those who thrive on such junk',[8] – the first two instalments of the *Hellraiser* franchise remain firm fan favourites, particularly *because* of their distinctly bleak and abject imagery.

The *Hellraiser* sequels have been a mixed blessing for Barker; they not only launched his film career but also extended Barker's audience beyond his core readership. *Hellraiser III: Hell on Earth* (1992) relocates Pinhead to 1990s New York City, moving the material further away from its distinctly British setting and cast of character actors. The script and marketing strategy of *Hellraiser III* clearly attempted to align Pinhead alongside then lucrative American slasher villains such as Freddy Kruger, abandoning Barker's narrative rules and instead favouring Pinhead as nothing more than another unbound serial killer. This modification, coupled with the insertion of occasional wise-cracks, signals the tonal shift the later instalments of the franchise would take, altogether expending the dark vision of *Hellraiser* and *Hellbound* for dispensable one-liners. *Hellraiser: Bloodline* marks the end of Barker's direct involvement with the series and clearly demarcates the franchise's descent towards its current repository in direct-to-DVD sequel hell; its director, Kevin Yagher, an established special effects make-up artist known for his Freddy Krueger's make-up, insisted on an Alan Smithee credit,[9] and it was also the last of the films to be given a theatrical release. When one takes stock of the later films in the franchise, it gives the distinct impression that they are all at the expense of Barker's original tale, rather than furthering it. The franchise still has a cult following in horror circles today but it never regained the power of its exciting debut. The first three *Hellraiser* films were highly ambitious considering their frugal production budgets, and succeeded to dazzle with powerful use of make-up, bizarre yet beautiful creatures, and gothic storylines, remaining influential today for their mood and S&M-inspired design. As noted by *Hellraiser* expert Paul Kane, 'it is the look of [the Cenobites] that captivates. At the time, audiences had never seen characters like these.'[10] The problem, then, with the *Hellraiser* series has largely been one of public perception; its visuals were tantalising for some and too extreme and disgusting for others. It is one of the more graphic and surreal horror films of the late 1980s, a Grand Guignol spectacle without the mordant wise-cracks of its contemporary slasher counterparts. It wasn't funny, it wasn't ironic, and it took itself very seriously. To those unfamiliar with Barker, the film's poster and video-box cover were striking, but may have severely stifled people's perception of him and his work. For many who found Barker through *Hellraiser*'s success (particularly on the VHS rental market – after all, Pinhead is one of the most recognisable horror icons in film), he would never really develop beyond this role as a gore maven, and was, like Wes Craven, distrusted when he tried.[11] Barker had personally moved on from the *Hellraiser* film franchise to focus on other creations that challenged his growth as a writer and artist. What he did next confounded all expectations.

The all-consuming roles of the writer/director on *Hellraiser* did little to slow Barker's remarkable publishing pace: in 1988 Barker published the novella *Cabal* (which was quickly adapted to the screen and was the second film to be directed by Barker, re-titled as *Nightbreed* (1990)), and made a significant departure from the horror genre with the publication of two of his ambitious dark fantasy novels, *Weaveworld* (1987) and *The Great and Secret Show* (1989). This sharp transition from splatterpunk horror to dark fantasy affirmed Barker's desire to cast off his generic 'shackles', and emboldened him to embrace the transformative powers of dark fantasy, rather than merely attempt to replicate his earlier horror material. Barker's biographer Douglas E. Winter deems this generic hybridisation to be the genesis of Barker's route into 'anti-horror', which he claims is not to horrify readers but to invite them to imagine worlds beyond Manichean absolutes associated with horror fiction. Anti-horror is defined by Winter as 'pushing the reader into a realm of ambiguity, forcing us to confront the real world, outside and within – a place of possibilities, some dark and dangerous, others bright and beautiful, and all of them liberating.'[12] Barker's works do straddle this territory which questions rather than reinstates societal values and norms, but his works are certainly invested in the tactics of horror and gothic fiction; the horrific and the fantastical merge in his writing in order to offer unease, occasional disgust, and the necessary disruption of the status quo. In *Weaveworld*, Barker permits a glimpse of a fantastical hidden world secreted within the fabric of a forgotten carpet, its filigree detailing a realm populated with powerful races and hidden magical arts. This novel marks the successful transition into what would later become a signature strand in Barker's work – an artist's call for the human need for fantasy. In the contemporary moment of the 1980s, with its prevailing materialism and empty acquisitiveness, *Weaveworld* stands apart as a defence for the need to nurture one's own creative inner-world – to see the magical that is hidden in the everyday experience – and to reject the nihilism that attempts to extinguish its spark. His novella, *Cabal*, continues this thematic enchantment with the fantastic as it disrupts the everyday world in its celebration of the creatures of Midian. In its refreshing vision of diverse gothic pluralism, it is the tyranny of the normal that ultimately destroys the shadow city of monsters. The monsters of Midian are driven underground by those who police the boundaries of society – psychiatrists, the police force, all of them instigators of societal rules and regulations – causing the Night Breed (the occupants of Midian) to rise up in this defiant celebration of queer difference. Barker is, and remains, firmly on the side of the expelled monsters.

For the next five years, Barker's fiction grew with an increased emphasis on the *dark fantastique* (as he terms it), creating and blurring multiple worlds of vast complexity. *The Great and Secret Show* (1989) and *Everville* (1994), the first two books of the Art (it has been projected as a trilogy awaiting conclusion), hinge upon existentialism and transcendance, debating rationality and evil in the pursuit of power, enabling fantastical leaps into imagined spaces and dreamy rivers of memories and magic, and culminating in an epic battle to ascend to a higher plane of power and philosophical enlightenment. Themes of reconcili-ation between fantastical dominions continued with Barker's self-proclaimed favourite novel, *Imajica* – a novel that divides his readership in its intense and densely layered universe and opaque narrative. Barker likes to reconfigure realities and completely immerse himself in a world of fantastic fiction, which some reviewers found difficult to bear, especially when many readers expected similar materials from a branded horror writer. During this exploration of dark fantasy material, Barker had numerous appearances on talk shows in early 1990 to promote *The Great and Secret Show*. These appearances include *People are Talking*, *Good Morning America*, and *What's Up, Dr. Ruth* (with special guest director, Wes Craven), during which, while trying to underscore his move away from his earlier works such as *Hellraiser* or *Books of Blood*, the discussion still largely emphasised his relationship with and ongoing contribu-tions to the horror genre. For the uninitiated, it may have seemed confusing or even contradictory for an author to oscillate between two genres so readily. Barker may have begun the necessary work to erase such rigid generic boundaries in his fiction, but it did come at a critical price. Respected by both friends and critics for his commitment to his authorial vision over rigid publishing catego-risation, he defended his generic fluidity when probed on the issue: 'my mind is not divided like a bookshop… What does the terminology matter? The urgency of the story is what drove me to write these passages in the first place. The rest is just packaging.'[13] Nevertheless, this new terrain led to mixed reviews and concerns about Barker's blurring of styles. In some reviews, critics espoused near-exhaustion in reading his complex vision of multiple layers of reality, enriched with riddles, contradictions, or philosophical quiddities. Ken Tucker, in his review of *The Great and Secret Show* for *The New York Times Book Review* praises elements of the novel for its breadth and 'its vast, loopy sprawl … it is nothing so much as a cross between "Gravity's Rainbow" and J.R.R. Tolkien's

"Lord of the Rings," allusive and mythic, complex and entertaining', [sic] but also calls for some restraint in his title, 'One Universe at a Time Please'.[14] For those who yearned for Barker the horror prodigy, Tucker succinctly articulated an evident and growing frustration.

By late 1989, Barker had his own frustrations too. His new film *Nightbreed* (1990) was eviscerated in the editing suite by 20th Century Fox, who demanded Barker's original cut be shorn from a lengthy 150-minute running time down to an overly lean (and narratively confusing) 90-minute film. This prompted the film's editor Richard Marden to leave the project in protest. While contending with studio demands and losing support to complete his film, and having run considerably over-budget, Barker became increasingly frustrated with the process of filmmaking on the whole. At each turn, *Nightbreed* was failing to materialise as desired, and suffered in part because Fox studios resolutely objected to Barker's central premise that the monsters were the heroes of the film. This friction between author/director and studios Morgan Creek and Fox caused needless narrative confusion in the theatrical cut of the film, and ultimately damaged their film product. The film also received a list of cuts from the MPAA (Motion Picture Association of America), which necessitated further trimming to achieve a contractually obligated R-rating. To add insult to injury, upon release in February 1990, Fox studios erroneously branded *Nightbreed* as a slasher film rather than a dark fantasy film in its promotional material. The film, caught up in a series of bitter arguments between director and studio executives, in the end also failed to find its intended audience at the box office. It was a war between corporate branding and an idealistic filmmaker, provoking the fair question if the studios had actually understood the script at all beyond the author's brand name. This was a particularly difficult period for Barker as he discovered the limitations and committee demands of making a film under the control of a major Hollywood studio. The film, in Barker's view, had been compromised from all sides, leaving him with a sour aftertaste about the industry. Barker's film would later be resurrected and re-edited to include a rough-cut restoration of lost footage and key scenes, which screened at numerous film festivals in 2012, and was retitled as *Nightbreed: The Cabal Cut*. In 2014, following international interest in *The Cabal Cut*, Barker supervised the release of his definitive version under the title *Nightbreed: The Director's Cut*.[15]

Following his grievances with the original production and release of *Nightbreed* (which Barker believed was amplified by his distance from the machinations of Hollywood as a then London resident), he decided to commit fully to his film career by permanently relocating to Los Angeles. Consequently, to increase his stake in future film projects and to have a controlling and influential voice, Barker also began his own production company, Seraphim Inc. Opting to produce rather than direct his next film project, an adaptation of 'The Forbidden' from *Books of Blood*, Volume 5, retitled as *Candyman* (1992), the film also relocated the urban legend tale from a dilapidated council estate in Liverpool to the infamous Cabrini-Green housing project in Chicago, injecting Barker's English version of the tale with a distinctly American flavour. Directed by Bernard Rose, *Candyman* achieved generally favourable critical reviews and strong commercial success, with Barker's name boldly brandished on the marketing material. *Candyman*, as with *Hellraiser*, would also go on to suffer inferior sequels led by marketing demands, again without input from its author.

Barker also opened up his work to a younger audience in the 1990s. This foray into young adult literature with the publication of *The Thief of Always* (1992), a highly imaginative fable that shimmers with Barker's signature dark creations, was certainly a diverse passage for the established horror/dark fantasy author; more importantly, this opportunity fulfilled a long-held personal desire. Barker had previously attempted to write a young adult fantasy novel, *The Candle in the Cloud*, before embarking upon his studies at the University of Liverpool in the early 1970s, and wrote another young adult novel *The Adventures of Mr. Maximillian Bacchus and His Travelling Circus* later in the decade but to no immediate avail (it was eventually published in 2009). Despite his experiments to break free from his status as a caged horror writer since the late 1980s, held in a strange stasis by the expectations of fans and readers desperate for him to return to the violent creations of splatterpunk, Barker nurtured the creative opportunity to finally publish a young adult novel. A highly unusual move at the time, HarperCollins was also hesitant of this venture, and, predicting massive losses on the project, bought the licensing for $1.[16] Published with Barker's own ink-on-paper illustrations, demonstrating his enviable ability to convey a dreamscape and touching tale through two distinct art forms on the same page, *The Thief of Always* pared back his more ambitious visions of other worlds and philosophical transcendence in favour of a simple but haunting fable. The novella would prove to be one of his finest tales. This softening of Barker's horrors neither dampened his vision nor compromised his material; if anything, the young adult fiction spark that began with the success of *The Thief of Always* would inform the next fifteen years of his work in writing and painting for his ambitious *Abarat* series (2002; 2004; 2011–).

Following the commercial success of Bernard Rose's film *Candyman* (on which Barker served as executive producer), Barker was prompted to direct what would become his final feature film. *Lord of Illusions*, based on his short story 'The Last Illusion' from *Books of Blood*, Volume 6, achieved moderate critical and commercial success with his film noir gothic tale of a magician and a cult leader whose shared Faustian pact entwines their fate in a nihilistic dance of magic and immortality. Featuring a strong cast including Scott Bakula, Famke Janssen and Kevin J. O'Connor, the film was nevertheless compromised by the studio (MGM/United Artists), though not to the same wounding extent as the scarring tussle over *Nightbreed*. The studio feared the film was too marginal, too generically hybrid as a film noir horror, and therefore lacking the desired 'Barker' commercial horror angle upon which they sought to profit. The resulting requested cuts (carried out by Barker) were less jarring to the tone of the film, but nonetheless recall the compromising conditions which seemed to dominate his involvement with film studios. It was another clash between artistic vision and economic projections, which Barker knew he couldn't win if he wanted to secure a theatrical release. It was agreed that they would release an unexpurgated director's cut of the film for the Laser Disc/DVD (and eventually Blu-Ray) markets. Pressed for more of the same *Hellraiser*-style gore, his film adaptations as a director all intended to serve horror fans. The problem clearly lay in his bifurcated public roles as a moderately successful horror director, and as an author and artist whose generic shift beyond the shackles of horror fiction had left him somewhat adrift. In sum, casual horror audiences struggled with Barker the novelist who occasionally worked within the genre, but was not willing to simply repeat similar material. Deciding to remain within the creative field of filmmaking largely as a producer, Barker continues to be an active collaborator, working on diverse films – including Bill Condon's Oscar winning *Gods and Monsters* (1998),[17] a drama based on *Frankenstein* (1931) director James Whale – within and beyond the field of horror cinema.

Barker spent the remainder of the 1990s writing three very different and timely novels, with an evident biographical influence. In the personal and moving *Sacrament* (1996), he withdraws from the more mythological elements of earlier works to emphasise the complexities and the importance of our place in the world at the precipice of ecological crises and human pandemics. It is also considered to be Barker's first openly gay novel, though this came as little surprise to those familiar with his works, and it was not a facet of his personal life that was hidden or suppressed. Barker explores themes of extinction and ecology, celebrations of individuality and the complexity of family life, the pain of loss, and the AIDS crisis. Though *Sacrament* is not considered one of his most lucrative titles, it is often regarded as one of his most emotive and personal. This was quickly followed by *Galilee* (1998), a sprawling saga concerning two warring families, the Gearys and the Barbarossas, charting their stormy, jealous, and fantastically entwined fate. The novel's quixotic mixture of phantasmagoria, prophecy, sexual trysts, and supernatural romance, enveloped in a strange family narrative recalls the Mayfair Witches trilogy by Anne Rice; their similarities lie in the gothic roots of family sagas imbued with secrets, birth rights, sacred knowledge, and the erotic magnetism of their central mysterious male characters – Rice's spectral and mysterious Lasher, and the titular black Adonis Galilee (inspired by Barker's then spouse, the photographer David Armstrong).

By the late 1990s, with so many published books, films, and tie-in products which carried his unique brand name (like Stephen King, Barker became an established brand in his own right through his market visibility), the BBC commissioned *Clive Barker's A-Z of Horror*, a six-part television series broadcast in late 1997/early 1998 which focused on the history and themes of the genre.

The series was hosted by Barker and was visually strong in scope and content, giving rise to a comprehensive tie-in book (featuring Barker's art) compiled by Stephen Jones. It remains a cultish series for Barker fans as it has never been made available on DVD. Soon after this, HarperCollins published an anthology of Barker's material, collecting both well-known and unknown passages and musings by the author. Part homage and part celebration of his literary diversity, the narrative compendium, *The Essential Clive Barker* (1999), is thematically arranged to unveil his broad appeal across his extensive body of work. The move was ultimately a clever marketing decision; in its unification of thematic touchstones throughout Barker's fiction, the book evidenced Barker's maturation in a fluid and broad manner, eliding his firm roots in horror fiction to the more liminal material of the *dark fantastique*. For both publishing and promotional purposes, this mosaic of extracts from novels, short stories, and plays sought to successfully overcome Barker's multiplicity by marrying his authorial imprint with universal thematic concepts, complete with each segment introduced by Barker. Though it is a collection almost entirely comprised of previously published material, it is best understood when considered as a Barker primer, providing a veritable map to navigate his terrain.

Contrary to many prolific authors in the digital age, Barker writes all of his novels by hand, believing that each word must earn its place on the page. It is staggering to believe that, as the author of numerous lengthy novels, he would continue this practice throughout his career. Alongside these voluminous handwritten manuscripts, he has become increasingly devoted to crafting accompanying paintings and sketches for his works; he was always been a talented and privately compulsive artist but in the terrain of young adult fiction, this skill is explicitly showcased and celebrated. The bold and colourful paintings which would chart the world of the Abarat, a magical archipelago filled with wondrous creatures, revealed the enormous undertaking each book demanded of Barker as both an artist and author. The *Abarat* series eschews some of his earlier darkness in favour of hope and discovery, as heroine Candy Quackenbush ventures into this mysterious land to trace her mystical origins and to vanquish the forces of evil that threaten this hidden kingdom. At present, the three books of the series, *Abarat*; *Abarat: Days of Magic, Nights of War*; and *Abarat: Absolute Midnight*, in turn explore the richness of this fantastical and dense terrain – in every corner or crevice of the island world, there are strange new sights or creatures at which to marvel. Currently awaiting completion with two more instalments in the series (recently expanded from a quartet to a quintet), *Abarat* was critically praised upon publication in 2002 and the rights were promptly purchased by Disney for a film franchise. The film project at present appears to be all but abandoned, and, in hindsight it may have proven to be simply too strange and demanding a vision for Disney studios. The other issue could be Barker's own pace in producing the books, which was too slow for a film franchise investment. For the young readers enthralled by the *Harry*

Potter saga during the same period, Rowling's ability to publish her series at a staggering rate proved that children would foster a deep love for the novels, growing up reading all of her beloved books in quick succession throughout their adolescence. Barker's pace, in contrast, bred impatience in some corners of his fandom. Reviewing the first book for the *Guardian* in 2002, China Miéville warmly notes its curious beauty as a novel, and as a piece of Barkerian art: 'Above all, [*Abarat*] is a deeply lovely catalogue of the strange. Islands carved into colossal heads, giant moths made of coloured ether, words that turn into aeroplanes, tentacled maggot-monsters: they dance past like a carnival, a true surrender to the weird, vastly more inventive than the tired figures that visit some bespectacled boy-wizards.'[18] *Abarat* could never contend with J.K. Rowling's boy wizard Harry Potter, precisely because it is too sublime and odd when compared to the boarding school adventures of a young boy wizard. Rowling's series had a distinctive hook, a source of narrative pattern recognition underpinned by a Manichean prophecy and English school-days nostalgia, and was humorously set in parallel with reality; Barker delights in abandoning reality from the outset in his series.

Alongside the intense creative period dedicated to crafting the *Abarat* series, Barker also authored a gothic *roman-à-clef* ghost story and scathing critique of Hollywood. *Coldheart Canyon* would ultimately prove to be a literary catharsis, a Boschian nightmare of sex and illusion, a sub-textual articulation of Barker's frustration with and deep love for the film industry and its complex, and often distasteful, history. Its cast features incorrigible players in any salient Hollywood nightmare: immoral publicists and heads of studios; drug-addicted actors; ruthless agents; entitled prima-donnas; complete with a taste for sexual sadism and depravity, horrific plastic surgery, and vying for the limelight by any means necessary. The novel is a rare creation in Barker's fiction; it is a hybrid fever-dream, rooted in gothic excess, erotic hallucination, and celebrity satire.

Above all, the act of writing is, for Barker, both compulsion and catharsis – he *needs* to write. Following *Coldheart Canyon*, which did not gain the expected critical traction it deserved, Barker returned to creating the flourishing world of the *Abarat* books and paintings, while editing an enormous 4,000 page handwritten manuscript for *The Scarlet Gospels* (2015).[19] With so many projects now demanding his attention, Barker suspended the process of completing the (then) final edit of *The Scarlet Gospels* to finish the short novel *Mister B. Gone* in time for a Halloween release in 2007. It is evident from the novel's epigraph that Barker is mired in a cycle of creation and destruction – 'Burn this book', its opening pages instructs the reader. It is reasonable to imagine that the act of continually rewriting and editing *The Scarlet Gospels* inspired the 'demon-in-the-book' narrative, complete with its destructive opening instruction and the power of the printing press, all of which feed into the tale of Jakabok Botch, the first-person demon narrator of a forbidden and dangerous tale. Trapped within the pages of the novel itself, Jakabok demands that the book be destroyed, lest its words utterly corrupt the reader. The power of writing is central to this novel; the underestimated lasting influence and magical qualities of the printed word captured via Gutenberg's printing press provide a means of immortality. The forbidden gothic book becomes a metafictional form of amusement and contamination in *Mister B. Gone*; addressing the reader directly, we hold the forbidden object in our hands, through which Barker's storyteller directly calls out to us to insist upon his destruction. The idea speaks to the frustrations and rewards found in the act of creation – an author can live eternally through the text, and be damned by it. With the business of Hell requiring completion, Barker finally returned to the book that had been troubling him since the late 1990s – the evolution of his tale of Hell itself, *The Scarlet Gospels*.

When Barker was designing and pitching his *Books of Abarat* series to Harper Collins in the late 1990s, he simultaneously began planning and pitching a short story collection of violent, pseudo-pornographic tales entitled *The Scarlet Gospels*. His long-time publishers, HarperCollins, were enthralled by the pitched *Abarat* series, but feared that the extremely strong and graphic content in his outline for *The Scarlet Gospels* would backfire, and subsequently declined to publish the proposed collection. This version of the book was to be extremely erotically charged in both content and artwork, arranged around Biblical themes and illustrated by Barker, but was put on indefinite hold. Determined to return to write the tale of Pinhead's demise, albeit with a manuscript that shifted significantly in scope and word count over the following decade, Barker relent-lessly pressed on: the title tale morphed from a short story within a collection of tales, only to be later revised as a mammoth manuscript focusing on this one story, which was eventually edited down into a fully realised novel. In all, it took close to fifteen years, numerous rewrites and exhaustive drafts before *The Scarlet Gospels* was eventually published with St. Martin's Press in 2015. *The Scarlet Gospels*, in its final published form, does read as a truncated novel stemming from a much grander vision, but its publication was nevertheless largely welcomed by critics who hailed the return of their prodigal son back into the fold of horror fiction.[20] In late 2015, reassuring his fans that he still has much to say about horror in the contemporary world, Barker informed fans via his social media outlets that he intends to work on web-based horror site material inspired by Creepy Pasta and its viral urban legends, including Slenderman, for a series of short films. Once again, Barker adapts with new technology and media to interrogate contemporary dark fantasies.

Barker's contribution to fiction, film, and the arts has produced a rich tapestry, ripe for scholarly analysis. In comparison with other authors, such as Stephen King, it is odd to note that Barker has been strangely fixed and glossed over in academic circles. It is tempting to speculate that this subdued scholarly response has been in part due to Barker's desire to focus his works through different media while oscillating between the genres of horror and the *fantastique*, and publishing for both adult and young adult audiences. To be a pioneer in this terrain has cost Barker many of the accolades he so richly deserves. Scholars who have championed Barker's work in the 1990s laid the foundations for many of the authors in this collection. Gary Hoppenstand's book *Clive Barker's Short Fiction* (1994) is an exceptional work on Barker's *Books of Blood* and serves as an exemplary scholarly primer on Barker's themes and metaphors. Linda Badley's excellent studies on horror fiction and film – *Film, Horror and the Body Fantastic* (1995) and *Writing Horror and the Body: The Fiction of Stephen King, Clive Barker, and Anne Rice* (1996) – strongly emphasise Barker's influence in popular horror studies, prizing his reading of the body as a text in horror fiction, and equating his importance with more established American gothic and horror authors Stephen King and Anne Rice. At the time of Badley's second publication in 1996, Barker's academic inclusion in its subtitle felt wholly justified; it would have been entirely within reason to predict a surge in Barker studies following his meteoric rise in horror studies. Since then, however, the massive shift in Barker's work has resulted in academic analyses of his material featuring sporadically in scholarly circles, garnering occasional analysis in articles and books, and of those published, most tend to favour analyses of his earlier fiction and films. The web-based Barker archive (www.clivebarker.info), run by dedicated Barker archivists and authors Phil Stokes and Sarah Stokes, has proven to be an invaluable resource for research, and for its meticulous inclusion of interviews, exhibitions, and images spanning Barker's whole career. To date, this new collection is the only book that completely dedicates itself to the scholarly analysis of Barker's works since Hoppenstand's analysis of the *Books of Blood*. This book builds upon the excellent foundational scholarly work by Hoppenstand and Badley, Douglas Winter's detailed biography, and others who have published on his work in spite of overwhelming scholarly neglect, and boldly aims to present and provoke new critical horizons in Barker's multiple arenas of creation. Barker has moved on in his creative voyage, and as scholars in the field, we must chart his new discoveries too.

This re-evaluation is not exhaustive, nor does it aim to be – this book begins the process of opening up spaces of enquiry, interrogating new ideas and scholarly engagement with Barker through his multiple and often difficult works rather than merely cataloguing their inception and reception. Barker has been so exhaustive in creating books and sagas, paintings, sketches, working with new media, comic books, video games, and other recent material, including his fluid meditation on time *Chiliad: A Meditation* (2014) and erotic poetry collection *Tonight, Again* (2015), that it would be simply impossible to analyse all of his creative outlets in one volume. His origins in art-theatre have also not been included in this study, remaining an interesting facet of inquiry for other critics to explore. Furthermore, to be completist is not the aim of any scholar in this work; it is the interrogation of Barker's valuable contributions – his ideas, his most influential materials, and continued multi-faceted engagement with horror and *fantastique* fiction and film since the *Books of Blood* – that warrants our critical attention. There is much to admire in this book's diverse and occasionally contradictory readings of Barker and his texts, as these selected critical interrogations yield multiple interpretations. This approach also foregrounds Barker's complexity; his works endure because of the debates and disruptions they present for numerous scholars, critics, and readers.

In the first part of the book, which examines Barker's earlier fiction and its place within British horror fiction and socio-cultural contexts, Darryl Jones' chapter '"Visions of another Albion": the *Books of Blood* and the horror of 1980s Britain' explores Barker's particular manifestations of 1980s British cultural anxieties, examining how selected tales from the *Books of Blood* are exemplary in their response to the frustrations and political radicalism of the period. Ripped from the headlines of Thatcher's divided Britain, Jones captures the vivid and contemporaneous essence of Barker's stunning debut. Kevin Corstorphine, in his chapter '"Marks of weakness, marks of woe": the *Books of Blood* and the transformation of the weird' examines several of Barker's seminal short stories within the context of the weird tale, and the liminal expression through which Barker distinctly marks his own horror style. Indebted to his roots in the theatre and to the Grand Guignol, Corstorphine traces Barker's own interest in subversive transformations, and how this is uniquely expressed in his horror stories from *Books of Blood*. Edward Timothy Wallington carefully unpicks the subtle stitching of Barker's second novel *Weaveworld* in his chapter 'When fantasy becomes reality: social commentary of 1980s Britain in Clive Barker's *Weaveworld*'. Through close reading and political analyses, Wallington finds palpable cultural anger directed at Thatcher's Britain and explores the novel's core themes of dark magic, enslavement, and 1980s materialism, heralded by the forces of evil in the thinly veiled guise of Mrs Thatcher and her government. Aiming to rally those who stand defiant of Thatcher's polarising vision of neoliberal British conservatism, *Weaveworld* is revealed to be a savage indictment of 1980s British politics, and the power of fantasy as critical social commentary.

Part II explores Barker's transition from author to filmmaker, and how his vision has been translated, captured, and occasionally compromised in its adaptation from page to the screen. As an author-turned-director, and author of adapted material for the screen, Barker's own relationship with the filmmaking process, according to Harvey O'Brien in his chapter 'The joyless magic of *Lord of Illusions*' is a complex source of artistic compromise and growing frustration. O'Brien explores Barker's last film as a director and as his explicit farewell to cinema; a rejection of its limitations and empty illusions, reading Barker's anxieties and disillusionment about the filmmaking process, and the human condition, through Nix, the film's antagonist. O'Brien considers whether Barker has truly found his artistic happiness through painting rather than the compromised medium of cinema to realise his vision. Bernard Perron, in his chapter,

'Drawing (to) fear and horror: into the frame of Clive Barker's *The Midnight Meat Train* and *Dread* comic and film adaptations', explores two adapted Barker works that focus on the power of observation and the act of looking. The framing of the films mirror those of graphic novels in their construction, and invite the viewer to consider and explore the explicit framing of the film and its comic adaptations. In these adaptations of Barker's work in comic book form, Perron finds there is freedom to create images wholly beyond the limitations of film. Brigid Cherry's chapter, 'Beauty, pain and desire: gothic aesthetics and feminine identification in the filmic adaptations of Clive Barker', argues that Barker's pleasurable brand of horror cinema affects female viewers in a very specific way, and, using fan testimony to critique Barker's unique contribution to horror cinema and fan culture, Cherry demarcates specific traits in Barker's inspiring works which hold considerable sexual appeal. Indeed, as Cherry proposes elsewhere, 'Barker's work contains features which can be potentially read as feminine and queer, positioning them within traditions of the Gothic, the melodrama and the fantastic (primarily in the shape of the fairy tale)',[21] which actively contributes to such strong responses from his female fans and audiences.

In Part III of the book, Barker's works are examined through the critical lenses of queer culture, desire, and brand recognition. In his chapter 'Clive Barker's queer monsters: exploring transgression, sexuality, and the other', Mark Richard Adams explores Barker's contributions to positive queer representations in the horror film, and the evident symbolic coding for monsters and otherness in Barker's films. In exploring Barker's three films as director – *Hellraiser*, *Nightbreed*, and *Lord of Illusions* – Adams analyses the films through their unique codifications of queered otherness, the proud rallying call for a queer community, and the complex expression of homosexual romance, within this informal Barkerian trilogy. Tony M. Vinci interrogates the metaphysical expressions of blackness and the power of race and transformative flesh in 'Breaking through the canvas: towards a definition of (meta)cultural blackness in the fantasies of Clive Barker'. Exploring the political and cultural revolution frequently expressed in fantasy fiction, and Barker's unique contribution to this field in *Imajica* (1991), Vinci's chapter critiques the socio-cultural function of fantasy fiction as a means to explore dissatisfaction with the contemporary moment, and, through his analysis of *Imajica*, offers insight into the subversive and transformative nature of blackness as a shifting signifier for radical change and revision within Barker's fantasies. Concluding Part III, Gareth James' '"A far more physical experience than the cinema affords": Clive Barker's Halloween Horror Nights and brand authorship', explores Barker as an auteur and horror brand. His horror installations at Universal Studios, *Freakz* (1998), *Hell* (1999), and *Harvest* (2000), specifically enabled Barker to call upon his previous artistry in the theatre to create an auteur-led interactive environment, including Barker's preoccupation with mazes (as filmic, literary, and literal spaces), to generate an affective horror experience for the theme park visitor. James also explores how this installation series contributes to Barker's branding more generally in horror culture.

The final part of this collection, 'Legacy', considers Barker's complex and multi-layered marks in the field, exploring and re-evaluating his works. In so doing, all three authors evaluate his specific place and unique contributions as an author addressing the fissures between modernity and postmodernity, realism and non-realism, splatterpunk and 'anti-horror', and finally between horror, fantasy, and the gothic mode. In '"What price wonderland?": Clive Barker and the spectre of realism', Daragh Downes considers an evident and frustrating thread in Barker's fiction from the *Books of Blood* to his later epic fantasies, plus the author's disregard or abandonment of his gripping realist frameworks in favour of non-realist secondary worlds and magical sensationalism. Barker's storytelling, for Downes, becomes evidently flawed once he embarks upon the fantasy epic, where his descriptive vagaries become exhausting and problematic conflations of the *fantastique*. For Downes, this is Barker's own weakness as an author, and one which articulates the precise issues Barker has grappled with in a vast career spanning genres and publication labels, and confounding readers' expectations. At the expense of realist strategies, Downes finds Barker has escaped into the hall of mirrors of fantasy and missed the opportunity to express his true excellence in a more realist mode. Analysing Barker's more recent fiction through Douglas Winter's framework of 'anti-horror', Xavier Aldana Reyes contends in his chapter, 'Clive Barker's late (anti-)horror fiction: *Tortured Souls* and *Mister B. Gone*'s new myths of the flesh', that Barker's central preoccupation remains focused on the body as the site for transformation and transcendence in recent works. In his detailed study of the novelette *Tortured Souls* (2014) and *Mister B. Gone*, Aldana Reyes posits the transformation of the body in *Tortured Souls* extends the metaphysical flesh-as-text for which Barker is celebrated, while *Mister B. Gone* transmutes the body of its trapped demon protagonist into the very leaves of a cursed book, extra-diegetically authored by Barker (breaking the 'fourth wall') through the diegetic voice of the cursed demon Mister B. The body and the book become sites of transformation, subjectivity, and power. The final chapter in this collection, 'The Devil and Clive Barker: Faustian bargains and gothic filigree' by Sorcha Ní Fhlainn, claims that Barker's obsession with revisiting, rereading, and reusing specifically dark and disturbing authorial patterns, posits his work firmly within the gothic mode. For Ní Fhlainn, many of Barker's works – *The Damnation Game*, *The Hellbound Heart*, *The Thief of Always*, *Coldheart Canyon*, and *The Scarlet Gospels* – explicitly invoke that most gothic of arrangements, the Faustian pact. For Barker, the infernal is ever-present, and enables him to reimagine gothic eruptions which break through the surface of everyday banality, in turn revealing a hybridisation of gothic and fantasy fiction. Despite seldom describing his own fiction as nearing the gothic form, save for one novel, Ní Fhlainn contends that Barker consistently calls upon and is narratively indebted to the gothic mode, its aesthetics and rich literary tradition.

The aim of this volume, and the work of its contributing scholars, is to provoke and excite, and to invite you to (re)discover, explore, and address Barker's works filtered through a range of critical and often diverse lenses. Many authors disagree or contradict one another, giving rise to a rich multi-focal reading of Barker's fiction and films. Across his multi-faceted, polymathic career, Barker's material, artistic modes, and cultural influence has changed, uniquely demanding academic scrutiny. This book is an invitation, a Barkerian doorway, a path towards understanding Barker's own place within popular fiction and popular culture, examining the power, the contradictions, and occasional limitations of his own unique brand. There is much to discover about this dark imaginer; 'we have such (in)sights to show you!'

Notes

1 Clive Barker, *Open to Question*, BBC Two, 8 December 1987, https://www.youtube.com/watch?v=ZOqaKgrbjfQ. Date accessed: 15 December 2015.
2 Douglas E. Winter, *Clive Barker: The Dark Fantastic* (London: Harper Collins, 2001), p. 13.
3 This infamous endorsement came about, according to Douglas Winter, at the World Fantasy Convention in Ottawa, Canada, in October 1984. King was reacting to new and emerging writers in the field and commented that perhaps Clive Barker was the future of horror. King later formally endorsed Barker on publications with 'I've seen the future of horror … and his name is Clive Barker'. For more on this, see Winter, *Clive Barker: The Dark Fantastic*, p. 171.
4 As a child who frequented video stores a lot in the 1980s, the video box for *Hellraiser* was a source of genuine intrigue and terror – the cover captured my imagination and burrowed under my skin, leaving an indelible impression. In later years, as a university student working in a video store, I used to give *Hellraiser* pride of place in the classic horror section. Today, the famed poster adorns the wall of my study.
5 Roger Ebert, Rev. of *Hellbound: Hellraiser II* (Dir. Tony Randel, New World, 1988), 23 December, 1988. *Roger Ebert Online Archive*. www.rogerebert.com/reviews/hellbound-hellraiser-ii-1988. Date accessed: 15 January 2016.
6 Roger Ebert, Rev. of *Hellraiser* (Dir. Clive Barker, New World, 1987), 18 September, 1987. *Roger Ebert Online Archive*. Available at: www.rogerebert.com/reviews/hellraiser-1987. Date accessed: 15 January 2016.
7 Doug Bradley recalls Barry Norman's visit to the set and his encounter with Barker on the set of *Hellbound: Hellraiser II*, in the exhaustively detailed documentary *Leviathan: The Story of Hellraiser and Hellbound: Hellraiser II* (Dir. Kevin McDonagh, Cult Film Screenings, 2015). The documentary also includes brief clips of Norman's reviews of *Hellraiser* and *Hellbound: Hellraiser II* on his BBC Film series.
8 Variety Staff, Rev of *Hellbound: Hellraiser II* (Dir. Tony Randel, New World, 1988), *Variety*, 31 December 1987. http://variety.com/1987/film/reviews/hellbound

-hellraiser-ii-1200427565/. Please note: Dates on this website are incorrect as published by *Variety*. *Hellbound: Hellraiser II* was not released until December 1988 in USA.

9　Alan Smithee (or Allen Smithee) was the official pseudonym used by film directors (from 1968 to 2000) who wished to publicly disown their film project. In order to officially use the credit, they had to evidence to the Directors Guild of America (DGA) that their creative control over the film had been compromised.

10　Paul Kane, *The* Hellraiser *Films and Their Legacy* (Jefferson, NC: McFarland, 2006), p. 40.

11　This is not the only instance when a horror director tries to shift genres and is distrusted for it. Wes Craven, a celebrated horror maestro known for the *Nightmare on Elm Street* and *Scream* series, directed the moving drama *Music of the Heart* (1999), proving that typecasting can be broken. Craven noted in interviews that he had to fight hard to direct the project because of his reputation as a horror director.

12　Winter, *Clive Barker: The Dark Fantastic*, p. 191.

13　Clive Barker, 'An Introduction: Private Legends', *The Essential Clive Barker* (London: Harper Collins, 1999), pp. 5–6.

14　Ken Tucker, 'One Universe at a Time Please', Rev. of *The Great and Secret Show* by Clive Barker, *The New York Times Book Review*, 11 February 1990. www.nytimes.com/1990/02/11/books/one-universe-at-a-time-please.html. Date accessed: 14 January 2016.

15　*Nightbreed: The Cabal Cut* (2012) restored scenes and sequences that were feared lost, but unfortunately varied in quality (some scenes were sourced from VHS, others from degraded film stock). This full restoration composite, with a running time of 155 mins, was completed by Russell Cherrington and Mark Miller, which provided audiences with a completist version of *Nightbreed* and screened at numerous international film festivals. Following the rekindled desire to save and re-distribute *Nightbreed* as Barker intended, a modified, restored, and recut version (which differs from *The Cabal Cut*) was released in 2014, adding 20 mins to the 102 min theatrical cut.

16　Winter, *Clive Barker: The Dark Fantastic*, p. 354.

17　In his Oscar acceptance speech for Best Adapted Screenplay (71st Academy Awards held in March 1999), writer and director Bill Condon thanked Clive Barker, who served as Executive Producer on *Gods and Monsters*, for his support in making the film.

18　China Miéville, 'Candy and Carrion', Rev. of *Abarat* by Clive Barker, *Guardian*, 19 October 2002. www.theguardian.com/books/2002/oct/19/sciencefictionfantasyandhorror.clivebarker. Date accessed: 1 March 2016.

19　Phil and Sarah Stokes, 'A Spiritual Retreat: The Seventeenth Revelatory Interview', 26 March 2007. www.clivebarker.info/intsrevel17.html. Date accessed: 14 January 2016.

20　Michael Marshall Smith gave *The Scarlet Gospels* a gleeful review for the *Guardian* upon publication (Rev. published 13 May 2015), welcoming Barker back to the horror fold, and praising his ability to remain at the peak of his generic form.

Unfortunately, Horror fan sites subsequently featured reviews which differ in opinion, with many expressing their disappointment with the uneven novel.

21 Brigid Cherry, 'Imperfect Geometry: Identity and Culture in Clive Barker's "The Forbidden" and Bernard Rose's *Candyman*,' in Richard J. Hand and Jay McRoy (eds), *Monstrous Adaptations: Generic and Thematic Mutations in Horror Film* (Manchester: Manchester University Press, 2007), p. 51.

Part I

Origins

2 Clive Barker, untitled.

1

'Visions of another Albion': the *Books of Blood* and the horror of 1980s Britain

Darryl Jones

The *Books of Blood*, first published in six volumes in 1984 and 1985, collectively add up to the most important work of British horror fiction of the 1980s. Together, the stories gathered across these volumes are often cited as revolutionising modern horror: my 1994 collected edition of Volumes 1–3 comes proudly emblazoned with two cover blurbs by Stephen King: 'I have seen the future of horror … and his name is Clive Barker' (on the front cover), and 'What Barker does makes the rest of us look like we've been asleep for the last ten years' (on the back).[1]

Formally and aesthetically, the *Books of Blood* are clear products of their time. The short-form horror fiction anthology was enduringly popular in postwar Britain, a familiar feature in bookstores and public libraries, and increasingly so on television from the mid-1960s. Published in 30 annual volumes between 1959 and 1989, and altogether selling some 5.6 million copies, Herbert Van Thal's *Pan Books of Horror Stories* series was one of the most distinctive British publishing phenomena of the postwar decades.[2] Their lurid covers were a familiar presence, particularly in working-class homes (we had two volumes at home as I was growing up in the 1970s – Volume 1 and Volume 19), and the *Pans* provided a point of entry into adult horror fiction (or into adult fiction, or into the adult world) for two generations of postwar readers. It was through Van Thal's selections that many readers first encountered a variety of classic and, increasingly, modern horror writers (Stephen King's 'Graveyard Shift', for example, appeared in 1980's Volume 21). Clive Barker's own experience of encountering the series as a schoolboy is entirely typical:

> I then moved on to 'The Pan Books of Horror Stories' which I just devoured – I thought they were wonderful. Then I would retell these stories to my friends, probably elaborating outrageously as I went along. … It did become something of a preoccupation with me. I was a podgy, slightly shortsighted schoolboy – a classic wimp … However, I knew these imaginative areas where I had some kind of power. I could tell stories to people and they would listen.[3]

The Pan Books of Horror Stories was the most notable but hardly the only long-running horror short-fiction anthology series of the era. The rival *Fontana Books of Great Ghost Stories*, for example, ran through 20 volumes from 1964 to 1984, under the editorship first of Robert Aickman (who had been suggested for the job by his friend Herbert Van Thal) and then of R. Chetwynd-Hayes, and offered, at least under Aickman's editorship, a notably exclusivist, conservative canon of largely British supernatural fiction, with a strong emphasis on Victorian and Edwardian writers.

These print-medium anthologies were in turn complemented by a series of high-profile horror-anthology television series. These series were particularly fecund across the 1970s, when any reasonably regular viewer of BBC or ITV would quickly have encountered, for example, *Dead of Night* (1972), Brian Clemens' *Thriller* (1973–76), Nigel Kneale's *Beasts* (1976), *Supernatural* (1977), *Armchair Thriller* (1978–80), *Tales of the Unexpected* (1979–88), or *Hammer House of Horror* (1980). One particularly significant regular feature across the entire decade was the annual *Ghost Stories for Christmas* series, broadcast, often on Christmas night, between 1971 and 1979, and most famously including Lawrence Gordon Clark's versions of classic ghost stories by M.R. James.

For anyone with even a passing interest in the genre, then, the short-form horror anthology was culturally inescapable in the postwar decades. The schoolboy Clive Barker, we have seen, was particularly captivated by the *Pan Books of Horror Stories*. For the adult Clive Barker, struggling to make his reputation as a writer, theatre director, and filmmaker, Kirby McCauley's 1980 anthology *Dark Forces: New Stories of Suspense and Supernatural Horror* was most significant.[4] Like the *Pan* and *Fontana* series, one of the most startling things about *Dark Forces* for a literary scholar is its eclecticism, its disavowal or perhaps blissful ignorance of traditional aesthetic categories and canonical hierarchies. Thus, the firmly literary Isaac Bashevis Singer, by 1980 already a Nobel laureate (he won the Nobel Prize for Literature in 1978), found himself rubbing shoulders in *Dark Forces* with established genre titans like Ray Bradbury, Robert Bloch, Richard Matheson, or Robert Aickman, with the current genre heavyweight champion Stephen King, with a host of minor and minorish genre writers (including Ramsey Campbell), and with a smaller group of literary unclassifiables including Joyce Carol Oates, the gothic illustrator Edward Gorey, and the conservative political theorist and man of letters Russell Kirk. In part, it was the sheer heterogeneity of *Dark Forces* which seems to have attracted Barker: 'I'll have a go at that', he later recalled thinking. 'I'll put on 23 different hats and do everything I always wanted to do in horror fiction.'[5]

If the *Books of Blood* are aesthetic products of their time, then they are also, and *a fortiori*, its ideological products. It is often argued that British history entered its decisively contemporary phase in 1979, with the election of Margaret Thatcher and the ending of the postwar consensus: 'Everyone was agreed', writes the historian of modern Britain Alwyn W. Turner, 'that the political and social consensus that had dominated Britain since the war had come to an end, but there was no certainty what would take its place in a new settlement'.[6] If 1979 constituted a paradigm shift in British political discourse, then a cultural materialist critic would expect a concomitant shift in cultural discourse, and most particularly in artistic practice. My argument in this article is that the *Books of Blood* are one manifestation of this shift, and that they constitute British horror's most interesting response to the Thatcher decade. If, as Stephen King's reactions suggested, the *Books of Blood* were revolutionary works, then this in part reflects the fact that they were the products of revolutionary times.

What did it mean to write British horror in the 1980s? Cultural production grows out of history and context – not entirely, and not in a simplistic way; but we need to view culture as a product of its time. This much is obvious. Furthermore, as a student of popular culture, and of horror in particular, I firmly believe that these forms of production offer oblique or displaced metaphorical or symbolic articulation of prevalent cultural anxieties.

Barker has spoken and written often about his 'perfectly sane upbringing' in the Liverpool of the 1950s and 1960s, and of 'the sheer banality of growing up in a town that was not of great interest to me' – though he has also described his home town as 'that fine but distinctly haunted city'.[7] Barker is a Liverpool writer, but in complex and nuanced ways – he is not, like writers as otherwise different from one another as Roger McGough and Alan Bleasdale, an *avowedly* Liverpudlian writer, for whom the city provides a source, an inspiration, and a subject. There are no named Liverpool locations of any kind in the *Books of Blood*, nor any explicit references to the city itself: 'The Forbidden', which I discuss at the end of this chapter, is generally thought to be set in Liverpool, and one can infer a Liverpudlian setting from the proximity of the university and cathedral in the story, but it is never named. Indeed, with a few notable exceptions (such as the rural folk horror tale 'Rawhead Rex' and the nightmarish school story 'Pig Blood Blues') those British-set stories in the collections tend, when their locations are identifiable at all, to be set in London. However, just because the stories do not engage with any of their contexts – historical, cultural, socio-political, geographical, biographical – in a straightforward manner does not mean that these are not valid interpretive contexts from which to study the stories. It does, however, mean that we should not expect ready parallels or easy answers.

By the 1980s, when the *Books of Blood* were published, Liverpool was at the sharp end of British postwar, post-industrial decline, a city blighted by deprivation and unemployment. In the fevered summer of 1981, riots broke out all over Britain. The reasons for these riots are complex, but clearly directly related to the economic policies of the Thatcher government which, in its uncompromisingly ideological macroeconomic crusade to control inflation through severely limiting the money supply, wreaked social havoc, creating conditions of runaway unemployment, which reached a postwar peak of

3,000,000 early in 1986, having risen by a staggering 836,000 in the *annus horribilis* of 1980 alone, the largest rise in a single year since the depression nadir of 1930.[8] One in eight of the British workforce was unemployed, and the traditionally Labour-voting former industrial heartlands of the North of England, Scotland, and Wales were hit disproportionately hard.[9] It is little wonder that in the eyes of many, Thatcher, far from enacting economic policy, was in fact waging class war.

Race war, too, according to some. In 1979, the Monday Club was formed, a right-wing pressure group with considerable support on the back benches of the Parliamentary Conservative Party. The Club's policy on immigration, according to a leaked memo, was uncompromisingly Powellite, and this in spite of the fact that Enoch Powell himself, the tormented political prophet of British racial disharmony in the late 1960s and 1970s, had by this time gone over to the Ulster Unionist cause: 'An end to New Commonwealth and Pakistani immigration, a properly financed scheme of voluntary repatriation, the repeal of the Race Relations Act, and the abolition of the Commission for Racial Equality; particular emphasis on repatriation.'[10] The New Cross fire of 18 January 1981, in which thirteen black teenagers died at a house party, was widely believed at the time to have been the deliberate work of racists – and while most commentators now accept that the fire was probably accidental, it is certain that insensitive police handling of the event sowed long-lasting seeds of bitterness in the community. A few months later, the 1981 riots broke out across a series of British urban communities with large black populations, most notably Brixton in South London (10–11 April) and Toxteth in Liverpool (3–6 and 27–28 July). The Toxteth riots were sparked by the arrest of Leroy Alphonse Cooper, whom police believed to have stolen the bicycle he was riding (it was in fact his own); the police in turn found themselves under attack by a group of forty black youths, with events quickly spiralling out of control into a full-scale riot. Interviewed by the *Liverpool Echo* on the 30th anniversary of the riots, Cooper himself provided an astute socio-political analysis of the events:

> We are talking about a community [Toxteth] established in this city since the days of the slave trade, here since the 1700s.
>
> With Margaret Thatcher, the vice was tightening on the working class, people were made to feel like second and third class citizens in their own country. We had between 70 and 80 per cent unemployment amongst young men between 16 and 30 in this area.
>
> The riot was a symptom of there being something really wrong with our society. We smashed our own community up, we destroyed our own homes. There had to be something wrong. It was like a blistering, weeping spot in the middle of your face which one day just explodes.
>
> The community had a foot on its neck for years. I think the riots were basically historical chickens coming home to roost.[11]

In the wake of the Toxteth riots, the Secretary of State for the Environment, Michael Heseltine, visited Liverpool, and was apparently horrified by what he saw, recommending a large-scale programme of urban renewal, to the cost of £270 million. Heseltine's recommendations resulted, amongst other things, in the highly symbolic redevelopment of the Albert Dock area, an endeavour which, in turn, led to the creation of a series of public–private 'Enterprize Zones' in Britain's inner cities. The report to the Cabinet in which Heseltine made these initial recommendations was entitled *It Took a Riot*.[12]

In a 1986 interview with Nick Hasted for *Creature* magazine, Clive Barker said:

> I don't worry about running out of ideas. I feel that there are always plenty – the newspapers are packed with thoughts and ideas. The question is whether you can push them to their limits and find out what they really mean. And the thing about good horror fiction, I believe, is that it doesn't just give you the story, it also gives you the subtext of the story.[13]

Sometimes, the stories in the *Books of Blood* draw clearly – if obliquely, grotesquely, or fantastically – on contemporary issues and events, of precisely the kind that any reader of a newspaper in the early 1980s would have encountered. In Volume 4's opening story, 'The Body Politic', human hands sever themselves from their wrists, rise up, and kill their owners. (Even those readers of newspapers not interested in the politics of the early 1980s might have recognised a contemporary frame of reference from the very opening sentence, as the protagonist of 'The Body Politic' is named 'Charlie George' in honour of the Arsenal and England footballer, who in 1980 lost a finger in a bizarre gardening accident.) From its very title onwards, the story articulates a barely encoded political metaphor. Good horror, Barker affirms, 'gives you the subtext of the story', and it does not require an advanced degree in literary hermeneutics to work out what is going on here: the entire story reads like a slice of British social history from around the period of the 1981 riots, drawing on the racism, unemployment, and urban despair which contributed to making the summer of 1981 such an inflammatory one. The *political* use of hands as a synecdoche for industrial labour and through that for economic alienation has a fictional prehistory dating back at least as far as Charles Dickens' *Hard Times* (1855), which repeatedly uses the term 'the hands' to denote Coketown's industrial workers, as this is the only part of them that has any use-value according to the dominant utilitarian philosophy of which the novel offers a sustained and devastating critique. For Barker the severed hands are doubly political, signifying both disenfranchised post-industrial youth and the decolonised subjects of the former British Empire. Colonel Christie, a former military officer now reduced to working as a nightwatchman, is 'a racist and proud of it. He had nothing but contempt for the blacks who thronged the corridors of the YMCA, mostly young men without suitable homes to go to, bad lots that the local authority had dumped on the doorstep like unwanted babies' (4: 14).[14] Christie's hands are severed by his own 'Kukri knife, given to him by a Gurkha during the war'; as he lies bleeding to death, 'A portrait of the Queen fell from its hook and smashed beside him' (4: 14, 15). The hands mount a full-scale attack on the YMCA, in a passage narrated from the perspective of Boswell, a Rastafarian, the story's representative of the Black British communities so centrally affected by the 1981 riots, on which the story comments obliquely ('The Body Politic' also includes a cameo from an inadvertently murderous punk). The story's closing line is a double-edged comment, referring both to the apocalyptic possibilities of a potential future in which body parts rebel against a centralising human consciousness, coming into an agency of their own, and to the postwar demise of the British *imperium*: 'He waited, heart in mouth, for the fall of Empire' (4: 33).

The riotous body politic is a recurring image throughout the *Books of Blood* – one might even go so far as to say that it is the collection's controlling metaphor, and certainly a central tenet of the 1980s 'body horror' movement with which Barker was closely associated. Volume 1's 'In the Hills, the Cities' is identifiably a work of the 1980s, a late-Cold War fable in which a pair of British lovers on holiday in Yugoslavia happen upon a ritual in which the inhabitants of rival cities, Popolac and Podujevo, strap themselves together, seemingly in their thousands, to form a pair of battling giants.[15] From the opening sentence, the story situates itself within a British political context: 'It wasn't until the first week of the Yugoslavian trip that Mick discovered what a political bigot he'd chosen as a lover' (1: 122). More than this, Mick's lover is a Thatcherite political commentator, 'to the Right of Attila the Hun' (1: 122):

> Judd was a journalist, a professional pundit. He felt, like most journalists Mick had encountered, that he was obliged to have a position on everything under the sun. Especially politics … because everything, according to Judd, was political. The arts were political. Sex was political. Religion, commerce, gardening, eating, drinking and farting – all political. (1: 122)

Mick and Judd encounter Vaslav, a local who explains to them the significance of the ritual of the giants: 'It is the body of the state … It is the shape of our lives' (1: 141). The Thatcherite Judd dismisses this as 'metaphor … Trotskyist tripe' (1: 143). The city-colossus is certainly a metaphor, and its realisation means that within the economy of the story it is certainly not 'tripe'. As with his use of riotous hands, Barker draws here on a rich seam of metaphorical representation of the body politic in corporeal form. The body politic is often, as here, bodied forth as a human giant, as in the celebrated frontispiece illustration to Thomas Hobbes' *Leviathan*, in which the giant of the state is revealed as comprised of a multitude of tiny homunculi, or Frankenstein's Monster, the one man made of many men, an embodiment for many readers of the power of the subjugated masses, or Demogorgon, the unstoppable monster of the people who finally overthrows Jupiter's unjust autocracy in Percy Shelley's *Prometheus Unbound*. As a former student of English and Philosophy at Liverpool University, it seems likely that these images and texts are explicit influences on 'In the Hills, the Cities', as is Dickens on 'The Body Politic'.

In her book *Writing Horror and the Body: The Fiction of Stephen King, Clive Barker, and Anne Rice*, Linda Badley offers a rather different political interpretation of 'In the Hills, the Cities': 'Popolac is a revision of the science fiction cliché of society as a machine by way of Michel Foucault's vision of power embodied and harnessed through a network of forces and relations, economic, social and political.'[16] Badley's book was published in 1996, at a time when, for institutional criticism, the turn towards critical theory seemed axiomatic. The Foucauldian model for understanding and thinking through power-relations, particularly as articulated in *Discipline and Punish*, was surely irresistible for many critics at the time, most especially those operating within the US academy. For those of us reading Barker in Britain during the 1980s and 1990s, the reality lay nearer to home, and thus it seems to me more likely, given the anti-Thatcherite political context within which the story operates, that the giants, far from signifying the kinds of power-relations of Foucauldian human instrumentalism suggested by Badley's interpretation, are nearer to a celebration of the anarchic, uncontrolled power of mass humanity, the *demos* asserting its terrifying agency (the *Demogorgon*) in a left-wing fantasy of riot:

> They [Popolac] became, in the space of a few moments, the single-minded giant whose image they had so brilliantly re-created. The illusion of petty individuality was swept away in an irresistible tide of collective feeling – not a mob's passion, but a telepathic urge that dissolved the voices of thousands into one irresistible command. … They saw only through the eyes of the city. They were thoughtless, but to think the city's thoughts. And they believed themselves deathless, in their lumbering, relentless strength. Vast and mad and deathless. (1: 139)

Judd is killed when a cottage, trampled by the out-of-control colossus of Popolac, collapses onto him; for Mick, Popolac affords an encounter with the sublime, or even the numinous, and he climbs on board: 'He was a hitchhiker with a god: the mere life he had left was nothing to him now, or ever. He would live with this thing, yes, he would live with it – seeing it and seeing it and eating it with his eyes until he died of gluttony' (1: 148).

My argument here, then, is that the riotous fleshly mutability of so many of the stories of the *Books of Blood* is avowedly and consciously a gesture of political radicalism. The political nature of 1980s body horror was thoroughly explored by its most articulate practitioner, David Cronenberg, who is in some ways Barker's transatlantic counterpart, and who brings to his work a fully worked out and consistent philosophy:

> I don't think the flesh is necessarily treacherous, evil, bad. It is cantankerous, and it is independent. The idea of independence is the key. It really is like

colonialism … I think to myself: 'That's what it is: the independence of the body, relative to the mind, and the difficulty of the mind accepting what that revolution might entail.'[17]

Of all the stories in the *Books of Blood*, it is Volume 2's 'Jacqueline Ess: Her Will and Testament' which engages most explicitly with the theme of fleshly mutability. The story is, in part, a feminist fable, a kind of 1980s reimagining of Betty Friedan's *The Feminine Mystique*, as Jacqueline Ess, a middle-class York housewife existentially bored and unsatisfied with her marriage and her place in society (the story opens with her suicide attempt) discovers that she has the power to reshape human flesh according to her will. Her first exercise of power is on the body of her patronising doctor: 'She stared at his wide shoulders, his narrow hips. A fine figure of a man, as Ben [her husband] would have called him. No child-bearer he. Made to remake the world, a body like that' (2: 60). From the outset, then 'Jacqueline Ess' deconstructs the relationship between gender, power, and the body, through the literal, graphic deconstruction and reconstruction of the flesh. Jacqueline finds herself thinking 'Be a woman':

> She willed his manly chest into making breasts of itself and it began to swell most fetchingly, until the skin burst and his sternum flew apart. His pelvis, teased to breaking point, fractured at its centre … It was from between his legs all the noise was coming; the splashing of his blood; the thud of his bowel on the carpet. (2: 60)

In classic 1980s fashion, when Jacqueline wants to learn how to use and control her new-found power, she turns to Titus Pettifer, a corporate raider:

> He ran more monopolies than he could count; his word in the financial world could break companies like sticks, destroying the ambitions of hundreds, the careers of thousands. Fortunes were made overnight in his shadow, entire corporations fell when he blew on them, casualties of his whims. This man knew power if anyone knew it. He had to be learned from. (2: 68)

Figures like Pettifer were Thatcherite icons in the 1980s: the corporate raider James Hanson, for example, whose firm Hanson plc acquired a multibillion dollar portfolio through leveraged buyouts, was a notable Tory backer, given a life peerage by Thatcher in 1983.[18] If anything, as a work of the 1980s 'Jacqueline Ess' is rather prophetic, as it was published some two years before the 'Lawson Boom' of 1986, in which the British economy became very largely dependent on its corporate and financial services as opposed to its manufacturing base (a dependency which remains strong to this day), a boom precipitated by the deregulation of the City of London in the 'Big Bang' of 27 October 1986, in which the London stock exchange was radically overhauled, its practices comprehensively modernised. Indeed, as Graham Stewart implies, Pettifer's model of conducting business was to prove perhaps Thatcherism's most influential legacy:

By the twentieth century's end, aggressive corporate takeovers were routinely identified as among the central and distinguishing components of the 'Anglo-Saxon model'. Such tussles for control had become frequent in the seventies, but it was the feverish deal-making of the eighties that made them a principal characteristic of the British way of doing business.[19]

As with the doctor, Titus Pettifer's encounter with Jacqueline literally deconstructs him, remaking him in an altogether different form, casting him in an altogether different light:

> 'You are an animal', she said. ...

> [Pettifer's] hands knotted into paws, his legs scooped up around his back, knees broken so he had the look of a four-legged crab, his brain exposed, his eyes lidless, lower jaw broken and swept over his top jaw like a bulldog, ears torn off, spine snapped, humanity bewitched into another state. (2: 83)

The politics of 'Jacqueline Ess' – anti-patriarchal, anti-capitalist – are largely clear and consistent, though they are troubled and perhaps seriously compromised by the story's close, which finds Jacqueline tied to an Amsterdam pimp's bed, 'Her body ... seething, her shaved sex opening and closing like some exquisite plant, purple and lilac and rose' (2: 87). While Barker seems to be aiming for some kind of transcendence at the story's very end, as Jacqueline and her lover Oliver Vassi literally die and melt into one another's arms – in one of the story's numerous corporealisations of figures of speech, here with perhaps a dash of Angela Carter's *The Sadeian Woman* – I have to say that I find this politically problematic, potentially playing into the traditional sexism of much pulp fiction.[20] However, ending 'Jacqueline Ess' in this way does avoid another potential political pitfall, the typological tendency of 1980s popular culture to produce, in its representations of powerful women, facsimiles of Margaret Thatcher. As Turner suggests, these mini-Thatchers proliferated across British popular culture in the early 1980s: patrician canine mistress Barbara Woodhouse; Mrs Bridget McClusky (Gwyneth Powell), martinette principal of Grange Hill Comprehensive School from 1981 to 1991; Detective Inspector Maggie Forbes (Jill Gascoigne) in *The Gentle Touch* (1980–84); Inspectors Jean Darblay (Stephanie Turner) and Kate Longton (Anna Carteret) in *Juliet Bravo* (1980–85). Turner correctly notes that 'Even the nightmarish, over-controlling mother of Ronnie Corbett's character in the sitcom *Sorry!* [1982–88] (played by Barbara Lott) had a hint of Thatcher about her.'[21] Shortly before she kills Pettifer, Jacqueline has an epiphany:

> Still the words came: the same dirty words that had been thrown at generations of unsubmissive women. Whore; heretic; cunt; bitch; monster.
>   Yes, she was that.
>   Yes, she thought: monster I am. (2: 82)

Whatever it is that Jacqueline Ess turns into at the end of her story, she does not turn into Margaret Thatcher.

'In eighties Britain', Graham Stewart argues, 'a surprisingly violent cultural battleground proved to be a tussle over architecture.'[22] If architectural post-modernism is Thatcherism given literal concrete form, then more than any other artistic medium, it was architectural modernism that gave aesthetic form to the ideological aspirations of the postwar consensus. In the words of the historian of postwar British architecture Robert Elwall, this was to be the nation's means of 'building a better tomorrow'.[23] As Alan Powers suggests, what distinguished modern British architecture was its particular *social* vision in the service of the state, its aspiration to build 'the "Just City"': 'the application of creative and liberal social thinking to the design of buildings and cities was arguably Britain's most distinctive contribution to the modern movement worldwide. ... Left-wing attitudes accompanied a shift in the architect's own role from gentleman practitioner to employee of a public organization.'[24] One of the major challenges facing the 1945 Attlee government, and its successors right up to the 1970s, was a wholesale reimagining of Britain's urban housing. The Victorian slums so characteristic of British cities were certainly overcrowded, insanitary, and unsafe, and many of these densely populated areas had been badly damaged by German bombing. The influence of Corbusier and of International Style Modernism, as well as the ease and relative cheapness of system-building, led to the ubiquity of the tower block as *the* symbol of postwar British social architecture.

At first, high-rise building seemed an entirely proper modern solution to Britain's housing problems. As Lynsey Hanley writes:

> The 1950s and 60s offered local authorities a monumental chance to show off to their voters: these futuristic-looking tower blocks were visible signs of progress, signalling the death of the slums and the final victory of the worker, who had not only work for life but a penthouse flat overlooking the city he helped to make prosperous.[25]

It was not only forward-looking socialist idealists who championed the tower block. Even the young John Betjeman – on his way to becoming an uncom-promising and highly influential proponent of Victorian architecture – initially advocated a large-scale programme of skyscraper-building to solve the nation's housing and commercial problems: 'Two dozen skyscrapers, though they would obviously dwarf St. Paul's, would not take away from its beauty if they were beautiful themselves.'[26]

By 1979, almost 50% of the population of Britain lived in council housing.[27] But the inadequacies of the system-built tower-block housing estate soon became very obvious. Residents may have moved into modern, clean homes, but they found themselves cut off from traditional communities and, often, far removed from amenities. The absence of individual gardens proved unexpectedly damag-ing: as Paul Barker suggests in his book *The Freedoms of Suburbia*, suburban living, much derided by Modernist architects and theorists, may in fact be perfectly attuned to British psychological life: 'I cast doubt on the wisdom of too much planning. There is no harm in just allowing things to happen. The pleasures of sheer chance should not be undercut. This is how most of our towns were created.' He quotes with approval the verdict of the design writer John Gloag in his essay on 'The Suburban Scene': 'You can't impose theories of living on the English.'[28]

Furthermore, these towers were often built to a shockingly poor standard, as graphically demonstrated in the case of Ronan Point in Newham, East London, which partially collapsed on 16 May 1968 after a gas leak caused an explosion, leading to the destruction of load-bearing walls which had been rapidly and cheaply erected according to the Larsen-Nielsen method of system-building, and which were held in place by rapidly rusting rivets, and had gaps filled with newspaper rather than concrete. Ronan Point was less than two months old.[29] Six further Larsen-Nielsen method tower blocks were subsequently demolished, condemned as 'death traps'.[30]

Even when they were soundly built, tower blocks could often seem deliberately inimical to human contentment. Ernö Goldfinger's monumentally dystopian Trellick Tower in West London was the tallest social housing in Europe when it was opened in 1972.[31] By the end of the decade, blighted by violent crime, it became known as 'the Tower of Terror'.[32] While this subsequent social collapse was not exactly a design feature, nor with hindsight should it be surprising, as Goldfinger deliberately designed his brutalist behemoths to look as intimidating as possible. They were built according to the aesthetics of terror. Even Goldfinger's highly sympathetic biographer, Nigel Warburton, acknowledges this in describing Trellick's slightly smaller East End twin, Balfron Tower:

> The massive scale of this bush-hammered concrete tower … gives[s] this the impression of being a modernist fortress, an effect heightened by the drawbridge-like entrance to the building. The boiler-tower overhang could be a modern allusion to the castle parapets designed for pouring oil onto anyone laying siege below. … The overall effect, particularly when approaching the building at night – when it is lit from above – is dramatic and uncompromising. Its aesthetic appeal from the outside is that of the sublime rather than the beautiful. There is nothing quaint or homely about the exterior.[33]

The architectural historian James Dunnett concurs, offering an admiring account of the building in even more dystopian terms: 'It is as though Goldfinger, from among the Functionalist totems, had chosen as an inspiration the artefacts of war. … At night the estate is illuminated by the merciless beam of powerful arclights mounted on the summit of the slab.' The overall effect of Balfron Tower is 'a delicate sense of terror', 'a terrible beauty'.[34] In thus consciously invoking the aesthetics of the sublime for his architecture, Goldfinger was also consciously invoking one of the most influential theories of horror, Edmund Burke's *Philosophical Enquiry* (1757):

Whatever is fitted in any sort to excite the ideas of pain, and danger, that is to
say, whatever is in any sort terrible, or is conversant about terrible objects, or
operates in a manner analogous to terror, is a source of the *sublime*; that is, it is
productive of the strongest emotion which the mind is capable of feeling.[35]

Given that, in these extreme cases, their brutalist architecture seems deliberately
designed on the principles of oppression and terror – embodying in concrete
a nightmarish Orwellian version of the British state – it is little wonder that
Hanley concludes: 'There is one phrase in the English language that has come
to be larded with even more negative meaning than "council estate", and that
is "tower block".'[36]

Unsurprisingly, then, the high-rise estate became a recurring component
of dystopian visions of postwar British social breakdown. Thamesmead in
south-east London was used as the location for Stanley Kubrick's *A Clockwork
Orange* (1973), Alan Clarke's football hooligan drama *The Firm* (1989) – 'a key
text on the subject of Thatcher's Britain', according to the great film critic Philip
French[37] – and the Aphex Twin's nightmarish *Come to Daddy* (1997). In 1985,
the geographer Alice Coleman's *Utopia on Trial: Vision and Reality in Planned
Housing* offered a scathing critique of the high-rise estate, singling out Broadwater
Farm in Tottenham for particular criticism, as, later, did Anne Power's *Estates
on the Edge* (1997).[38] On 6 October 1985, a London policeman, Keith Blakelock,
was hacked to death by knives and machetes in a riot at Broadwater Farm
following the death of a black woman, Cynthia Jarrett, who suffered a heart
attack while the police were searching her home.

The high-rise estate, then, was a common locus of fear and horror in postwar
Britain, in both fact and fiction. Published in 1985, the same year as the
Broadwater Farm riot, 'The Forbidden' is one of the key stories in the *Books
of Blood*. *Candyman*, Bernard Rose's 1992 adaptation of the story, relocated
the action to the notorious Cabrini-Green housing project in Chicago, whereas
Barker's original location, though unspecified, is firmly British. The film's act
of cultural translation serves to highlight one important fact, which is that
'The Forbidden' is fundamentally a story about life lived under intolerable
conditions of urban deprivation, in which social bonds have dissolved. Its
protagonist is a postgraduate sociological ethnographer researching a PhD
entitled 'Graffiti: The Semiotics of Urban Despair' (5: 2).

The story opens with a familiar critique of architects and town planners, part
of an ongoing discourse of anti-Modernism that accompanied postwar inner-city
social housing from its inception – exactly the kinds of critiques articulated, in
measured form, in the books by Coleman, Power, Hanley, and Paul Barker:

Like a flawless tragedy, the elegance of which structure is lost upon those suffering
in it, the perfect geometry of the Spector Street Estate was only visible from the
air. Walking in its drear canyons, passing through its grimy corridors from one
grey concrete rectangle to the next, there was little to seduce the eye or stimulate
the imagination. What few saplings had been planted in the quadrangles had

long since been mutilated or uprooted; the grass, though tall, resolutely refused a healthy green.

No doubt the estate and its two companion developments had once been an architect's dream. No doubt the city-planners had wept with pleasure at a design which housed three [hundred] and thirty-six persons per hectare, and still boasted space for a children's playground. Doubtless fortunes and reputations had been built upon Spector Street, and at its opening fine words had been spoken of its being a yardstick by which all future developments would be measured. But the planners – tears wept, words spoken – had left the estate to its own devices; the architects occupied restored Georgian houses at the other end of the city, and probably never set foot here. (5: 1)

As Barker here correctly suggests, architects were often criticised for designing social housing in which they themselves would not dream of living. Peter and Alison Smithson, for example, were the uncompromising architects and social theorists for whose work the term 'brutalism' was first coined, by the architectural critic Rayner Banham.[39] The Smithsons were, in David Kynaston's words, 'defiantly uncuddly'.[40] Robin Hood Gardens, their social housing estate in Poplar, East London, has drawn enormous criticism since its opening in 1969: the Pevnser architectural guide to East London describes Robin Hood Gardens as 'ill-planned to the point of inhumane', and in 2008 the *Guardian* reported that 'The tenants and Tower Hamlets council [its owners] want the place down, and now. … Eighty per cent of Robin Hood's residents want the estate demolished and rebuilt along more humane lines so they can stay in the neighbourhood'.[41] When the Smithsons chose to build a house for themselves, the location was not urban, let alone deprived: in 1962 they built Upper Lawn Pavilion in the rural idyll of Tisbury, Wiltshire.[42] While Ernö Goldfinger did elect to live in Balfron Tower for two months after its opening, this gesture has been the subject of very different interpretations: Warburton acknowledges that this was 'a publicity stunt', but understands it as 'the opportunity to make a public commitment to the virtues of high-rise living', a gesture which Hanley dismisses as 'gubbins'.[43] Goldfinger's own house was in one of London's most exclusive addresses, Willow Road, Hampstead, looking out over the Heath.

Like Thamesmead, Trellick Tower, or Broadwater Farm, the Spector Street Estate has been left to rot:

This was – or had been – the site of the estate's amenities. Here was the children's playground, its metal-framed rides overturned, its sandpit fouled by dogs, its paddling pool empty. And here too were the shops. Several had been boarded up; those that hadn't were dingy and unattractive, their windows protected by heavy wire mesh. (5: 16)

Compared to this despairing account of wasted lives and urban devastation, the supernaturalism of 'The Forbidden', its attempt to frame its subject within an overarching narrative of urban legends, seems decidedly secondary, if not irrelevant. The Spector Street Estate, and the social, political, and aesthetic decisions that have conspired to turn it into an urban hell, is real locus of horror in 'The Forbidden'.

On 29 March 1981, just a few days before the Brixton riots, the first London Marathon was staged, an event which drew almost 7000 competitors (the number now exceeds 35,000). Once again, Clive Barker had been reading the newspaper – or watching television – and responded with 'Hell's Event'. The story is a Manichean restaging of the London Marathon. At stake is the possibility of Satanic rule on Earth. Unknown to himself, Cameron, a socialist athletics coach, and his protégé Joel, a champion athlete and 'the best-loved black face in England' according to 'One of the tabloids' (2: 36), find themselves competing in the marathon against the forces of Hell, as represented by Voight, a white South African who calls Joel a 'Black bastard' (2: 52) (the story's racial politics are righteous, but not sophisticated). The event is brokered by Gregory Burgess, MP – technically, we are told, an 'Independent', but certainly not a socialist: 'I serve Hell, Mr. Cameron. And in its turn Hell serves me' (2: 45). In 1981, many people thought the same about Thatcher's government.

While following the action of the marathon, Cameron gets lost in London and inadvertently finds his way into an icy cavern which houses a Satanic temple: he has a moment of epiphany, and sees 'Visions of another Albion' (2: 42). This is a self-consciously Blakean moment, an apprehension of the numinous underlying quotidian reality, of a kind which is repeated throughout the *Books of Blood*.

But, for those of us living through 1980s Britain, it is worth remembering that Clive Barker's 'other Albion' was also, obliquely but nevertheless recognisably, our own country. A generation down the line, the *Books of Blood* painfully embody this country of ideological fault lines, with its divisive racial politics, its decaying built environment, its abandoned urban working class, its troubled conceptions of gender and sexual identity, and its new forms of capital and power, even more starkly than might have appeared to a reader at the time, caught (as this one was) *in medias res*. They are the authentic dark imaginings of the British 1980s.

Notes

1 Volumes 1–3 were published by Sphere in 1984, and volumes 4–6 in 1985. For this article, I am using the 2-volume anthology editions: *Clive Barker's Books of Blood*, Volumes 1–3 (London: Warner, 1994); *Clive Barker's Books of Blood*, Volumes 4–6 (London: Warner, 1994).
2 For the sales figures for the *Pan Books of Horror Stories*, see Johnny Mains, *Lest You Should Suffer Nightmares: A Biography of Herbert Van Thal* (Bargoed: Screaming Dreams, 2011), p. 21.

3 Barker, interviewed by Stephen Jones, in 'Clive Barker: Anarchic Prince of Horror,' *Knave*, 15:5 (1987), reproduced in www.clivebarker.info/childhood.html. Date accessed: 12 April 2015.

4 Kirby McCauley, ed. *Dark Forces: New Stories of Suspense and Supernatural Horror* (New York: Viking, 1980).

5 'Clive Barker: Banking on Blood,' *Locus*, 19:7, Issue 306 (July 1986), reproduced in www.clivebarker.info/ints86.html. Date accessed: 12 April 2015.

6 Alwyn W. Turner, *Rejoice! Rejoice! Britain in the 1980s* (London: Aurum, 2010), p. xvii. See also, for example, Dominic Sandbrook's four-volume history of modern Britain, which covers the years 1956–79; David Kynaston's ongoing series of postwar British histories (four volumes to date) plans to cover the years 1945–79, the years of the postwar consensus.

7 Bill Babouris, 'Addicted to Creativity,' *Samhain*, 70 (November 1998); Curt Schleir, 'The Future of Horror is Here: His Name is Clive Barker,' *Inside Books* (November 1988); Clive Barker, 'Ramsay Campbell: An Appreciation,' *1986 World Fantasy Convention Programme*. All reproduced at www.clivebarker.info/childhood.html. Date accessed: 12 April 2015.

8 Andy McSmith, *No Such Thing as Society: A History of Britain in the 1980s* (London: Constable, 2011), p. 6; Turner, *Rejoice!*, p. 11. For an excellent account of Thatcherite monetarist economic policy and its socio-political consequences, see Graham Stewart, *Bang! A History of Britain in the 1980s* (London: Atlantic, 2013).

9 For this figure of one in eight unemployed in the early 1980s, see Stewart, *Bang!*, p. 82.

10 McSmith, *No Such Thing as Society*, p. 86. Of all contemporary historians of 1980s Britain, McSmith takes the strongest line in blaming the 1981 riots directly on race relations: his chapter on the riots (pp. 86–110), on which I draw heavily here, takes its title from Linton Kwesi Johnson's dub poem 'Inglan is a Bitch'.

11 Marc Waddington, 'Leroy Cooper: The Toxteth Riots were a Wake-Up Call and Did Some Good,' *Liverpool Echo*, 4 July 2011. www.liverpoolecho.co.uk/news/liverpool-news/leroy-cooper-toxteth-riots-were-3369244. Date accessed: 13 April 2015.

12 Stewart, *Bang!*, p. 98.

13 Clive Barker, interview with Nick Hasted, *Creature*, 5 (1986), reproduced in www.clivebarker.info/ints86.html. Date accessed: 12 April 2015.

14 Page and volume numbers for the *Books of Blood* are given hereafter in the text.

15 Podujevo is an actual former Yugoslavian city, in what is now modern-day Kosovo. Popolac is fictitious, its name clearly a variant on 'people', 'popular', 'populace'.

16 Linda Badley, *Writing Horror and the Body: The Fiction of Stephen King, Clive Barker, and Anne Rice* (Westport, CT: Greenwood Press, 1996), p. 76.

17 Chris Rodley, ed. *Cronenberg on Cronenberg* (London: Faber and Faber, 1997), p. 80.

18 For Hanson, see Stewart, *Bang!*, pp. 397–8. Hanson plc was the subject of a high-profile 1980s advertising campaign, branded as 'A company from over here [the UK] that's doing rather well over there [the US].'

19 Stewart, *Bang!*, p. 396.

20 See Angela Carter, *The Sadeian Woman: An Exercise in Cultural History* (London: Virago, 1979). More overtly, the American edition, published by Pantheon, was entitled *The Sadeian Woman and the Idea of Pornography*.

21 Turner, *Rejoice!*, p. 7.

22 Stewart, *Bang!*, p. 262.

23 Robert Elwall, *Building a Better Tomorrow: Architecture in Britain in the 1950s* (Chichester: Wiley-Academy, 2000).

24 Alan Powers, *Britain*, 'Modern Architectures in History' series (London: Reaktion, 2007), pp. 53–4.

25 Lynsey Hanley, *Estates: An Intimate History* (London: Granta, 2007), p. 104.

26 David Kynaston, *Austerity Britain, 1945–51* (London: Bloomsbury, 2007), p. 29.

27 Hanley, *Estates*, p. 98.

28 Paul Barker, *The Freedoms of Suburbia* (London: Frances Lincoln, 2009), pp. 10, 64.

29 For Ronan Point, see Hanley, *Estates*, pp. 106–11; Dominic Sandbrook, *White Heat: A History of Britain in the Swinging Sixties* (London: Abacus, 2007), pp. 660–2.

30 Hanley, *Estates*, p. 110.

31 Nigel Warburton, *Ernö Goldfinger: The Life of an Architect* (London: Routledge, 2005), p. 164.

32 Hanley, *Estates*, p. 113.

33 Warburton, *Ernö Goldfinger*, p. 156.

34 James Dunnett, 'A Terrible Beauty …', in James Dunnett and Gavin Stamp (eds), *Ernö Goldfinger: Works I* (London: Architectural Association, 1983), p. 7.

35 Edmund Burke, *A Philosophical Enquiry into the Origin of Our Ideas of the Sublime and Beautiful*, ed. with an Introduction by Adam Phillips (Oxford: Oxford University Press, 1990), p. 36.

36 Hanley, *Estates*, p. 97.

37 Philip French, 'The Firm,' *Observer* (20 September 2009): www.theguardian.com/film/2009/sep/20/the-firm-film-review. Date accessed: 24 April 2009.

38 Alice Coleman, with the Design Disadvantagement Team of the Land Research Unit King's College London, *Utopia on Trial: Vision and Reality in Planned Housing* (London: Shipman, 1985); Anne Power, *Estates on the Edge: The Social Consequences of Mass Housing in Europe* (Basingstoke: Macmillan, 1997).

39 Dominic Bradbury, *The Iconic House: Architectural Masterworks since 1900* (London: Thames & Hudson, 2009), p. 160.

40 David Kynaston, *Modernity Britain: Opening the Box, 1957–59* (London: Bloomsbury, 2013), p. 317.

41 Bridget Cherry, Charles O'Brien, and Nikolaus Pevsner, *The Buildings of England: London 5: East* (New Haven: Yale University Press, 2005), p. 356; Simon Jenkins, 'This Icon of 60s New Brutalism Has its Champions. So Let Them Restore It,' *Guardian*, 20 June 2008. https://www.theguardian.com/commentisfree/2008/jun/20/architecture. Date accessed: 26 April 2015.

42 For Upper Lawn Pavilion, see Bradbury, *The Iconic House*, pp. 160–3.

43 Warburton, *Ernö Goldfinger*, p. 157; Hanley, *Estates*, p. 112.

2

'Marks of weakness, marks of woe': the *Books of Blood* and the transformation of the weird

Kevin Corstorphine

One does not die in dreams. (Artaud)[1]

3 William Blake, 'The Ghost of a Flea', 1819–20.

Clive Barker's writing has been indelibly marked by Stephen King's enthusiastic endorsement calling him 'the future of horror'. While there is much in the various stories that comprise the *Books of Blood* to suggest this, it is a rather misleading term, and has been confounded repeatedly by his exploration of the fantastic and imaginative over a focus on the gory splatterpunk/body horror that made his reputation. This is a reputation also founded, of course, on the film *Hellraiser*, which cemented Barker in the public imagination as a purveyor of transgressive, sexually charged horror fiction. This perception, driven by market forces and fan culture, partly obscures the content of his early work, which is more varied and widely interesting than is often credited. This chapter will argue the importance of seeing *Books of Blood* in a broader context of horror and 'weird' fiction, and re-evaluate its meaning in the light of recent developments in fiction, with a focus on China Miéville's 2010 novel *Kraken*.

Barker's work is influenced as much by visual art as it is literature. In this context I would like to consider William Blake's painting *The Ghost of a Flea* (1819–20). Blake would meet with his friend, the occultist John Varley, to hold séances, where they would attempt to summon spirits which Blake would draw. Blake, of course, had visions of angels and ghosts throughout his life. On one such occasion in 1819 they were apparently visited by a spirit which Blake had encountered thirty years previously when it turned up in his house, making him run outside in terror. In this miniature the flea itself appears as a tiny creature on a stage, but it is dwarfed by another figure; Blake's personification of the flea as a bestial, even vampiric, humanoid. Blake is one of Barker's great influences, and the way in which Blake sees the world here in many ways prefigures Barker's own visionary consciousness. The figure treads the boards, theatrically, aware of its own sense of drama and threatening presence. This monster displays absolute evil and yet absolute humanity, and it works by tapping into what Freud would later call the uncanny. Echoes of this creature are seen throughout Barker's early work: Mahogany the Butcher, Rawhead Rex, the Candyman, and of course *Hellraiser*'s Cenobites. *The Ghost of a Flea* uses the horror mode more overtly than Blake's other work, but is no less visionary for its grotesque excess. The purpose of this chapter is more to trace a line of artistic purpose than to provide a taxonomic definition, but it will be useful to lay out the territory before proceeding to a closer analysis of the stories.

Roz Kaveney provides a useful distinction between what she describes as 'dark fantasy', aligned with Barker's later work, and horror:

> Part of the difference is that the central aim of horror is to create catharsis by confronting the reader with a world in which the worst thing happens to the characters with whom we identify, whereas the protagonist of dark fantasy comes through that jeopardy to a kind of chastened wisdom.[2]

This is a point of view corroborated by Barker himself, who in his 1998 introduction to *Books of Blood* reflects that in his more recent fiction he has 'felt an ever stronger need to explore images of redemption rather than damnation'.[3] Although more than a trace of the horror can be found in his later work, the *Books of Blood* stand as a period piece of a particular time in horror fiction, the largely defunct term 'splatterpunk' (not one embraced by Barker) encapsulating the transgressive excess that Paul M. Sammon has associated with the Reagan/Thatcher era; a transgression that can be read, as Gary Hoppenstand puts it, as, 'a fictive backlash against the 'vicious' conservative political state'.[4] Kaveney claims that the 'only conceivable response was a hedonism of damnation, a relishing of the exquisite pain of one's own destruction'.[5]

Barker's later move to the United States also means that they engage more closely with British culture and identity than subsequent fiction; something important to a consideration of their legacy within a literary tradition. There is an element of so called 'dark fantasy', then, yet the term is limiting, and no more useful than Barker's own repeated invocation of the more elegant terminology of the *fantastique*, deriving from the French tradition, and specifically the polymath Jean Cocteau, another of Barker's key influences.

This brings us to the term 'weird', which has recently come back into fashion, in defiance of Barker's comments that, 'the old definitions are laughably stale, as witness several recent essays on the so-called *weird tale*'.[6] There is perhaps an interesting ideological difference in this, as S.T. Joshi would later rubbish much of Barker's work, somewhat unfairly, in *The Modern Weird Tale*, where he claims that: 'He is in many ways a herald of the complete and possibly irremediable decadence of the field'.[7] Joshi justifies this mainly on the grounds of Barker's lack of explication of supernatural phenomena, something which Hoppenstand sees no problem with due to Barker's 'construction of the supernatural as metaphor and horror as literary subtext of the human condition'.[8] This contrasts with Hoppenstand's view of Stephen King, who he characterises as 'safe' due to his narrative technique and characterisation:

> When he should turn outward, addressing society as a critic, he regrettably only turns inward to the tormented soul, to the self-centered protagonist. King's characters are the troubled adolescent, the abused spouse, the self-doubting writer. Thus, when King introduces *the scare* to his story, the horror is safely contained within the character. King is a comfortable read.[9]

One major difference here is that Hoppenstand places the blame of this 'safe' or conservative mode of horror at the feet of H.P. Lovecraft, as the early twentieth century's most influential horror author and, through his 'Supernatural Horror in Literature' (1927), an important critic and constructor of a canon. Lovecraft himself uses the term 'weird' to denote, in typically overblown fashion, 'a malign and particular suspension of those fixed laws of Nature which are our only safeguard against the assaults of chaos and the daemons of unplumbed space'.[10] Here there is an echo of Thomas De Quincey's essay on *Macbeth*, where the knocking at the gate following Duncan's murder signifies the return to a 'natural' mode of being, as oppose to the quasi-dreamspace where regicide has

taken place against the laws of hospitality and loyalty to divine right. He says
that at this moment:

> Another world has stepped in; and the murderers are taken out of the region of
> human things, human purposes, human desires. They are transfigured […] the
> knocking at the gate is heard […] and the re-establishment of the goings-on of
> the world in which we live, first makes us profoundly sensible of the awful
> parenthesis that had suspended them.[11]

For De Quincey, the sublime terror produced by Shakespeare is in the suspension of the laws of nature within the space of fiction. Lovecraft's version of this
might seem dramatic, but it occurs within a work of literary criticism, and
literary techniques are his focus. A convicted rationalist, he actually buries
quite a subtle paradox within this statement. If the laws of nature are indeed
fixed, then they are surely adequate to safeguard against what is then logically
impossible. The trick of the weird tale turns out to be not so different from
other fiction; that is to enable the concept formulated by De Quincey's contemporary Coleridge to take place: the willing suspension of disbelief. It is the
purpose of doing so that is the politically charged issue at stake here.

Hoppenstand traces the legacy of King's conservatism to Lovecraft: 'his
work is ripe with paranoid reflections of ethnicity and social class; his horror
fiction often mirrors an inner dread of outer social forces'.[12] This is, of course,
going too far for King's own broadly liberal outlook, but is in complete opposition
to Barker's radical social politics. One story that exemplifies these politics, as
well as the essence of the weird, is 'The Body Politic', published in Volume 4
of the *Books of Blood*. This story is based around one instance of what Joshi
refers to as Barker's 'serious conceptual difficulties'.[13] The premise is simple,
absurd, yet compelling. The protagonist, Charlie George, becomes increasingly
troubled by a feeling of distance from his hands, which have become independent
of his mind, and plot to overthrow their host body. The right hand claims to
be the Messiah, and severs the left so that it can gather an army. In the end it
is Charlie who sacrifices himself for the sake of humanity, throwing himself,
and of course 'Right', from a rooftop with a Biblical flood of hands in hot
pursuit. The story, however, does not end with a closing of this particular
Pandora's Box. Having fractured the idea of the unity of the body, Barker
concludes with an open-ended questioning by another character, Boswell:

> And did his eyes envy their liberty, he wondered, and was his tongue eager to
> be out of his mouth and away, and was every part of him, in its subtle way, preparing
> to forsake him? He was an alliance held together by the most tenuous of truces.
> Now, with the precedent set, how long before the next uprising? Minutes? Years?
> He waited, heart in mouth, for the fall of Empire.[14]

This is extraordinary writing for what masquerades as a whimsical exercise
in the weird. It uses the body, and bodily horror, in order to question the unity
of the self, something that engages directly with late twentieth-century 'high'

literary debates and themes. In keeping with Hoppenstand's earlier point, its focus is also centrifugal, gesturing towards wider society with its invocation of 'Empire'. We might bear in mind that this story was published just after the Falklands War, itself an example of real-world bloody horror conducted in the name of imperial nationalism, defying Joshi's point that Barker's work is marred by 'excessive violence that serves no aesthetic purpose, and, in general, simply a lack of depth and substance'.[15] Joshi detects a lack of subtlety in Barker that prevents him from reaching the grandeur of the true weird tale, yet Barker's dismemberment and flayings belie the consistent artistic vision that runs through his work.

There is a real misunderstanding of Barker's gory excess as cheap sensationalism designed to increase a certain target market. Yet were this true, he would surely have continued to mine the vein of horror that others continue to do with endless sequels to the *Hellraiser* series, for example, while in fact Barker pursues his interests in fields as diverse as epic fantasy, children's literature, and painting. It can hardly be surprising that Barker consistently rejects such potentially valid terms as 'splatterpunk', designating a particular trend, when he is a resolutely unfashionable author in outlook, even when fashion happens to coincide with this vision. Although he acknowledges the literary Gothic (Poe perhaps foremost), Barker's background is grounded in the theatre, and again the influence of the French avant-garde shows itself in his love of the Parisian Grand Guignol of the early twentieth century. These interests, however, are linked, as Poe was a major influence on the Grand Guignol and his work was adapted for the stage on many occasions, having previously been translated and expounded by the likes of Baudelaire and Mallarmé. It is revealing that Barker includes a treatment of the Grand Guignol in *his A-Z of Horror* (series broadcast on BBC in 1997); and in the accompanying book, directed at a popular audience, he makes a case for the need of academic attention to horror, and to re-evaluate the terminology:

> Horror elicits far more complex responses than gasps and giddiness. It can shame us into recognizing our own capacity for cruelty; it can arouse us, making plain the connection between death and sexual feeling; it can inspire our imaginations, removing us to places where our most sacred taboos may be challenged and overturned.[16]

The legacy of the Grand Guignol can be seen here. Barker is making two points about horror. The first is that he sees it as artistically valid, by observing that an act of self-reflection takes place at the same time as the reader or viewer takes part, as opposed to being a passive spectator. Secondly, he associates horror with the transgressive, and indeed takes it almost for granted that challenging orthodox beliefs is a positive thing. His allegiance, then, is clearly to the avant-garde as much as the populist, an aspect of Barker that is at odds with the popular conception of his work, and indeed to the conception of horror fiction laid out by Stephen King, who says, 'when we discuss monstrosity, we are expressing our faith and belief in the norm and watching for the mutant. The writer of horror fiction is neither more nor less than an agent of the status quo.'[17] Barker addresses this same question of monstrosity by claiming that, 'the abomination [...] is a necessary part of the human story. It defines what the best in us despises, and reminds us how close we come to it in our forbidden thoughts.'[18] These views, though, are not as opposed as they might appear, as both authors place emphasis on the importance of confronting the unpleasant aspects of the human condition in a kind of therapeutic sense, as one might expect from writers immersed in a post-Freudian culture.

A perfect example of the monstrous abomination can be found in 'Rawhead Rex', from Volume 3 of *Books of Blood*. This comes perhaps closest in Barker's work to the kind of 'conservative' outlook favoured by Stephen King. The eponymous monster is the embodiment of evil, raping women and eating human flesh, with a particular fondness for babies. It is freed from its prison in the earth by an unwitting farmer, and wreaks havoc on the village of Zeal, 'forty miles south-east of London, amongst the orchards and hop-fields of the Kentish Weald.'[19] It is not an invading force, however, but rather its history has been intertwined with humans since time immemorial. Joshi dismisses the story due to its lack of believability. He criticises the 'half-baked anthropology'[20] on which the premise lies, as if providing scientific grounding is of primary importance to what is unashamedly a tale of the macabre. It is difficult to remove the suspicion that Joshi's objections are simply those of taste, based on Barker's lack of restraint and reliance on 'pure sensation'.[21] Some of this is, of course, valid, but it is interesting where this objection stems from. It marks a break in the 'weird' that will become important later in this discussion. 'Rawhead Rex' can be seen as precisely the kind of intervention into the laws of nature that Lovecraft found so compelling. The creature violently disrupts everyday life and causes the villagers to band together, very much like the characters that populate King's many fictional small towns in Maine. Declan Ewan, the church verger, becomes an acolyte of the creature, and is killed at its hands in an echo of Renfield in *Dracula* (1897). The message is similar to Stoker's novel: loyalty, community, and courage in the face of adversity are essential to the individual character, and indeed, to England.

Barker's true purpose in this, however, is to play around with psycho-sexual symbolism in a way that would make Lovecraft blush. Rawhead Rex is a rampaging figure of violent masculinity with its, 'shoulders twice as broad as a man's; lean, scarred arms stronger than any human'.[22] It fantasises over past rapes and styles itself as a King: 'This place was his. Just because they'd tamed the wilderness for a while didn't mean they owned the earth. It was his, and nobody could take it from him.'[23] Evil here is identified with patriarchal authority, which seeks no justification other than right asserted through raw power. The creature is a tyrant, and acts as a grotesque exaggeration of the worst of masculinity. This is borne out by its aversion to the feminine. It abhors menstruation: 'She had the blood-cycle on her, he could taste its tang, and it sickened him. It was taboo, that blood, and he had never taken a woman poisoned by its presence.'[24] It is eventually defeated by a stone statue of a pagan fertility goddess (albeit having its head smashed in by it); a statue that arouses men and draws them to its presence with phallus as divining rod. Rawhead Rex could even be read as a satire of contemporary schools of feminist thought (Andrea Dworkin's *Intercourse* would be published just after the story, in 1987) with one female victim wondering if the creature is just, 'some vile menstrual nightmare […] some rape-fantasy out of all control.'[25] The monster's masculinity is even undermined by a profusion of imagery of the feminine grotesque: 'He looked from eye to eye, and then down to the wet slits that were its nose, and finally, in childish terror, down to the mouth. God, that mouth. It was so wide, so cavernous, it seemed to split the head in two as it opened.'[26] With its teeth, 'two rows on each jaw, two dozen needle-sharp points,'[27] it is both phallus and *vagina dentata*, superego and id, and Barker is almost comically unrestrained in his use of imagery. Despite the excess, however, the target of his critique (misogyny and arbitrary power) appears to be sincere, although it would be a gross oversight not to acknowledge that this revels in the tongue-in-cheek humour appreciated by horror fans and so often missed by critics of the genre.

Barker's humour plays both to this audience and yet has a certain streak of surrealism running through it, derived perhaps from his background in theatre. Antonin Artaud's concept of the 'theatre of cruelty' may have encompassed more than the kind of bodily excess that Barker writes about, yet there is something very evocative in his call for a return to the epic and mythic in theatre, which can involve grotesque spectacle, 'fiery, magnetic imagery,'[28] as part of its artistic intentions:

> In the same way as our dreams react on us and reality reacts on our dreams, so we believe ourselves able to associate mental pictures with dreams, effective in so far as they are projected with the required violence. And the audience will believe in the illusion of theatre on condition they really take it for a dream, nor for a servile imitation of reality. On condition it releases the magic freedom of daydreams, only recognisable when imprinted with terror and cruelty.[29]

Artaud's conception of a new theatre harks back to the willing suspension of disbelief, but appeals to the concept of a dream space in which this occurs. Applying this idea to short stories, there is something reminiscent of Poe's ideas in 'The Philosophy of Composition' (referring to his long poem 'The Raven'), where he places emphasis on 'unity of impression'[30] derived from reading in one sitting, to avoid the break when, 'the affairs of the world interfere.'[31] The terror and cruelty of the *Books of Blood*, then, can be seen as a means to break through the mundane and the everyday to access the freedom of dreaming.

This is artistic and experimental writing wearing the skin of genre fiction. It is this break with reality that has directed much of Barker's later fiction and has put him in the position of influencing the so-called 'New Weird'.

Jeff Vandermeer, in his introduction to the 2008 anthology *The New Weird*, which includes 'In the Hills, the Cities', from Volume 1 of the *Books of Blood*, attempts to define the term. Vandermeer himself is sceptical of its status as a 'movement', yet his working definitions remain useful:

> New Weird is a type of urban, secondary-world fiction that subverts the roman-ticized ideas about place found in traditional fantasy […] New Weird has a visceral, in-the-moment quality that often uses elements of surreal or transgressive horror […] New Weird fictions are acutely aware of the modern world, even if in disguise, but not always overtly political […] New Weird relies for its visionary power on a 'surrender to the weird' that isn't for example, hermetically sealed in a haunted house on the moors or in a cave in Antarctica.[32]

This is all largely descriptive and quite broad, but serves the anthologist's purpose in bringing together an interesting collection of stories. The most perceptive of these definitions, though, is the idea of the 'surrender to the weird'. Lovecraft's fiction, for example, fits this model, with the horrors limited to small towns ('The Shadow over Innsmouth'), strange houses ('The Dreams in the Witch House'), or indeed in an Antarctic cave as alluded to by Vandermeer (*At the Mountains of Madness*). Barker's 'surrender to the weird' can explain where it breaks from the classic weird, and also Joshi's objections to his style. Hop-penstand, who surrenders critically to this strand of the weird, identifies it in 'The Body Politic', where the swarm of hands breaks free of any possibility of narrative denial:

> Underpinning the tremendous physical and emotional horror of the story is a sense of wonder. In addition to being a terrifying spectacle, the army of amputated – and subsequently liberated – hands is also a miraculous vision, something unique and bizarre, something beyond the commonplace drudgery of everyday life.[33]

Like Blake's *Ghost of a Flea*, Barker's use of horror is a starting point for an imaginative journey. Vandermeer too sees this as a strength and claims that, 'in many of Barker's best tales, the starting point is the acceptance of a monster or a transformation and the story is what comes after'.[34] This sympathy for the monster, and a sense that the horrific is not only acceptable, but somehow longed for, is a key component of the *Books of Blood*. Horror and pain are transformed through fiction into something transcendent. This is exemplified in perhaps the most overtly 'urban' story, 'The Forbidden'.

Published in Volume 5, and subsequently forming the basis of the film *Candyman* (1992), 'The Forbidden' is widely considered to be set in Barker's native Liverpool, and does not flinch from depicting the grimy reality of the contemporary world. The protagonist, Helen Buchanan, is a student working on a PhD thesis entitled 'Graffiti: The Semiotics of Urban Despair'.[35] She becomes obsessed with the dilapidated Spector Street Estate and in particular the urban legends that circulate about a figure called the Candyman, whose slogan of 'sweets to the sweet' (she can't recall the source: the hysterical and lovesick Ophelia in Shakespeare's *Hamlet*) is sprayed in a boarded-up maisonette beside a mural of a grinning head, to which the bedroom door serves as the mouth:

> Much of its power lay in its context, of course. That such an image might be stumbled upon in surroundings so drab, so conspicuously lacking in mystery, was akin to finding an icon on a rubbish-heap: a gleaming symbol of transcendence from a world of toil and decay into some darker but more tremendous realm.[36]

This might read as a manifesto for Barker's writing. 'The Forbidden' takes a joy in the supernatural and a scathing attitude towards the depravity of everyday life. A child is murdered, her throat slit, and the community offer the corpse up on a bonfire for the Candyman. It is tempting to read the figure of the Candyman as fictional even within the narrative, in which case they themselves have killed the child out of superstition and ignorance, and Helen has been driven into delusion by becoming too obsessed with the story, as with Jane Austen's parodic *Northanger Abbey*, where Catherine Morland is overtaken by the fantasies she projects from reading gothic novels. The Candyman, like Rawhead Rex, is portrayed as a kind of rapist bogeyman, albeit more sophisticated in his approach. He is the grooming child molester feared by every community, but exaggerated into a grotesque fantasy, with yellow skin, blue lips, and gleaming ruby eyes. He is very much a product of the deprived/depraved community that worships him. He is specifically composed of the daily atrocity peddled by tabloid newspapers. Helen muses that:

> People were facile. They needed these shows and shams to keep their interest. Miracles; murders; demons driven out and stones rolled from tombs. The cheap glamour did not taint the sense beneath. It was only, in the natural history of the mind, the bright feathers that drew the species to mate with its secret self.[37]

We should not, perhaps, confuse this contempt with the overall narrative voice, given that Helen is portrayed as somewhat ludicrous in her middle-class intrusion into a community she does not begin to understand. It does, however, evoke Artaud's theatre of cruelty once again. He complains that the public have turned away from theatre, 'to the cinema, music-hall and circus to find violent gratification whose intention does not disappoint them'.[38] He points out that, 'the masses today are thirsting for mystery',[39] which is very much the case in this story. 'It is useless', he claims, 'to accuse the public's bad taste while it slakes its thirst with inanities, as long as we have not given the public a worth-while show'.[40] Helen finds comfort in the Candyman, and an escape from the world. She is seduced by him, and yet this is undercut by disruptive feminine imagery. At first she walks out of the mouth without realising it is behind her, a kind of birth into a new world. Eventually she crawls into the bonfire, which acts as a womb-space, both comfort and death. Her sense of self is annihilated and absorbed into storytelling. Her final thought is a desire to be seen by her husband, not to be saved, but so that he would have, 'something to be haunted by. That, and a story to tell.'[41] She continues the mythology she had intended to study, stepping into the narrative hinted at by the Candyman: 'You weren't content with the stories', he says, 'with what they wrote on the walls. So I was obliged to come.'[42]

There is a sense here that writing is powerful, that it can imagine worlds into being. This is echoed in the framing tale 'The Book of Blood'. Simon McNeal makes the mistake of faking his powers as a medium, leading the dead to actually come for him to tell their stories, carving their words into his very flesh. The Book of Blood is a human being, and the dead tell their stories to relieve themselves of the tale, a very Romantic conceit derived from Coleridge's 'Rime of the Ancient Mariner'. Only death is final, fixed. The last line in 'The Book of Blood (a postcript): On Jerusalem Street', and indeed the entirety of the *Books of Blood*, is that, 'only the living are lost'. In death our stories, however bizarre or grotesque, are set in stone whereas in life we are forever becoming. This is played out in Volume 2's 'Jacqueline Ess: Her Will and Testament', where even the flesh is malleable, transformed at will by a woman who has discovered hidden depths of power at her lowest ebb, through an attempted suicide. Jacqueline discovers that she can twist and mould flesh with her mind, and uses this to destroy a patronising doctor and then her adulterous husband, by folding and crushing the physical substance of their bodies. There is something of Plath's 'Lady Lazarus' here in her devouring grandeur, and she becomes irresistible to men, including one powerful billionaire who actively seeks the horrific death she provides. Determined not to serve men, she twists him into a grotesque beast:

> She had killed his nerves: he felt no pain. He just survived, his hands knotted into paws, his legs scooped up around his back, knees broken so he had the look of a four-legged crab, his brain exposed, his eyes lidless, lower jaw broken and swept up over his top jaw like a bulldog, ears torn off, spine snapped, humanity bewitched into another state.[43]

The human body is taken apart and reshaped into something of a different order. Through Jacqueline Ess, the reader is invited to contemplate the human form in a visceral and direct fashion, reflecting back on what the essence of humanity might be, if the flesh, as well as identity, is something potentially fluid and shifting. Indeed, age and disease perform this function continually, if not in such an exaggerated fashion, and Barker repeatedly returns to the idea of these real-life horrors as something to be explored and dissected, as if trying to make sense of them. This can be seen in 'Son of Celluloid' from Volume 3, where a mortally wounded criminal crawls into a movie theatre and the malignant tumour in his stomach causes the films to become reality. The cancer takes on a consciousness of its own: 'It was a filthy thing, a tumour grown fat on wasted passion.'[44] The bodily collides with the narrative, as Hollywood's glamorous fictions are brought to life by this 'dreaming disease'.[45]

Vandermeer claims that in Barker's work, 'body transformations and dislocations create a visceral, contemporary take on the kind of visionary horror best exemplified by the work of Lovecraft'.[46] This sense of vision is what informs the 'New Weird' writers such as China Miéville, an admirer of Barker. His 2010 novel *Kraken* bears interesting comparison to Barker, in not just its themes but its unashamed surrender to the weird. *Kraken* follows Billy Harrow, a curator at the Natural History Museum in London who is on duty when the prized giant squid exhibit is stolen. Billy is drawn into a world of squid worshipping cultists (teuthists), who do battle with Londonmancers (wizards who can shape the city to their will) and various enemies including the Tattoo, who is a living face tattooed into the back of a living man, and Grisamentum, who has turned himself into ink, hoping to merge with the ink in the giant squid and become a god. The squid, as Miéville toys with, has been associated with the mythic harking back to Tennyson's poem 'The Kraken', Jules Verne's *Twenty Thousand Leagues Under the Sea*, and Lovecraft's Cthulhu Mythos. Attempted thefts of the squid have been deadly, however, as it is guarded by a creature called the angel of memory, or mnemophylax:

> Each museum of London constituted out of its material its own angel, a numen of its recall, mnemophylax. They were not beings, precisely, not from where most Londoners stood, but derived functions that thought themselves beings. In a city where the power of any item derived from its metaphoric potency, all the attention poured into their contents made museums rich pickings for knacking thieves. But the processes that gave them that potential also threw up sentinels […] In the Museum of Childhood were three toys that came remorselessly for intruders – a hoop, a top, a broken video-game console – with stuttering creeping as if in stop motion […] And in the Natural History Museum, the stored-up pickled lineage of the evolved was watched by something described as of, but not reducible to, glass and liquid.[47]

The memory angel, a monstrous creature made of the imaginative 'stuff' of accumulated imagination, is reminiscent of Blake's Flea, and indeed of Barker's Candyman, who is brought into being by the fears and desires of the people living on the Spector Street Estate. Like the hands of 'The Body Politic' these entities are 'derived functions that thought themselves beings'.[48] The idea is clearly ludicrous, but evocative in its imaginative power. They are given life by the impressions and feelings of visitors to the museums. In fact the very exhibits hold a fetishistic power and are thus targets for would-be magicians. Again, the mundane is transformed by the imagination into something powerful by virtue of 'metaphoric potency'.[49] Miéville, like Barker, is very much concerned with the power of narrative, whether in written fiction or the fictions we weave around our own lives. There is an element of Lewis Carroll's *Alice's Adventures in*

Wonderland (1865) in both the plot device of discovering a hidden world adjacent to the everyday, and with its free play of absurd imagery. Miéville, however, notably avoids positing these shadowy worlds as separate from contemporary London, but emphasises the modern, urban elements, which of course involves this complete surrender to, or acceptance of, the weird as narrative fact and not dismissible as a dream or alternative dimension. This is in keeping with Michael Moorcock's views set out in his essay 'Epic Pooh'. Here, Moorcock attacks the popularity of Tolkien, and accuses him and fellow writers such as C.S. Lewis of promoting an overly sentimental view of pastoral England:

> While there is an argument for the reactionary nature of the books, they are certainly deeply conservative and strongly anti-urban, which is what leads some to associate them with a kind of Wagnerish hitlerism [sic]. I don't think these books are 'fascist', but they certainly don't exactly argue with the 18th century enlightened Toryism with which the English comfort themselves so frequently in these upsetting times. They don't ask any questions of white men in grey clothing who somehow have a handle on what's best for us.[50]

In contrast, Miéville's writing is left-leaning, and radical in tone. He describes himself as a 'revolutionary socialist'[51] and points out his admiration for the surrealists, who he says, 'examine questions of power and oppression in the very *form* of their work'.[52] Rather than make a claim for high art, however, Miéville claims allegiance to the form of pulp writing, which he sees as compatible with his Marxist ambitions. This embracing of popular culture, *contra* Adorno, can also be seen in Barker's unashamed use of 'exploitation' fiction to convey some quite complex messages about politics and about literature.

Many of the stories in *Books of Blood* are influenced by film and theatre, but the most obviously self-reflexive literary story is in Volume 2's 'New Murders in the Rue Morgue', a homage to Poe. Barker identifies Poe as the progenitor of the school of transgressive fiction that he revels in: 'After Poe, the thrust of *fantastique* fiction would never for me be a matter of conventional folks setting their Christian values against some fretful, haunted darkness, but a celebration, however perverse, of that darkness.'[53] This unofficial sequel to Poe's tale of an escaped killer Orangutan playfully toys with ideas of fiction and reality from the beginning. The conceit is that the protagonist, Lewis Fox, is a great nephew of Poe's Detective C. Auguste Dupin. In the world of the story, Dupin was real, and his stories passed on by his brother in a drunken night in Richmond, Virginia, to a young Edgar Allan Poe. Lewis has become an old man, and cannot remember whether the Rue Morgue was invented or has since been destroyed, yet he decides that, 'the distinction was academic. What did it matter what was true and what invented? In his head all of it, the half-lies and the truths, were one continuum of personal history.'[54] He has come to Paris to help a former lover, Catherine, whose brother Phillipe has been accused of brutally murdering a young woman. It transpires that the real killer, as in Poe's original, is an ape, but this one is a gorilla that Philippe has taught to act like a human. It wears clothes and shaves its face in an attempt to deny its true lineage. The ape's other efforts betray a hint of ambiguous sexuality, as it, or perhaps rather he, leaves an overpowering smell of perfume wherever he goes, and 'his gait was mincing'.[55] For Lewis, fiction and reality collide in the awful revelation of monstrosity, and he commits suicide by jumping into the freezing Seine. Characteristically for Barker, though, the horror is not contained. The ape is not destroyed, but lives to continue its efforts to live as a man, seemingly starting a new life with a prostitute who accepts him in return for a supply of drugs:

> In mid-morning, a young woman with red hair, her arm linked into that of a large ugly man, took a leisurely stroll to the steps of the Sacre Coeur. The sun blessed them. Bells rang.
>   It was a new day.[56]

This brave new world is one where a gorilla can become a human by acting as one. The Parisian setting is an appropriate one to this kind of existentialist thinking. Barker takes a radically open view throughout his work of human (and apparently gorilla) freedom. The true enemy is not the monster, but the forces of conformity that threaten the will of the individual. Although Lewis appears to be the hero of this story, his time has come to an end and he is destroyed only through his inability to adapt to the new paradigm he sees before him. This critique of the ways in which convention shackles the human spirit is as important to Barker as it was to Blake.

The title of this chapter refers to Blake's 'London', the first two stanzas of which are worth quoting from here:

> I wander thro' each charter'd street.
> Near where the charter'd Thames does flow
> And mark in every face I meet
> Marks of weakness, marks of woe
>
> In every cry of every Man.
> In every Infant's cry of fear.
> In every voice; in every ban.
> The mind-forg'd manacles I hear[57]

Clive Barker's *Books of Blood* do not shy away from dwelling on the weakness and suffering of the human condition; in fact they revel in it. There is a sense here of looking atrocity in the eye and not flinching, of a deep responsibility to tell stories. There is also an attack on conventional ways of thinking that keep people in their place: an attempt to shatter the 'mind-forged manacles.' To return to *The Ghost of a Flea* we can see how here, as in Barker, the everyday is transformed into the monstrous, but the monstrous is again transformed into something unexpected. There is always movement, and always flow. For Barker the human subject is always becoming something new, shedding skin if needs be. The *Books of Blood* are often filled with despair, but there is hope:

a faith that scarred and marked though we may be, we can always add to the story, even if it means etching new chapters onto flesh. The power of writing, and of the imagination most importantly, is to awaken us to these possibilities.

Notes

1 Antonin Artaud, 'Theatre and the Plague', *The Theatre and its Double*. Trans. Victor Corti (Montreuil, London and New York: Calder, 1993), p. 7.
2 Roz Kaveney, 'Dark Fantasy and Paranormal Romance', in Edward James and Farah Mendlesohn (eds), *The Cambridge Companion to Fantasy Literature* (Cambridge: Cambridge University Press, 2012), p. 217.
3 Clive Barker, Introduction to *Books of Blood*, Volumes 1–3 (London: Sphere, 1998), p. x.
4 Gary Hoppenstand, *Clive Barker's Short Stories: Imagination as Metaphor in the* Books of Blood *and Other Works* (Jefferson, NC and London: McFarland, 1994), p. 14.
5 Kaveney, *The Cambridge Companion to Fantasy Literature*, p. 217.
6 Clive Barker, Foreword to Hoppenstand, *Clive Barker's Short Stories*, p. 2.
7 S.T. Joshi, *The Modern Weird Tale* (Jefferson, NC and London: McFarland, 1994), p. 116.
8 Hoppenstand, *Clive Barker's Short Stories*, p. 44.
9 *Ibid.* pp. 12–13.
10 H.P. Lovecraft, 'Supernatural Horror in Literature', in Stephen Jones (ed.), *H.P. Lovecraft, Tales: A Miscellany of the Macabre* (London: Gollancz, 2011), p. 426.
11 Thomas de Quincey, 'On the Knocking at the Gate in *Macbeth*', in Robert Morrison (ed.), *On Murder* (Oxford: Oxford University Press, 2006), pp. 6–7.
12 Hoppenstand, *Clive Barker's Short Stories*, p. 16.
13 Joshi, *The Modern Weird Tale*, p. 117.
14 Clive Barker, 'The Body Politic', *Books of Blood*, Volumes 4–6 (Volume 4) (London: Sphere, 2011), p. 33.
15 Joshi, *The Modern Weird Tale*, p. 132.
16 Clive Barker, Introduction to Clive Barker and Stephen Jones, *Clive Barker's A-Z of Horror* (London: BBC Books, 1997), p. 16.
17 Stephen King, *Danse Macabre* (London: Warner, 1993), pp. 55–6.
18 *Clive Barker's A-Z of Horror*, p. 20.
19 Barker, 'Rawhead Rex', *Books of Blood*, Volumes 1–3 (Volume 3), p. 36.
20 Joshi, *The Modern Weird Tale*, p. 118.
21 *Ibid.* p. 116.
22 Barker, *Books of Blood*, Volume 3, p. 43.
23 *Ibid.* p. 45.
24 *Ibid.*
25 *Ibid.* p. 50.
26 *Ibid.* p. 42.
27 *Ibid.* p. 45.

28 Artaud, 'Theatre and Cruelty,' *The Theatre and its Double*, p. 64.

29 Artaud, *The Theatre and its Double*, p. 65.

30 Edgar Allan Poe, 'The Philosophy of Composition,' *'The Raven' and the Philosophy of Composition* (San Francisco and New York: Paul Elder & Company, 1907), p. 4. Archive.org. https://archive.org/details/ravenandphilosop00poeerich. Date accessed: 27 July 2012.

31 Poe, *'The Raven' and the Philosophy of Composition*, p. 4.

32 Jeff Vandermeer, 'Introduction,' in Ann Vandermeer and Jeff Vandermeer (eds), *The New Weird* (Tachyon: San Francisco, 2008), p. xvi.

33 Hoppenstand, *Clive Barker's Short Stories*, p. 106.

34 Vandermeer, *The New Weird*, p. x.

35 Barker, 'The Forbidden,' *Books of Blood*, Volumes 4–6 (Volume 5), pp. 1–37 (2).

36 Barker, *Books of Blood*, Volume 5, p. 12.

37 *Ibid*. p. 32.

38 Artaud, *The Theatre and its Double*, p. 64.

39 Artaud, 'No More Masterpieces,' in Artaud, *The Theatre and its Double*, p. 56.

40 Artaud, *The Theatre and its Double*, p. 57.

41 Barker, *Books of Blood*, Volume 5, p. 37.

42 *Ibid*. p. 31.

43 Barker, 'Jacqueline Ess: Her Will and Testament,' *Books of Blood*, Volumes 1–3 (Volume 2), p. 83.

44 Barker, 'Son of Celluloid,' *Books of Blood*, Volumes 1–3 (Volume 3), p. 32.

45 *Ibid*. p. 32.

46 Joshi, *The New Weird*, p. x.

47 China Miéville, *Kraken* (London: Macmillan, 2010), p. 178.

48 *Ibid*.

49 *Ibid*.

50 Michael Moorcock. 'Epic Pooh,' Revised edition. *Revolution Science Fiction*. www.revolutionsf.com/article.php?id=953. Date accessed: 30 July 2012.

51 China Miéville and Joan Gordon, 'An Interview with China Miéville,' *Science Fiction Studies*. Vol. 30 (2003), p. 360.

52 *Ibid*. p. 365.

53 Clive Barker, 'Edgar Allan Poe.' *Independent* magazine. 30 November 1991. *Revelations: The Official Clive Barker Website*. www.clivebarker.info/essaysb.html. Date accessed: 30 July 2012.

54 Clive Barker, 'New Murders in the Rue Morgue,' *Books of Blood*, Volumes 1–3 (Volume 2), p. 123.

55 Barker, *Books of Blood*, Volume 2, p. 136.

56 *Ibid*. p. 150.

57 William Blake, 'London,' in David Bindman (ed.), *William Blake: The Complete Illuminated Books* (London: Thames & Hudson, 2001), p. 410.

3

When fantasy becomes reality: social commentary of 1980s Britain in Clive Barker's *Weaveworld*

Edward Timothy Wallington

When Clive Barker's *Weaveworld* was first published in 1987, it was quite understandably consigned to the genre of fantasy/horror, and the book is undoubtedly a remarkable and thrilling example. However, when read from a different perspective, the tale transcends the immediate limitations of its genre to provide a thought-provoking and evocative reflection on the times in which it was written. These were the 1980s, and the decade was marked by a number of dramatic and unprecedented events: Margaret Thatcher was at the helm of the British government with her monetarist fiscal policies, austerity measures, and the call for a return to core values; sexual equality had gained considerable ground from the tentative gains made in the 1960s and 1970s; and the country found itself under siege from a terrifying and seemingly invincible disease in the form of AIDS, which randomly decimated people from all sections of the population. A close reading of the story shows how these elements are woven into its fabric, and that various features of Thatcherism find expression in its characters.

The era of the Iron Lady, Margaret Thatcher, began in the late 1970s, and as the first female prime minister of Britain, she held office for an unprecedented three uninterrupted terms from 1979 to 1990. Her political and fiscal policies caused such a commotion that she joined the hallowed ranks of those in history whose names have been honoured with their very own -isms. In this case, the country was honoured with a liberal dose of Thatcherism. How then did Thatcherism cause such a seismic shift in British life?

Historian David Marquand suggests that Thatcher's economic policy was the principal agent of change.[1] Struggling with a weak economy, the nation and its services were under severe strain for adequate funding by the 1970s. After the so-called winter of discontent,[2] many sections of the nation seemed weary of industrial action and welcomed Thatcher's unsentimental and pragmatic approach, which shifted the emphasis firmly into the hands of market forces and placed the nation in accordance with economic principles more closely associated with North America than Europe. Perhaps a unique twist of Thatcherism was the way in which economic responsibility embraced a brand of moral rectitude described by Marquand as 'vigorous virtues'. The holders of this faith were 'upright, self-sufficient, energetic, adventurous, independent-minded, loyal to friends and robust against enemies'.[3] Thatcher was on a crusade to re-educate the nation in accordance with so-called timeless Victorian values and to wean it from the nanny state that had emasculated its people.

So it was that services were cut, while government assets were sold and privatised, including telephone services, British Gas, British Aerospace, and Britoil. Education was not exempt, and, according to Shirley Letwin, the new regime 'treated individuals not as independent, self-sufficient agents … but as instruments of production'.[4] Thatcher biographer Peter Riddell adds that in the employment field, 'women and ethnic minorities … suffered particularly',[5] an observation reinforced by Peter Leese.[6] Industrial action was crushed to ensure maximum rationalisation and profitability, while methods for dealing with illegal or obstructionist picketing became swift and efficient: 'The police were far better organized than ever before, with the National Reporting Centre to coordinate police movements and intelligence and a high degree of latitude given to the police in the handling of pickets, however violent the methods used', according to Morgan.[7]

The confrontational attitude expressed in this approach may have been partly responsible for the intense hatred directed at Thatcher from various sections of the country. Doctor and impresario Jonathan Miller found her 'loathsome, repulsive in almost every way', and was revolted by 'her odious sub-saccharine patriotism, catering to the worst elements of commuter idiocy', as suggested by Hughes.[8] The popular conception of the Thatcher years was perhaps most perfectly enshrined in Employment Secretary Norman Tebbit's immortal phrase 'On yer bike!' which has, of course, since joined 'Let them eat cake' as an eternal symbolic raspberry blown at a nation's poor by a sneering and heartless ruling class. The sobering message was, according to Letwin, 'that people living in cardboard boxes might be at least in part responsible for their plight'.[9] Leese concludes that Britain in the 1980s is encapsulated in Peter Greenaway's 1989 film *The Cook, the Thief, His Wife & Her Lover*, in which a restaurant owned by a London East-end gang leader becomes the microcosm for a society that has lost its way.[10] The film was one of many examples of art responding to the new society that had crystallised in the 1980s. Clive Barker's *Weaveworld* was another such; in our tale of Cal and Suzanna's mission to save the magical Fugue and its people, there is an imaginative reworking of the new order that prevails.

Broadly speaking, the villains of *Weaveworld* are notable for their Thatcherite traits. Shadwell, for example, is in many ways a socialist's worst nightmare – He is a master of sales, a profession oft characterised by unscrupulous, indiscriminate, and manipulative techniques to create a perpetual need for intrinsically worthless

consumer items. In casting Shadwell in this role, Barker creates a grim personification of the inhumanity and emptiness generated by a slavish devotion
to material gain and the profit principle, one in which the strong prevail and
the weak are abused or discarded. Many readers in the 1980s were vocal in
their condemnation of a regime that subordinated human need to profitability,
a regime in which schools, universities and hospitals became forced to view
their students or patients as clients and to work out business plans to secure
the highest returns. For a section of the population that lamented the passing
of more humanitarian principles, Shadwell's villainous role as a nightmarish
door-to-door salesman seems particularly fitting and poignant.

The capitalistic profit principle is further vilified in the methods that Shadwell
employs. Through his association with the Seerkind Immacolata, he becomes
the owner of a jacket whose inner lining can present a prospective victim
with a magical image of their heart's desire and then deliver an illusion of it
in the material world. The image can be seen as a chilling indictment of the
unregulated free market, where the consumer is encouraged to see consumer
items as panaceas for deep-rooted psychological needs or torments. Cal's first
exposure to the jacket captures some sense of the villainy attached to such
materialism:

> This time he [Shadwell] fully opened the jacket, exposing the lining. And yes,
> Cal's first judgement had been correct. It *did* shine.
>
> 'I am, as I said, a salesman,' Shadwell was explaining. 'I make it a Golden
> Rule always to carry some samples of my merchandise around with me.'
>
> Merchandise. Cal shaped the word in his head. What a word that was:
> *merchandise*. [...] Jewellery, was it that gleamed there? Artificial gems with a
> sheen that blinded the way only a fake could. He squinted into the glamour,
> looking to make sense out of what he saw, while the salesman's voice went about
> its persuasions.[11]

Immacolata's desire to enslave the Seerkind does not share Shadwell's pursuit
of self-aggrandisement; however, we learn that she was originally inspired by
such an instinct, and the description we have of her formative years suggests
the kinds of demonising in which haters of Margaret Thatcher might indulge:
'her history became a round of blood-lettings, pursuits and further blood-lettings.
Though she was still known and worshipped by a cognoscenti, who called her
by a dozen different names – the Black Madonna, the Lady of Sorrows, Mater
Maleficorium – she became nevertheless a victim of her own strange purity
[Immacolata cannot stand to be touched, much less to have sex]. Madness
beckoned.'[12] The blood-lettings can be read as Thatcher's perceived assaults on
the unemployed, teachers, nurses, miners, and non-profit-makers in general.
Like Immacolata, Thatcher was worshipped by devoted followers who called
her The Iron Lady. She also partly mirrored Immacolata's loathing of sexual
contact through her association with Victorian sexual puritanism, which forbade

extramarital and recreational sex, whether in the flesh or in the media. If we then compound these parallels with the fanatical madness that opponents of both Immocalata and Mrs Thatcher imputed to them, it could be argued that this description of Immacolata presents a stylised description of Mrs Thatcher. Even the villain's witch status is chillingly reminiscent of a comment made about Mrs Thatcher by political writer Shirley Robin Letwin: 'The Times column-ist, Ronald Butt, who had earlier been an enthusiastic supporter, said that Thatcherism had become associated with witchcraft.'[13]

The desire for vengeance can be added to these bleak associations with Tory leadership in the 1980s. Kenneth Morgan considered that the intensity of the prime minister's mission was such that she 'appeared to see herself as the embodiment of revenge upon a whole generation of social engineers', and that, 'she committed to the view that "there was no such thing as society", only individuals and families.'[14] The Seerkind are very much a society, made up, in fact, of four family groups that co-exist harmoniously. Immacolata's, and later the Scourge's, intended revenge on them can thus be seen as a metaphor for the kind of pogrom that Thatcher declared against liberal town councils such as Liverpool and London, eventually to have them disbanded altogether.[15]

The fourth villain, Hobart, is a classic Thatcher goblin. A policeman provides the perfect partner in crime to a salesman in a novel written during the Thatcher years when many had come to see the police force as the strong right arm of the prime minister, the one she used to suppress miners, teachers, nurses, and minorities. Hobart enters the story with a reputation for using law-enforcement to suppress otherness, and we soon see him flexing his muscles in the inter-rogation rooms of the police station with Suzanna and Jerichau. In his assault upon a woman and a black man, both stereotypical victims of police in the Thatcher years, and in his blind missionary zeal to remove dissident elements from society, Hobart steps into a caricatured role as the patriarchal racist police bully with a dash of fascistic dementia, the type that many associated with Mrs Thatcher's regime. Shadwell is quick to see the policeman's true nature: 'The inspector was probably insane, but that was all to the good. And he had one particular aspiration which Shadwell knew he might one day need to turn to his own ends. That was, to lead – as Hobart put it – a righteous crusade.'[16] Like a masculine version of Mrs Thatcher, Hobart is on a mission to save the country from moral and social decline. Moreover, Hobart's underlings, the other police officers, are depicted as witless buffoons unable to exercise moral judgement or think for themselves. Those who remember the series *Spitting Image* might recall the scene in which Mrs Thatcher is seated at the head of the table in a restaurant with members of her cabinet. After ordering raw meat for herself, the waiter asks 'and what about the vegetables?' 'They'll have the same!'[17] is Thatcher's dismissive reply. When confronted by magic from the Fugue, Hobart instructs his moronic underlings to deny their senses and perceptions and see only what he, their leader, sees. Their response is unquestioning obedience.

Conversely, Cal, Suzanna, and the Seerkind collectively represent the forces for good in the novel, and, significantly, they oppose the vigorous virtues championed by Mrs Thatcher. Cal is a lowly and unenthusiastic clerk for a city insurance firm; in fact, his disaffection is such that when experiencing upsets in his life, he thinks nothing of taking days off at his employer's expense. In contrast to the Thatcherite yuppie, he represents the withdrawn imaginative type who displays an unhealthy disregard for materialistic gain and professional advancement. In a brave new acquisitive world, Cal is a complex and introverted loner and outsider. Suzanna is similarly unconventional. Not only a professional sculptor, she is also the owner of a magical force called the Menstruum that, aside from its nominal association with female menstruation, can disable foes possessed of much greater physical strength. Later she begins an interracial affair with a black Seerkind man, a multicultural gesture signalling her opposition to the Thatcher mindset. Therefore, she is similar to Cal in that she possesses qualities that mark her as a deviant within the puritanical meritocracy of the 1980s.

As outsiders, however, the Seerkind represent some of the novel's most extreme examples. They are hedonistic, unfocused, strangely gifted and beyond any reasonable definition of a practical and materialistically oriented society. Not only are they nonconformist in appearance, but also displaced in time, with characters hailing from various moments in history. Apart from a brief section describing the death of Suzanna's Aunt Mimi, the guardian of the carpet and the Fugue, our first meaningful encounter with them takes place after Cal and Suzanna have had an early confrontation with Shadwell and Immacolata. Lying platonically in bed together, Cal and Suzanna are visited by five Seerkind who come to physical life from a fragment of carpet that the couple has left in the bedroom. Their names are exotic and bohemian: Lilia Pelicia, Frederick Cammell, Apolline Dubois, Jerichau St Louis, and Nimrod. Frederick turns out to be a portly but dapper rogue in his fifties, Apolline Dubois is a hooker, and Nimrod a lascivious man trapped in a baby's body, ever ready for a welcoming female bosom in which to bury his face. All are capable of working magical charms.

The Seerkind lifestyle, once it unfolds before Cal on his travels within the Fugue, also proves to be distinctly other in regard to the principles of Thatcher's regime. We saw that Mrs Thatcher had little regard for society, preferring instead the notion of a country founded upon individuals and families. The Seerkind, in contrast, are communal people, given to parties and gatherings in which they perform art, acrobatics, and storytelling for each other, with no other goal than bonding, inspiration, and delight. When they cajole the atrociously shy Cal into performing for them, all he can think to do is recite a poem written by his wild grandfather Mad Mooney. Instead of sneering at this contribution, however, they love his poem, and Cal begins to experience the joy of exuberance, openness, and company. For sheer recreation, the Seerkind also devour large quantities of a delicacy called giddy fruit, which is basically delicious juicy dope that grows on trees. In the eyes of responsible, progress-oriented, stoical conservatives they would be considered disreputable, scruffy, eccentric, and uncoordinated. Furthermore, they display a sublime indifference to time, efficiency, production, or Mrs Thatcher's vigorous virtues.

Their land, the Fugue, also provides an interesting symbolic contrast to the principles of Thatcherism. When Cal first arrives, he describes what he sees:

> Last time he'd set eyes on this place it had been from a bird's eye view [when he fell from the ledge at Mimi's house], and the landscape had seemed various enough. But from the human perspective its profusion verged on the riotous. It was as if a vast suitcase, packed in great haste, had been upturned, its contents scattered in hopeless disarray. [...]
>
> Amid this disorder, the most curious juxtapositions abounded. Here a bridge, parted from the chasm it had crossed, sat in a field spanning poppies; there an obelisk stood in the middle of a pool, gazing at its reflection.[18]

Although the landscape is described here as having been virtually packed when the Seerkind were under attack from the Scourge in the previous century, the strange, incongruous bundling together of beautiful scenes and objects seems indicative of the way the Seerkind conduct their lives and the ways they find of getting along with their neighbours, no matter how ostensibly incompatible they may appear. Cal is struck by this overriding principle of inclusion during his first gathering of Seerkind in the Fugue: 'There were negro and Caucasian faces, one or two with an oriental cast; there were some who boasted traits not quite human – one with Nimrod's golden eyes (and tail, too, presumably); another pair whose features carried symmetrical marking that crept down from the scalp; yet others who bore – either at the dictates of fashion or theology – elaborate tattoos and hair-styles.'[19]

What we seem to have here is a collective in racial, cultural, and spiritual harmony, a vision reflected in the distribution of both animate and inanimate objects. Such a vision bespeaks an expansiveness, tolerance, and plurality that many felt were being trampled by the Thatcher paradigm of individualism and family. On a less altruistic note, the setting also literally expresses the hedonism of its people. During Cal's second visit to the Fugue, when war has broken out between Shadwell's supporters and those fighting to save the Fugue, he is taken to Venus Mountain, on whose slopes a sleeper experiences sensual dreams and sensations. Cal's young Seerkind friend de Bono roguishly points out to him that, in the Fugue, it is 'the nearest thing we've got to a whorehouse'.[20]

Although less individually centred, the Women's Movement is a second agent of significant social change in the 1980s to be amply represented within the novel. Since the end of the Second World War, a number of important acts promoting equal rights for women had come into law. The Abortion Act of 1967 extended women's access to choose abortion, while the Equal Pay Act of

1970, according to Andrew Rosen, at least 'established the principle of equal pay for equal work'.[21] In 1975, the Employment Act prevented employers from denying female workers the rights of maternity, including leave of absence without penalty. Of course, these acts were merely part of a much wider shift in attitude towards gender equality, but they did put an official stamp on this cultural shift and indicated the degree to which the country had accepted it in more than words and feeling alone. Inevitably, such change found its way into various forms of art and more popular entertainment, and *Weaveworld* is no exception. In this novel, we see not only increased power for women, but also the ways in which this impacts men and how the landscape of sexual politics was being redrawn.

First, there is an apparent reversal of power in terms of how men and women relate in a non-sexual context. Appoline, the hooker, is aggressive and coarse, and when a young boy spits at her in the street, she 'spat back with impressive accuracy'.[22] She is also a decisive and vital character who takes the lead when the Seerkind become aware that the Scourge is once more in pursuit of them. These qualities are evident when she seeks out Suzanna and formulates a plan of action as her male counterparts fret aimlessly. Of the leading characters, moreover, the females are the ones that can boast the most intense magical powers, with both Immacolata and Suzanna in possession of the Menstruum, the force that enables them to take a physically dominant role on a number of occasions. The two leading males, Cal and Shadwell, are frequently awestruck by it, and, for all their attempts at either valour or villainy, they remain marginalised from those who can access the higher version of humanity, privileged only to the Seerkind. Where once the masculine hero might have bludgeoned his way into supremacy through muscle and firepower, this version of the 1980s male finds himself confused and partly emasculated by arts beyond his control. A second issue is sexual agency. Many female characters in books throughout the 1960s and 1970s had commonly shown us a new breed of woman who dared to say yes to sex outside marriage. *Weaveworld*, on the other hand, gives us examples of women who have the power to say no, and these fall on both sides of the good-versus-evil divide. Immacolata refuses to be touched, let alone mounted by Shadwell, whereas Suzanna is the one who decides that her relationship with Cal should remain platonic, not he.

The sexually active characters also seem to be predominantly female. Appoline, for example, appears to ply her trade as a prostitute as much through lust as necessity. Immacolata's spectral sister, the Magdalene, almost literally devours men, raping a succession of them throughout the story as a way of producing her brood of hideous children. In fact, the traditional symbol of male sexual power, the erection, is actively mocked on one occasion when she sets about Cal: 'He'd never felt such caresses, coaxed by agonizing degrees to the point of no return. His gasps became cries, but the lullaby [sung by the Magdalene as she rapes him] drowned them out, mocking his manhood with its nursery lilt. He was a helpless infant, despite his erection; or perhaps because of it.'[23] The traditional image of women being abused and discarded is thus inverted as the Magdalene relieves her helpless donors of their seed before spitting them out like cherry stones.

In love, the women also take charge. Cal's long-standing relationship with local girl Geraldine[24] is notable for the extent to which she plays the dominant role, nursing him back to health one time after a harrowing confrontation with the supernatural, and assuming responsibility for most practical matters and decisions during the period when they live together as a couple. Cal is clearly not the kind of alpha male we might, a generation ago, have expected as our hero, and it is hardly surprising that in love he is attracted to a woman who is decisive, capable, and supportive. Suzanna and the Seerkind Jerichau comport themselves in a manner similar to that of Cal and Geraldine. In their attempts to elude Hobart and his bully boys,[25] Suzanna decides when and where they will make their escapes as they move the carpet and themselves from town to town in a stolen car. As Geraldine did with Cal, she takes care of most of their practical concerns, while Jerichau assumes a more passive and sensitive role. This power dynamic between the two is reinforced when Jerichau is eventually abducted by Shadwell's entourage and tortured by Immacolata and her sisters. Suzanna nurses his shattered and dying frame in her arms, an act she later performs for Cal after he has dispatched the Scourge.

This is not to say that male figures do not perform acts of traditional heroism and villainy in the story. However, in doing so they are matched or even surpassed by female characters, and there is clear evidence that the John Wayne–Maureen O'Hara[26] model is inappropriate for Britain in the 1980s. Furthermore, as powerful female role-models such as Anita Roddick, Vivienne Westwood,[27] and Madonna gained prominence, it was inevitable that their influence should extend beyond women to men. Cal and Jerichau appear to express this influence by ceding the traditionally masculine role of couple leader to Geraldine and Suzanna respectively, a move that characterises them as so-called New Men. This revised version of manhood, which embraced household tasks traditionally associated with women, became a common feature in the 1980s.

Of the various changes that took place in this decade, no one who lived through it will ever forget the terror that spread across the country with the appalling advent of AIDS. In early 1983 a curious and mildly disturbing article tucked innocuously away in a corner of *Newsweek* described an affliction, thought to have originated in Africa, that had killed a number of people in New York, and for which there was no apparent cure.[28] Within a few years this same disease had achieved epidemic status, and in every British town huge colourless billboards presented dark, forbidding images alongside stark warnings lest we should all die of ignorance. It seemed as though Armageddon had arrived.

Perhaps the most striking allusion to AIDS in *Weaveworld* is the Scourge, which, as we have already seen, was originally an angelic spirit whose mission was to guard the Edenic garden where the original Seerkind were created and then lived. When the Seerkind escaped into the world, the Scourge remained at its post for thousands of years until the garden had withered to desert and its mind grew corrupted by insanity and hate. When aroused, it becomes an insatiable destroyer, and having made one attempt to annihilate the Seerkind at the end of the nineteenth century, it is provoked into a renewed assault by Shadwell in the later sections of the novel. The Scourge is a creature with hundreds of eyes that can incinerate people and objects at will. Its name, strength, and utter lack of compassion combine with the totality of its destructive mission to form a strong reference to the devastating and unstoppable disease in our midst that killed without prejudice on a biblical scale.

Its victims are also worthy of mention. In describing common perceptions to the disease, Angus McLaren notes that, 'AIDS was nature's vengeance on those who had tried to violate its laws.'[29] He goes on to add that, 'The enemy was the "other" – the addicts, immigrants and haemophiliacs – and it followed that those who felt themselves besieged thought of quarantines and forcible testing [...] The not-so-subtle message was that society needed to be protected as much from the deviant as from the disease.'[30] The deviant in *Weaveworld* are the Seerkind. They look weird, their speech is wrong, and they have strange powers that ordinary people – the Seerkind call them Cuckoos – do not possess. When Suzanna takes her first walk with Appoline and Jerichau, the latter innocently sets off other pedestrians' aura, that is, the colours that emanate from the head reflecting the colour of a person's soul. In a moment, there is a firework display of colours in the air, but rather than be overwhelmed with wonder, the public instantly turns on the small motley crew responsible and attempts to rend them limb from limb for revealing an unconventional image of beauty and truth. When the police arrive, members of the public shift the blame for violence on the three outsiders, and the police, recognising a group of freaks, are unequivocal in apprehending the villains:

> 'They started it, officer,' said one of the number, a balding individual who, before the blood had stained his knuckles and shirt, might have been a bank cashier.
> 'Is that right?' said the officer, taking a look at the black derelict [Jerichau] and his sullen mistress [Suzanna]. 'Get the fuck up, you two,' he said. 'You've got some questions to answer.'[31]

Once in the police station, Suzanna defends herself and Jerichau from brutality by using her inner force, the Menstruum, and is thereon classified by law enforcement as a terrorist.

Seen in this light, we have an indiscriminate killing machine, the Scourge, directing its fury on a group of disorderly and disreputable freaks. This appears to be the same scenario described by McLaren, in which the deviant being slain was as dangerous as the slaying disease. Barker appears to be presenting the public not only with its angel of death come to terrorise humankind, but also its inclination to deliver a chosen target for sacrificial retribution.

Another feature that seems to reflect the arrival of AIDS into the human consciousness is the revised view of sex. If books written between the 1950s and the 1970s displayed more liberal attitudes to sex, *Weaveworld* presents a partial *volte-face* in that we have an image of it as something dark, unpleasant, and debilitating, a force capable of birthing evil consequences. The activities of Immacolata's sister the Magdalene have already been described in part, and it is she who represents an ugly and frightening vision of human coupling. Cal, as we noted earlier, fell victim to her filthy embrace. A short time earlier, his friend Elroy met a similar fate at night while wandering in the garden shadows at a wedding party:

> On his second step, something grazed his face. He [Elroy, Cal's friend] stifled a cry of shock and put his hand up to find strands of matter in the air around his head. For some reason he thought of phlegm – cold, wet threads of phlegm – except that they *moved* against his flesh as if they were part of something larger. A heart-beat later this notion was confirmed, as the matter, which was adhering now to his legs and body, pulled him off his feet. He would have let out a cry, but the filthy stuff had already sealed his lips. And then, as if this were not preposterous enough, he felt a chill around his lower belly. His trousers were being torn open. He started to fight like fury, but resistance was fruitless. There was weight bearing down on his abdomen and hips, and he felt his manhood drawn into a channel that might have been flesh, but that it was corpse cold.
>
> He could not resist this pornography: his prick spat its load. He howled against the seal at his mouth. The pleasure was short, the pain that followed, agonizing.[32]

This is dirty, sinister sex that is all about abuse and which leaves the victim damaged and diminished; in fact, when the Magdalene transfers her affections to Jerichau later in the story, the prolonged encounter brings about his death.

The reproductive consequences of the Magdalene's embraces are doubly grim. The seed she purloins is quickly converted into vile, deformed children whose instinct is to kill, maim, and terrorise[33] at the behest of their mistress, Immacolata, and later their master, Shadwell. And although this nightmarish depiction of sex might be dismissed on one level as merely fantastic fiction, it expresses a revulsion, pessimism, and regret that were absent from many novels written in the previous few decades, when the so-called permissive society had steadily gained momentum. Given the horror and confusion that accompanied the country's knowledge of the AIDS epidemic and the tainted attitude towards sexual contact that followed in its wake, the degraded vision of sex as depicted in the novel mirrors a nation's fear and self-loathing at the appalling consequences of the free love it had so ardently embraced in the previous decade.

Granted, there are relationships in which sex is seen in a more positive light. The relationships between Cal and Geraldine, and of Suzanna and Jerichau do seem to contain love and affection. However, these positive feelings appear largely independent of physical intimacy, which occurs more as a bodily function; in fact, the sexual side of the two relationships ostensibly springs more from a spirit of 'why not?' rather than the rapturous excitement we might traditionally associate with new romance. In one section on the nature of Cal's relationship with Geraldine, the words 'comforting', 'convenient', 'natural', 'easy', 'down-to-earth', and 'unsentimental' are all used within the space of around six lines to describe their union. Geraldine is also 'as much companion as lover'.[34] Suzanna's relationship with Jericahu is marked by a similar lack of intensity in the moment. In their case, the relationship was an option marginally preferable to remaining friends and so inconsequential that 'Suzanna could not pinpoint the moment of decision'. Their coupling 'just seemed right', and again the word 'comfort' is used to explain the drive that brought them together.[35]

Apolline's bawdy interludes and the Magdalene's atrocities notwithstanding, mere comfort and convenience – going with the flow – seem the best that the story can offer in terms of sexual passion. Given the demise of the sexual revolution at the hands of our very own scourge – AIDS – it seems reasonable to assume that ardour for unrestrained sex in both fiction and life had cooled somewhat, and that these unspectacular displays of affectionate monogamy were more representative of a nation's sexual aspirations than the sophisticated and uninhibited hedonism of Nicholas Urfe in John Fowles' *The Magus* or Joe Bodenland in Brian Aldiss' *Frankenstein Unbound*. In the space of a decade, the sexual politics within science fantasy and novels of the uncanny had changed significantly.

Whatever our view of the 1980s may be, few would deny that this period saw the old order give way to the new, and that many of the changes entailed varying degrees of upset. If the trajectory from the late 1950s to the late 1970s had been one of expanding personal freedoms, better health, and a more assured and leisurely material comfort for large sections of the country, the 1980s heralded in a more austere meritocratic age of individualised material gain. It was an age that promised success in return for stricter personal habits and increased professional responsibility, and which may, at the twist of a stock market downturn or an injudicious one-night stand, strip the newly prosperous yuppie of both wealth and health at a stroke. In social terms, although the advances made for racial and sexuality equality in previous decades were still alive and, in some cases, gaining even more ground, many felt these to be under threat, which, in turn, created an atmosphere of unease.

This chapter has made the case that although Clive Barker has undoubtedly produced a remarkable novel of the fantastic, a genre that has traditionally transported readers from the mundane to the incredible, it also communicates this sense of unease and provides a fascinating commentary on the times in which it was written. On the surface, this might initially appear to be a paradox. Fantastic literature, by its very title, would appear to promise the most fanciful imaginings available to us in fiction. However, in many of the more interesting stories within the genre, there are layers of meaning in which we may recognise the confines of historical and cultural circumstance with keen and sometimes uncomfortable awareness. Such is the case in *Weaveworld*, and the novel has shown itself to be, on one level, a powerful medium for the concerns of a very specific set of cultural and political events. It is testimony to the claim that a novel can, through literary invention, serve as a historical document, not so much in terms of communicating the facts of an age, but rather its feel and atmosphere.

Notes

1 David Marquand, 'Moralists and Hedonists', in David Marquand and Anthony Seldon (eds), *The Ideas that Shaped Post-War Britain* (London: Fontana Press, 1996), p. 12.
2 In the winter of 1978–79, Britain suffered a series of devastating strikes.
3 Marquand, 'Moralists and Hedonists', p. 25.
4 Shirley Letwin, *The Anatomy of Thatcherism* (New Brunswick and London: Transaction Publishers, 1993), p. 376.
5 Peter Riddell, *The Thatcher Era And Its Legacy* (Oxford: Basil Blackwell, 1991), p. 151.
6 Peter Leese, *Britain Since 1945* (Hampshire: Palgrave Macmillan, 2006), p. 142.
7 Kenneth O. Morgan, *Britain Since 1945* (Oxford: Oxford University Press, 2001), p. 474.
8 David Hughes, 'High Abuse From the Left, Low Abuse From the Right', *The Telegraph*, 16 February 2009, p. 1. http://blogs.telegraph.co.uk/news/davidhughes/8594817/High_abuse_from_the_Left_low_abuse_from_the_Right_/. Date accessed: 18 September 2015.
9 Letwin, *The Anatomy of Thatcherism*, p. 314.
10 Leese, *Britain Since 1945*, p. 152.
11 Clive Barker, *Weaveworld* (London: Collins, 1987), p. 55.
12 *Ibid.* p. 152.
13 Letwin, *The Anatomy of Thatcherism*, p. 319.
14 Morgan, *Britain Since 1945*, p. 438.
15 In 1986 Mrs Thatcher abolished six large Metropolitan city councils on the grounds that they were inefficient and unnecessary. Critics argued that the move was politically motivated as the councils were predominantly left-wing. The most renowned of them was the GLC (Greater London Council) run by Red Ken Livingstone.
16 Barker, *Weaveworld*, p. 328.

17 *Spitting Image*, ITV (1984–86), https://www.youtube.com/watch?v=DPzzgE34YQY. Date accessed: 18 September 2015.

18 Barker, *Weaveworld*, pp. 233–4.

19 *Ibid.* p. 257.

20 *Ibid.* p. 475.

21 Andrew Rosen, *The Transformation of British Life 1950–2000* (Manchester and New York: Manchester University Press, 2003), p. 102.

22 Barker, *Weaveworld*, p. 182.

23 *Ibid.* p. 90.

24 Geraldine is Cal's official girlfriend. She is present in his life before the mysteries begin, and takes Cal back after he returns from them the first time. Their relationship eventually ends when Cal returns to take on the Scourge.

25 When the carpet unfolds for the first time, Cal, Suzanna, and Shadwell are all thrown into the strange land of the Fugue. The Fugue only comes out of hiding for a day, however, and when it weaves itself back into the carpet, Suzanna and Jerichau take possession of it and try to protect it from the clutches of Shadwell and Hobart. For this reason, they travel the country, staying in cheap hotels and living on their wits and always ready to move when Suzanna's instincts tell her that the pursuers are hot on their trail.

26 Movie actors John Wayne and Maureen O'Hara were a classic Hollywood team in a number of movies during the 1950s and 1960s, in which Wayne played the traditional strong, silent, and all-powerful male, while O'Hara would be the irrational, emotional beauty who needed to be tamed or rescued.

27 Anita Roddick founded the highly successful chain of environmentally friendly Body Shop stores in 1976. Vivienne Westwood gained fame for successfully marketing punk fashions from the late 1970s throughout the 1980s.

28 Walter Isaacson, 'Hunting for the Hidden Killers: AIDS Disease Detectives Face a Never Ending Quest,' *Newsweek* (122) 1, 4 July 1983, http://content.time.com/time/magazine/0,9263,7601830704,00.html. Date accessed: 18 September 2015.

29 Angus McLaren, *Twentieth-Century Sexuality* (Oxford: Blackwell Publishers, 1999), p. 196.

30 McLaren, *Twentieth-Century Sexuality*, p. 197.

31 Barker, *Weaveworld*, p. 187.

32 *Ibid.* p. 78. Italic added.

33 In the story, these children are called by-blows. They are born seemingly within hours of conception and bear a chilling resemblance to the abominations to be found in the hell paintings of Hieronymous Bosch. They might have four arms and no legs, organs without rather than within, and sacs of burning, venomous fluid hanging from their flesh. They begin as weapons of Immacolata, but Shadwell eventually commands their obedience.

34 Barker, *Weaveworld*, p. 317.

35 *Ibid.* p. 322.

Part II

Screening Barker

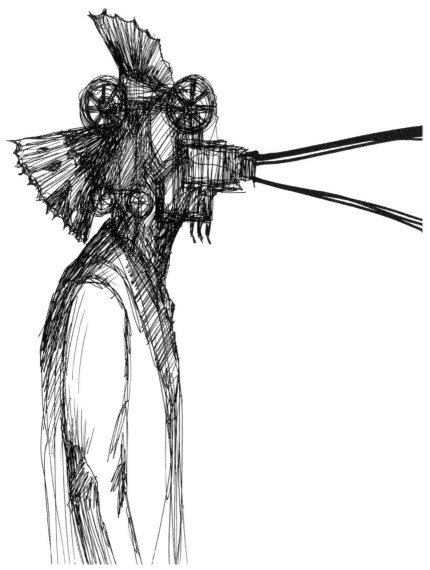

4 Clive Barker, 'Projecto', pre-2010.

4

The joyless magic of *Lord of Illusions*

Harvey O'Brien

Clive Barker found joy in painting at the age of 45, two years after the release of *Lord of Illusions* (1995), his third and last feature as a film director.[1] Speaking in the documentary *Clive Barker: The Man Behind the Myth* (2007), the artist described his encounter with the medium in a wistful voice: 'It was like opening a door into a whole new world. It was love at first sight. It was like "oh, Lord, why have I waited this long to open a tube of this paint?" It was like discovering I had another life waiting for me.'[2] That life was a life beyond film, a fourth artistic outlet for the writer of literature and theatre; one perhaps more suited to his idiom. Certainly painting evidently brought him joy, an emotion notably absent in *Lord of Illusions* even in the capacity of the affective dialectic of euphoria and dread characteristic of his work. Rather, *Lord of Illusions* is marked by self-deflating irony and skepticism amounting almost to a self-loathing that made it an apt cinematic swansong;[3] a farewell to a medium that seemed to have brought Barker nothing but trouble.

As a mainstream filmmaker,[4] Barker had started with something of an Orson Welles moment. From the triumph of *Hellraiser* (1987) came the disaster of *Nightbreed* (1990), which, like *The Magnificent Ambersons* (1942), was compromised and re-edited following studio interference.[5] Though also compromised in theatrical exhibition *Lord of Illusions* fared slightly better than *Nightbreed* immediately thereafter, receiving the benefit of a 'director's cut' for LaserDisc release in 1996. On the commentary track, reproduced on the later DVD issue of the film, Barker seems relatively pleased with the fact that audiences had a chance to see the film as he meant them to because of the unrated director's cut, and he describes the film with some affection, though he would later describe it has his 'least pure'.[6] Douglas Winter even reports on Barker's personal intervention with Blockbuster Video in the United States to stock the director's cut even though it was unrated and therefore against company policy.[7]

But *Lord of Illusions* is a particularly joyless film. It is not only dark; it is nihilistic. In what seems a conscious articulation of a disconnection between artist and medium, the film posits cinema itself as an insubstantial Phantas-magoria: a meaningless spook show that ultimately fails to enrich our perception of truth. In the film, cinema and magic are metonymistically intertwined, and both are 'debunked'. There is no magic, just more and deeper layers of illusion, delusion, and despair. Affectively, it works against the film *as* a film that the pleasure of image-based illusion should be so problematic when image based illusion is also being used to substantiate its thematic preoccupations, which are familiar Barker motifs of faith, corporeal transience, and desire.

The narrative attempts both to fuse and to subvert both *film noir* and horror, playing on and then undermining the audience's expectations of these genres and their ephemeral pleasures, drawing in and pushing away in the same gesture. It also both deploys and dismisses then cutting-edge computer-generated visual effects to problematise the status of the image – alternating between effects scenes depicting deliberately risible illusions and horrific images of 'real' magical power intended to be frightening. The resulting ontological uncertainty is not conducive to visual pleasure. Winter describes the film as 'a remarkable self-critique of the art and artifice of filmmaking,'[8] but arguably it is more than that: *Lord of Illusions* is a rejection and repudiation of cinematic illusion that is *in itself as a cinematic object* as nihilistic as its narrative. It is self-negating almost to Godardian proportions. It is therefore no surprise that when Barker picked up a tube of paint and began to express himself directly onto canvas that the mechanical, collaborative, and inevitably compromised world of film-making became a tertiary concern.

The irony of all this is that Barker has described writing itself as a form of magic,[9] and the writing of Clive Barker is typically as celebratory as it is unsettling. As Gary Hoppenstand puts it, 'his bottom line message to his readers is not so dark. In fact, it's quite optimistic.'[10] Barker describes hope and wonder in the crossovers between our world and realms of corporeal and spiritual possibility that are at once dangerous and potentially redemptive. This is the theme of 'The Last Illusion', the short story from Volume six of the *Books of Blood* nominally given as the point of departure for *Lord of Illusions*. In it Barker introduces his literary alter-ego, Harry D'Amour – a private investigator and baptised Catholic who finds himself continually drawn to the occult though he does not seek it out. Harry is hired by Valentin, the personal assistant of a deceased stage magician called Swann, for the unusual task of watching over Swann's dead body as it rests in its coffin. Actually, this is not so unusual in Irish Catholic culture, with its pagan antecedents, where 'waking' the body is a remnant of precisely what Harry D'Amour is *actually* doing, though he doesn't realise it – protecting the body from evil spirits that would claim it in the name of darkness.

It is eventually revealed that Swann was not just an illusionist. He had magical powers, granted to him by otherworldly forces known as the Gulfs, operating in the service of the Devil. As Valentin puts it, Swann was given 'the ability to perform miracles. To transform matter. To bewitch souls. Even to drive out God.'[11] In defiance of the Mephisthophelean temptations of this dark gift and his Faustian pact, Swann had elected not to use these abilities to wield power and corrupt humanity. Instead he had chosen to perform magic tricks in stage shows as if they were actual illusions, allowing people to enjoy the wonders of 'magic' without the necessity to acknowledge the instrumental power of angels or demons. For this, the Gulfs intend to claim Swann's soul and torture him for eternity.

D'Amour's intervention facilitates redemption. Though Swann's widow Dorothea is lost to the Gulfs because she sides with a demonic lawyer named Butterfield who torments Harry and Valentin (the latter, whom, incidentally, is revealed to be a demon himself – Swann's original tempter but latterly his friend and familiar), Swann's body is purged by fire and saved. The story concludes with the following affirmational observation: 'Things came and went away; that was a kind of magic. And in between? Pursuits and conjurings; horrors, guises. The occasional joy. That there was room for joy; ah! that was magic too.'[12]

The fact is that Harry D'Amour's perennial encounters with demonic forces are in themselves an affirmation of his belief in God – the comfort and the curse of knowledge. 'The Last Illusion' is a story of salvation: 'Dead, yes. Past saving? No', as Valentin says.[13] Swann's defiance of the Gulfs affirms the strength and worth of the human spirit, and his defiance had 'made his apologies to Heaven',[14] which makes Harry's defence of his soul doubly blessed.

Barker has stated in interviews that his intention in creating Harry D'Amour was to give audiences a protagonist who was basically good – a real hero.[15] In 1994, just as *Lord of Illusions* was going into production, Harry had featured as a major character in the novel *Everville* (1994), where he spoke the line 'God, I love the world.'[16] Though Harry encounters the 'truth' about Barker's Quiddity and the parallel realities that intersect with ours (which must put his Judeo-Christian world-view into some relief), he finds hope and beauty in human beings, and particularly in human prayer. After Harry destroys the demon of Wyckoff street (an *Exorcist*-like antagonist in an recurring memory that haunts him through both 'The Last Illusion' and *Lord of Illusions*, the details about which are revealed in *Everville*), Harry hears Hail Mary being recited by a woman and thinks to himself how beautiful it sounds: 'It would not turn death away, of course. It would not save the innocent from suffering. But prettiness was no insignificant quality, not in this troubled world.'[17] 'The Last Illusion' is a story about hope and joy. For the reader there is a sense of the value of a human being; of life lived in the light of spiritual transcendence and in defiance of limitation and constraint.

Lord of Illusions is almost the antithesis of 'The Last Illusion'. The characters have the same names and the broad outlines of the stories are similar, but where 'The Last Illusion' found 'room for joy', *Lord of Illusions* is entirely despairing. Why this is important, and not merely a matter of problems of adaptation or how

'the film is not as good as the book', is that it can be argued that the joylessness
and ontological confusion demonstrated by *Lord of Illusions* is symptomatic of
its director's falling out of love with the cinema. The film is a conscious and
much darker re-imagining of its source by the same originating artist working
in a different medium. Undoubtedly traumatised by making *Nightbreed*, Barker
as director takes on the persona not so much of Harry D'Amour or even of
Swann, but that of Nix, the film's antagonist, in his determination to demystify
cinematic processes and reveal the 'mud and shit' that lies under the human
skin; the delusions we continue to live by and the inevitable disappointments
we face when we finally confront the truth about reality. In *Hellraiser* the kinky
masochism of Pinhead's invitation to experience the limits of pleasure and
pain held some primal psychoanalytical appeal to the enthralled cinemagoer.
In *Nightbreed* we were explicitly invited to look beneath the skin both in literal
and cine-genre terms to see beauty and fellowship in those that are different
from us. In *Lord of Illusions* we are invited to stare into the abyss when we
look at other people, who dissolve into CGI renderings of viscera and sinew.

This is precisely what happens near the beginning of the film when Swann,
played by Kevin J. O'Connor, returns to the desert compound of Manson-like
cult leader Nix, played by Daniel Von Bargen, a real magician with real magical
powers, in order to kill him and save the young girl Dorothea who will later
become Swann's wife. Nix invites Swann to see the world 'as it really is' with
'a god's eyes', and plunges his fingers into Swann's face. This grants Swann
the power to perceive beyond the veil of the flesh, and to see his friends as
twisted masses of pulpy gore. Swann reels in terror, and as Nix opens his arms
and exhorts Swann to 'feel the power', he is shot and killed from behind by a
crying Dorothea.

In his analysis of the film, Jonathan F. Bassett observes that *Lord of Illusions*
is centrally concerned with death anxiety, and notes that in this very scene
what Nix does is force Swann to confront the reality of the human condition.
Writing from the perspective of what he labels 'terror management', Bassett
observes that the horror in *Lord of Illusions* stems from 'the power of the film
to make salient the unpalatable existential realities of corporeality and mortality'.[18]
There is not a lot of arguing with that, or with the presence or prevalence of
this theme in the film. In fact, the absolute nihilism of Barker's vision of human
flesh in *Lord of Illusions* is literally embodied in its antagonist's very name:
'Nix' – nothingness.

Nix is the lurking, malevolent force that threatens Swann's soul. In the film
it is *his* Faustian pact that is the point of contact with the darkness, and Swann
rejects *him* rather than the Gulfs, who do not feature. Nix's power is configured
in terms of messianic symbolism. He is the leader of a cult, preaching revelation
and purgation, which his followers misunderstand as salvation. He even dresses
in robes following his resurrection at the climax. Harry D'Amour's involvement
is actually more peripheral and accidental in the film than it is in the original
story. Hired to follow an insurance fraudster (illusion/con/trickery – we get

it), he encounters one of Swann's associates, a fortune teller named Quaid, who is being tortured to death by Butterfield (played by Barry Del Sherman), now no longer a neatly besuited lawyer as he was in 'The Last Illusion', but a gold pants-wearing gimp with shaved eyebrows.

Quaid's demise leads Harry to knowledge of Nix and of Swann, and also to Dorothea (played as an adult by Famke Janssen) who orders Valentin (played by Joel Swetow) to hire D'Amour (played by Scott Bakula) to watch over Swann while he is still alive. When Swann dies spectacularly during a David Copperfield / Las Vegas-style magic trick gone wrong, D'Amour finds himself in conflict with Butterfield and his skinhead sidekick, and gradually gets sucked deeper into the messianic/apocalyptic promise of Nix's return feared by Swann and the remnants of his team. Eventually it is revealed that Swann has faked his own death to hide from Butterfield and Nix, and it is Harry who galvanises him into action by shaming him for evading his responsibility to humankind. Butterfield nonetheless succeeds in resurrecting Nix after torturing Valentin to death, but the resurrected Nix rejects his fawning cult of followers, including Butterfield, in favour of Swann, whom he clearly still desires.

The relationship between Nix and Swann is romantically charged or at least highly sexualised. This is evident in the aforementioned confrontation scene where Nix tenderly strokes Swann's face and speaks in a tone of invitation, not threat, before plunging his fingers into him. The pervasive tone of Nix's engagements with Swann, both in the opening and closing scenes, is of one man trying to convince another to be with him. His acts of psychic and physical penetration are violent, but tinged with affection and with the ultimate aim of revelation. Nix speaks with sadness and regret as well as anger when he realises he has lost Swann. He speaks of wanting to keep each other company in the dark. He tells Dorothea that the grave is lonely, though life is worse, and after rejecting his other followers as worthless sheep he tells them 'Only Swann is worthy.'

As a Hollywood film from 1995, and therefore in the wake of *The Silence of the Lambs* (1991) and *Philadelphia* (1993), the queer element to this story is notable enough, particularly in the context of Harry Benshoff's analysis of homosexuality in the horror film in which he notes, 'Queer suggests death over life by focusing on non-productive sexual behaviours, making it especially suited to a genre which takes sex and death as central thematic concerns.'[19] This chimes quite neatly with Bassett's notion of death anxiety as a defining feature of the film, making the queered monster doubly abject. However, Benshoff quite likes Barker's work, particularly *Nightbreed*, which he dubs 'spectacularly queer',[20] and likes the challenge that the film represents to notions of prejudice around monsters and monstrosity as a queer metaphor. However, he also observes that there is a risk that 'he is simply producing more images of monster queers with which to frighten mainstream USA',[21] and this is patently true in *Lord of Illusions*.

Nix is certainly a negating character – a force of absolute despair resonating disappointment and disillusion. 'I was born to murder the world', he says. He describes himself to Dorothea as 'a man who wanted to be a god, then changed his mind'. 'I'm going to show the world who's waiting at the end, and I'm going to make it despair', he says. This almost hysterical queering is, to be fair, simply a reflection of a dark characterisation of romantic disappointment, but it also results in the kind of othering that becomes repellent in its very vehemence, producing the kind of 'monster queer' effect Benshoff is describing.

But even more so, given what Nix is actually doing – destroying illusion – trying to bring Swann over to the dark side where people get no pleasure from magical entertainment: this is Barker on cinema. After *Nightbreed*, he realises it doesn't love him, and he just doesn't love it anymore. He is grasping for contact with his audience through the barbed wire of the mechanical and industrial processes of cinema, the technical and creative methodologies of film, and he has found it all too much. There is no magic in this art. The film and the story make a distinction between real magic and stage illusion, the point being that the blurring of the boundaries between them – the realm of affective audience experience, if you will – is what gives us hope and inspires our imaginations. Swann brings joy to ordinary people by concealing the truth and giving them illusion: Nix brings despair by revealing it.

Magic doesn't tend to induce despair. Magic, like cinema, is a primarily mechanical process of misdirection and misrecognition in which the audience willingly participates with an anticipation of pleasure in engaging with the illusion. Magician Derren Brown tells us 'Magic isn't about fakes and switches and dropping coins in your lap. It's about entering into a relationship with a person whereby you can lead him, economically and deftly, to experience an event as magical.'[22] The gendering of that sentence is interesting given Brown's own queerness, and ties fairly neatly with the Swann/Nix dynamic in *Lord of Illusions*, but more broadly speaking, Brown is quoted by Annette Hill, whose exploration of the paranormal in contemporary media is focused mainly on precisely this consensual relationship between audience and magician or other purveyor of illusions.

Since its origins in the late nineteenth century, there has been a logistical, technological, and performative relationship between magic and cinema. Magician George Méliès was one of cinema's pioneers, while Soviet director Dziga Vertov used the visual metaphor of a Chinese conjurer to illustrate and describe the process of editing in a key sequence in *Man With a Movie Camera* (1929). Even the phrase 'the magic of cinema' is part of popular lexicon. In 1975 Orson Welles presented *F for Fake* (1975) – a documentary about hoaxes and fakery that was a playful interrogation of tropes of truth and lies of both cinema and magic as aspects of the human predilection for credulity and denial. Welles himself performs a number of conjuring tricks in the film as its on-screen narrator, and explicitly interlinks these tricks with his activities as a filmmaker.

Hill positions magic and paranormal entertainment firmly within cultural processes and contemporary technologies, and points out that in the late nineteenth and early twentieth centuries, performing magicians, including Harry Houdini, spent a great deal of their time publicly debunking the activities of spiritualists. Indeed, this was a frequent subject of early films, for example in Robert Paul's *Is Spiritualism a Fraud?* (1906) and the films featuring Houdini himself in which the admiration of his skills was as important as 'believing' in the effects. Hill accordingly observes that in exposing séances and spirit-manifesting routines as technical tricks, magicians had two aims – one to overthrow a primary competitor, and two to demonstrate their own technical skills, situating the emphasis on performance, performativity, and public culture instead of on the private and domestic sphere of spiritualism.

This is a keynote concern in *Lord of Illusions*, most explicitly stated in the scene where Harry D'Amour visits the Magic Castle in Los Angeles (the city of angels – a reference not incidental, of course) and confronts pretentious magic guru Vinovich (played by Vincent Schiavelli), who spouts aphorisms in a fake Eastern European accent. Vinovich proclaims that given a little preparation, he can reproduce any miracle from the Bible. According to him, the point of magic is to relieve the tedium of everyday lives, to entertain people with an exhibition that suggest the presence of the wondrous. 'It is more than entertainment' he says, 'We are opening up people's heads. We are bringing miracles back into their miserable little lives.' Vinovich states that he believes illusionists walk a path between 'divinity and trickery', which Harry puts in terms of 'Heaven and Hell' to question the moral ethos of the professional magician and in trying to understand the difference between what they do and what Nix and Swann could do. When Harry asks if the miracles are ever real, Vinovich definitively states 'No. They are always fake.'

5   Vinovich (Vincent Schiavelli) and the magicians at the Magic Castle in *Lord of Illusions*.

Vinovich explains that Swann's work was 'tainted by evil', but in one of the film's odd if entertaining self-contradictory twists, the narrative gravity of this pronouncement is undercut by Harry's debunking of Vinovich's persona. Making fun of the angry Vinovich who is storming out of the room Harry says 'Great accent, Brooklyn, right?' to which Vinovich yells, dropping the faux-Dracula and resorting to pure *New Yoik*, 'Fuck you, a'right.'

So, in repeating the Houdini effect – the debunking – what is Clive Barker doing with cinema? Gary Hoppenstand describes Clive Barker's philosophical aesthetic in related terms. He points out that Barker's insistence on finding instances of the miraculous and wondrous in everyday life not only locates his work within a grounded *realpolitik*, it also gives him distance and objectivity. His disbelief in the supernatural facilitates the exploration of horror as a purely metaphoric space: it's not so much about believing in the wondrous as understanding what it means. This is what, for Hoppenstand, marks him out as a writer of literature rather than a mere storyteller, and would, in those terms, put *Lord of Illusions* into the same aesthetic paradigm as *F for Fake*. But Welles' film was full of playful *jouissance*, and self-effacing (but not self-denigrating) irony and satire, inviting the audience to share complicity in the game Welles is playing. In the film's most famous feint, the director reveals that the preceding seventeen minutes of the documentary about art forgery have themselves been a fake, and teases the viewer with the fact that he had warned them he would only tell the truth for an hour. There's a literal twinkle in his eye as he speaks to the camera. He is the trickster and we are in his power because we chose to surrender to the illusion of truth in documentary form.

Hoppenstand notes the importance of audience engagement in Barker's work, particularly in theatre, and argues that his need for control is definitive in the affect of his aesthetic of disturbance. Barker introduces us to a rigidly controlled, identifiably real and human space, then reveals parallel and interconnected imaginative spaces that defamiliarise human reality: 'Nothing scares us quite so much as knowing that we really don't know the world we live in', Hoppenstand says.[23] This, to Hoppenstand, explains Barker's use of magic in 'The Last Illusion' where, as I said earlier, human truth triumphs over the 'formidable might', of magic.[24]

At the heart of all this is the dialectical ontology of illusion, and with it, as Hill and Brown note, the essential element of willing participation on the part of the audience, who know it is a trick but receive pleasure from the execution. As Hill puts it 'The premise of a magic trick consists of an effect and a method. Within the construction of a trick there is a basic design where the audience sees the effect without realising the method behind it.'[25] This is almost the same process that determines the affect of cinema itself. Many writings on cinema emphasise the psychoanalytic and perceptual double-bind upon which cinema operates, in which recognising the mechanics of the image doesn't necessarily delimit an engagement with it. Cinema is a liminal space; an imaginative frame in which we allow our brains to become what Gilles Deleuze describes as a 'centre of indetermination',[26] where something like Brown's necessity to be led, economically and deftly, to a magical experience is defined by various types and natures of cinematic practice, written about by psychoanalytical writing on cinema too voluminous to delve into in this forum but summarised by the same paradigm as the effect of magic.

The issue becomes particularly pointed in fantastic genres. Writing on science fiction cinema, Brooks Landon identifies what he terms an 'aesthetics of ambivalence',[27] which operates on this dual level of disavowal and wish-fulfilment. Particularly when special effects come into the equation, and particularly as time dates them, he argues, it becomes less a matter of whether or not the effects are convincing *per se*, which has more to do with the present moment of their technological production, as the function they serve to signal difference in the diegetic ontology and imagine possible futures. He speaks of the principle in physics described by O.B. Hardison known as the 'Horizon of invisibility':[28] where when a paradigm shift occurs in theoretical physics, the language of current science is frequently inadequate to describing what is seen because it has crossed over the epistemological horizon. Landon argues that the very visibility and even transparency of special effects in films that address future technologies or alternative realities thereby represents a conscious articulation of this kind of transcendence – a visualisation of the unseen and unknown that invites a response to the spectacle of the technology that has produced it not as counterpoint, but as celebration.

Patricia MacCormack goes even further in her *Cinesexuality* manifesto, a philosophical appeal for a fusion of cinematic and corporeal desire and imagination. MacCormack argues that cinema has the capacity to transcend descriptive, definitive categories of identity, gender, and sexuality in ways that create a liminal and libidinal space where our sense of reality is negotiable and navigable. For MacCormack, the blurring of ontological and cognitive boundaries through our consensual relationship with the cinematic image brings us to a cognitive plane where:

> Beyond dialecticism, cinema can be thought as involuting self and image on a libidinal plateau, twisting textures of intensity including, but not limited to, vague notings of visceral, genital, and cerebral pleasure. The dissipated, enfleshed self repudiates certain aspects of the body itself as signified, but the explicitly fleshy or visceral body is necessarily the libidinal and the cerebral corporeal.[29]

This sounds a bit Barkeresque, or maybe more Cronenbergian, but there's certainly something in it that feeds into Barker's deployment of magic as metaphor and the discourse on sexuality, denial, and identity with which *Lord of Illusions* is concerned. With its consciously deconstructive discourse on illusions of the self and the body, as well as magic and cinema, it does seem that *Lord of Illusions* should have produced something more joyously fluid and subversive like *F for Fake*, or even *Videodrome* (1983).

But *Lord of Illusions* doesn't work this way. It seems to want to, on some level, but it is a nervy film, trying almost too hard to subvert itself at every turn to the point where it stops being able to function, folding back on itself so many times and in so many ways that, like the badly realised Origami-man that materialises in what is supposed to be a major scene of fright and wonder, it simply disappears. In a way, the film is overly dialectical, and overly didactic, robbing it of the liminality, ambiguity, and aesthetic ambivalence MacCormack, Landon, and Deleuze are describing. Barker's assault on his audience is too vitriolic, perhaps reflecting his skepticism of popular narratives that lack a deeper truth. 'The audience wounds itself constantly. It wounds itself with the banality of its desires', he says[30]. *Lord of Illusions* is satirical, parodic, and subversive, but arguably it is actually too literal, too locked in each loaded critical moment to produce a cohesive cinematic object that can 'lead us' to the magical experience and beyond the deconstruction. Again, as Hill remarks of Derren Brown, the assertion of the effect of psychological processes and deconstructions of the paranormal do not take away from the entertainment: in fact, they enhance it. *Lord of Illusions* is a film so out of love with cinema, so angry, so disappointed, and so confused about what audiences actually want that it gets entirely lost in its own articulation and absolutely excludes the cinesexual pleasures described by MacCormack. It pushes us away so completely that we do as it asks and leave it.

In a key scene following the confrontation with Vinovich and the Magic Circle, Harry breaks into the repository of The Magic Castle with the aid of Billy Who, another professional magician, and discovers Vinovich's Nix files. However, their investigation is interrupted by the appearance of a fearsome monster with dangling claws, an exposed brain, and bulbous eyes. The scene is reminiscent of that marked by the appearance of the Castrate, a kind of lumbering tank-Demon, in 'The Last Illusion', but crucially, in the film, it is shown to be a bad special effect – a mechanically projected image of a clichéd 'scary monster' designed to frighten gullible burglars. Harry realises this and shoots the projector, then makes the deflating remark 'Hokey enough for you?' referencing the glitzy, over-the-top, absolutely fake world of professional magic that they have been investigating, but also, by inference, the 1950s-style B-movie beasties that this creature clearly parodies. But then, whither the Castrate, or the Nightbreed, or the Cenobites? What are we to make of Barker's attitude towards hokey monsters, especially in the context of this particular film and this image of cinematic illusion?

The difficulty here is that the film is not merely positing an ambiguity, or plotting an intersection between ontologies, it is actively undercutting itself when it engages in this nexus of representational discourse. The problem is compounded not long after this scene in another in which we are expected to engage with a similar manifestation of otherworldly forces, but this time 'for real'. Specifically, following a sexual liaison with Dorothea, Harry is menaced

6 and 7   Left: 'Hokey monster' from *Lord of Illusions* as example of 'bad' special
effect. Right: Butterball from *Hellraiser* as 'real' monster.

by a CGI fire-snake and a floating Origami-man. Again given the limitations
of technology at the time and Landon's note that it doesn't really matter, we
can't be overly hard on the fact that the CGI is poor, but what is awry in the
scene is the lack of empathetic reaction of horror, shock, or unease on the part
of the audience, upon which Barker is relying.

Harry is seen to be genuinely affected this time; he is both cautious and
frightened, emotionally justified by the narratively determined need to protect
the classic damsel in distress. What is odd is that Harry's previously demonstrated
skepticism seems to fly out the window in the face of what must be, presumably,
superior 'technology' (Swann's actual magic). The problem is that given the
deconstruction of the monster in the earlier scene, the audience is already
wary of the veracity of ethereal manifestations and cannot share Harry's unease.
When it is finally revealed that the snake and Origami-man were both manifestations of Swann's magic designed to scare Harry but not hurt him, it is merely
doubly distancing, as the audience is now being asked to conflate their narrative
and cognitive disavowal of illusion with their position as cinematic spectators.
This actually directs attention onto the quality of the special effects (which are
no better for this than the 'hokey monster') rather than away from them. It's
too much of an 'it's up your sleeve' moment for the 'magic' to work, and for
the effect to register before it is deconstructed. We begin from a position of
such detachment that there's nothing to engage with emotionally. Intellectually,
the point has already been made, rendering the scene narratively and thematically
repetitious, if not downright confusing.

It is interesting listening to the commentary on *Lord of Illusions* to hear
how Barker seems to have conceived of what he was doing in making the film.
He talks a lot about the audience, and about how audiences respond to horror
films. He says he wants to confound their expectations, to present them with
unfamiliar settings and to revise tropes. He is proud of the way the film takes
place mostly in daylight, for example, and of Harry D'Amour as a genuine
good guy rather than the usual hellbound heart. Tellingly though, he also talks
about preview audiences, and about the editing process by which the theatrical

cut of the film came to exclude several scenes of dialogue that articulate the ideas because the producers wanted to get to the big scares. Of course the problem is that Barker was hoping the scares would come less from big moments and more from creating a sense of unease because their expectations were being confounded. It is, in this sense, an ambitious failure.

In a sense, what is clear is that Barker is not entirely able to reach his audience in this medium. Through the haze of commercial requirements, industrial and managerial collaboration, and the expectations of the kind of median audience constructed by Hollywood managerial culture to engage first hand with films in their preview phase, Barker wants, on one hand, to treat the audience with respect, but on the other to force them to eschew their pleasures and stop wounding themselves with banality. He speaks quite a bit about horror audiences, both in the commentary track and in journalism around the time, collected online at www.clivebarker.info. In an interview in *The Dark Side* magazine in 1995 he noted:

> *Lord of Illusions* uniquely parallels something that's going on in my own art all the time. It deals with illusions and illusionists, and illusionists provide, for bourgeois audiences, narratives – they are, loosely speaking, narratives in the form of tricks or illusions – that seem to be pieces of frivolous entertainment but are, at root, extremely rich and dark tales of death and resurrection.[31]

This makes pretty clear that Hoppenstand's analysis is correct, and that Barker's conscious address to the audience radicalises his subversive approach. But again *Lord of Illusions* is a film that seems not to have faith in itself to the extent that the audience is not really given either the solid ground of the *realpolitik* or the spectacular pleasures of an aesthetics of ambivalence with which to engage precisely the dark and rich tales of death and resurrection Barker is trying to reach by way of shattering illusion. Though he is keen to express himself as an artist, the medium has let him down. He is not able to attain the ecstatic, cinesexual plane of the cinematic imaginary because he is so busy actively deconstructing it in what is an overly literal, and ultimately ham-fisted, way.

The genre-blending, in particular, is ineffective, as, although in theory the use of the investigative structure and debunking, demystifying activity of a private eye to deconstruct supernatural events makes sense, the, in his own words, 'hokey' way in which the *noir* scenes are photographed and played serve only as another kind of self-parody. A bit like Tim Burton's similar deployment of scientific discourse as an antidote to superstition in *Sleepy Hollow* (1999) four years later, the register seems to dissolve when the narrative wants to go someplace else, resulting in inconsistency rather than ambiguity. Though Barker has stated in interviews that he was very happy with Scott Bakula as Harry, again his neo-noir take on the wry private eye seems overly knowing and ironic, the point where we never fear for Harry's soul because Harry doesn't particularly seem to fear for it himself, not insofar as we can see it in terms of the actor's performance and the consciously ironic dialogue.

In contrast to the contemporaneous *X-Files* (TV, 1993–2002), it is tonally adrift as an investigator narrative. Harry D'Amour becomes here merely another floating cinematic signifier, a jumble of gumshoe clichés and half-realised satire and, ultimately, a secondary character. This robs the story of its moral heart. Harry's mission becomes exactly the same as Nix's – to destroy the illusion, and as we are distanced from Nix by the insistent queering and Harry by the irony, it is, as in the story, Swann who technically gives us the only glimpse of liberation and possibility in his line 'Flesh is a trap, and magic sets us free', which is the last line in the film, spoken in a flashback montage by Dorothea. But we don't feel free. We haven't seen magic. We haven't even seen flesh. We've been so aggressively confronted with our own subjectivity as postmodern film viewers immersed in the filmic imaginary that we haven't been allowed to *engage* with it, not even in terms of an aesthetic of ambivalence, a centre of indetermination, or a cinesexual rapture, let alone any kind of ideologically inclined political subversion/liberation that might, in Linnie Blake's words 'discourage an easy acceptance of cohesive, homogenising narratives of identity, national or otherwise',[32] and so we walk away from it, just as Barker did from cinema itself. Then he took up painting. It seemed to bring him joy.

Notes

1 Barker provides conflicting accounts of the exact beginning of this pursuit, noting at the public interview at the Irish Film Institute, 13 July 2011 (held in conjunction with the *Clive Barker: Dark Imaginer* conference hosted by the School of English at Trinity College, Dublin, 13 and 14 July 2011), that he began painting during *Nightbreed* as an outlet. Certainly we can infer that it had become a full-blown artistic activity after his film directorial career had stopped.

2 *Clive Barker: The Man Behind the Myth*, Sam Hurwitz, short promotional documentary on *The Midnight Meat Train* DVD (2007).

3 Pun intended. The doomed magician at the centre of the story is called Swann. I'm pretty sure Barker intended it to be a pun also.

4 Leaving aside his independent/experimental shorts *Salomé* (1973) and *The Forbidden* (1978).

5 Though unlike *Ambersons*, it would receive belated restoration and vindication.

6 Public interview at the Irish Film Institute, 13 July 2011.

7 Douglas Winter, *Clive Barker: The Dark Fantastic* (London: HarperCollins, 2001), p. 398.

8 Winter, *Clive Barker: The Dark Fantastic*, p. 403.

9 'Writing is a form of magic. Making art is a form of magic.' Clive Barker, *In Conversation* with Sorcha Ní Fhlainn, a special panel presented as part of the *Clive Barker: Dark Imaginer* conference, 14 July 2011, Trinity College, Dublin.

10 Gary Hoppenstand, *Clive Barker's Short Stories: Imagination as Metaphor in the Books of Blood and Other Works* (Jefferson, NC and London: McFarland, 1994), p. 14.

11 Clive Barker, 'The Last Illusion,' *Books of Blood, Omnibus Edition*, Volume 6 (Volumes 4–6) (London: Sphere, 1988), p. 30.

12 Barker, 'The Last Illusion,' p. 148.

13 *Ibid.* p. 112.

14 *Ibid.* p. 131.

15 See Michael Beeler, '*Lord of Illusions*: Filming the *Books of Blood*,' in *Cinefantastique*, Vol. 26:3, April 1995, www.clivebarker.info. Date accessed: 18 July 2014.

16 Clive Barker, *Everville* (London: HarperCollins. 1995), [Overseas Edition] p. 416.

17 *Ibid.* p. 624.

18 Jonathan Bassett, 'Death and Magic in Clive Barker's *Lord of Illusions*: A Terror Management Perspective,' *Studies in Popular Culture*, Vol. 32:1, Fall, 2009, pp. 69–70.

19 Harry M. Benshoff, *Monsters in the Closet: Homosexuality and the Horror Film* (Manchester and New York: Manchester University Press), 1997, p. 5.

20 *Ibid.* p. 260.

21 *Ibid.* p. 265.

22 Derren Brown, *Tricks of the Mind* (London: Channel Four Books), 2006, p. 36.

23 Hoppenstand, *Clive Barker's Short Stories*, p. 18.

24 *Ibid.* p. 164.

25 Annette Hill, *Paranormal Media: Audiences, Spirits and Magic in Popular Culture* (London and New York: Routledge, 2011), p. 137.

26 Gilles Deleuze. *Cinema 1: The Movement-Image* [1983], Trans. Hugh Tomlinson and Barbara Habberjam (London and New York: Continuum International Publishing Group, 2005), p. 64.

27 Brooks Landon, *The Aesthetics of Ambivalence: Rethinking Science Fiction Film in the Age of Electronic (Re)Production* (Westport, Connecticut, and London: Greenwood Press), 1992, p. 65.

28 *Ibid.* p. 153.

29 Patricia MacCormack, *Cinesexuality* (Aldershot and Burlington: Ashgate Publishing, 2008), pp. 1–2.

30 Clive Barker, *In Conversation*, 14 July 2011.

31 Maitland McDonagh, 'A Kind of Magic,' in *The Dark Side*, No. 45 April/May 1995, www.clivebarker.info. Date accessed: 18 July 2014.

32 Linnie Blake, *The Wounds of Nations: Horror Cinema, Historical Trauma and National Identity* (Manchester and New York: Manchester University Press, 2008), p. 14.

5

Drawing (to) fear and horror: into the frame of Clive Barker's *The Midnight Meat Train* and *Dread* comic and film adaptations

Bernard Perron

Be it through words, lines, colours, performance on stage, or live-action on celluloid, Clive Barker remains first and foremost a *dark imaginer*, an artist in the fullest sense of the term, creating dark and mesmerising images. The distinctive style that defines his work certainly comes from his initial inspirations. As Russell Cherrington, specialist of Barker's work and restoration director of *Nightbreed: The Cabal Cut* (1990/2012) has remarked: 'Barker had an affair with comics when he was young. He saw that words and images could go together.'[1] Barker himself has asserted earlier in his career that: 'I think the two major narrative impulses which brought me to the way I write were comics and movies, no doubt about that.'[2] In fact, it is difficult not to acknowledge that comics and movies have brought him to *the way he frames things*. Hence, it goes without saying that his literary works would and should be adapted both for the sequential art and the silver screen.

In this chapter, I will conduct a narrative and formal comparative analysis of two short stories of the *Books of Blood* (1984),[3] that is 'The Midnight Meat Train' (second story of Volume 1) and 'Dread' (first story of Volume 2), and their comic and film adaptations. 'The Midnight Meat Train' was adapted into a comic book by Chuck Wagner and Fred Burke in 1990 (Eclipse Books), and illustrated by Denys Cowan and Michael Davis.[4] Jeff Buhler wrote the screenplay of the film directed by Ryûhei Kitamura in 2008.[5] 'Dread' was adapted into a comic book by Fred Burke in 1992 (Eclipse Books), and illustrated by Dan Brereton. Anthony DiBlasi wrote and directed the movie in 2009. Clive Barker was involved as a producer in the making of both films. The goal of my close reading of the intertextual process at work between the words, the drawings, and the film frames is to demonstrate that Clive Barker's horror fiction not only gives birth to strong representations, but also questions our fascination for dark images. Furthermore, the two film adaptations are both marked by self-reflexive elements, which add to the play of attraction and repulsion. Since it is a fundamental act in the process of filmmaking, I'll explore the notion of framing.

To begin with, considering *The Midnight Meat Train* and *Dread* movies together is indeed relevant for many reasons. The films represent the two extremities of the horror fiction spectrum. If *The Midnight Meat Train* seems at first to be about following the trail of a very brutal serial killer slaughtering his victims with a meat hammer, then odd elements bring the story into the supernatural realm: the train's acceleration and deviation to an unusual track, the weird and sickening growths on Mahogany's torso, and, of course, the ancient flesh-eating creatures living under the city. Kitamura's direction is also very stylish, especially during the murder scenes, where the action is depicted through various camera movements, slow motions, singular camera angles, and CGI effects. As for *Dread*, DiBlasi's *mise-en-scène* is much more sober, watching the characters closely and showing their various liaisons through numerous shots and reverse-shots. Described by DiBlasi himself as a 'coming-of-age, psychological thriller with graphic bits of horror and sex throughout it',[6] the film explores the human mind as well as the emotional states a person can go through, and stays in the realistic sphere. Accordingly, although meat plays a central role in both stories, we are talking about human flesh in the first instance, and beef in the second one.

For my argument, even if it is an indirect one, the most important link between the two movies appears on the cover of the US Blu-ray of *The Midnight Meat Train* and on the cover of the UK DVD of *Dread*. In the first case, we read: 'Easily the best Clive Barker adaptation since the first *Hellraiser* film (Scott Weinberg, Cinematical)', and in the second one: 'One of the finest Clive Barker adaptations to date (shocktillyoudrop.com)'. With all the tribulations surrounding the theatrical release of *The Midnight Meat Train*[7] and the limited release of *Dread*, these two endorsements for the films' home distribution remain one of the best ways to prompt people to see them. Above all, they strikingly underline the notion of adaptation. And undeniably, this impulse toward cinema makes sense as Barker acknowledged in 1991: 'I said [to Hollywood studios] a couple of stories that haven't been optioned would make good movies. One of them is *Dread* which would make a very nice movie if it were handled properly.'[8] And in the audio commentary of the bonus features of *The Midnight Meat Train* Blu-ray, he says that for him it was an 'obvious candidate for a movie'. If the *Books of Blood* can or should be adapted on film,[9] it is because, '[Horror] Cinema so desperately needs stories.'[10] In a time where the horror film genre lacks inventiveness to the point of remaking not-so-old classics (like the slashers of the 1980s), Clive Barker's short stories become remarkable options because of their narrative arc, their imagery, and their use of confined and moving spaces (*The Midnight Meat Train* literally takes the reader and viewer on a roller coaster). Yet, when we think about how poorly *Rawhead Rex* (from the *Books of Blood*, Volume 3, screenplay by Clive Barker) was brought to the silver screen by George Pavlou in 1986,[11] or about the bad treatment that 20th Century Fox subjected *Nightbreed* to (the film adaptation of the 1988 Barker's novel *Cabal*, directed by Barker himself in 1990), we are reminded that literary adaptations to film are more often seen as a question of faithfulness or betrayal.[12] To adapt is to transpose from one media to another; it is ineluctable to transform and to appropriate the work of someone else.

In accordance with such an appropriation, on the one hand, the two comic adaptations follow the narrative line of the two short stories accurately. While they illustrate the action and give a face to the characters, they also condense Barker's work by cutting out descriptive sentences here and there. For instance, the reader knows much less about Leon Kaufman at the beginning of *The Midnight Meat Train* comic,[13] and has less access to Steve's feelings at the beginning of the *Dread* comic, than in the original narratives.[14] On the other hand, in order to make two feature films (and not short ones), Buhler and DiBlasi's screenplays expand Barker's stories while remaining true to them.[15] In Kitamura's movie, Leon Kaufman (Bradley Cooper) now has a girlfriend, Maya (Leslie Bibb), whom he wants to marry, and a good friend, Jurgis (Roger Bart), who introduces him to an important gallery owner (Brooke Shields) in order to help him succeed in his art. Mahogany (Vinnie Jones) is sick with an unknown disease. Meat becomes an even more important leitmotif as Leon is presented as a committed vegetarian, preferring to make the restaurant's owner where Maya works cook for him the tofu he brings in instead of steak. In DiBlasi's movie, Quaid (Shaun Evans)'s past, and source of dread, is both explained and shown. He plans a Machiavellian affair with a new character, Abby (Laura Donnelly); while she wants to hide her body and face half-covered by a port-wine stain (a capillary malformation in the skin) as much as possible, Quaid films her getting naked before sexual intercourse and broadcasts the image on campus. Stephen[16] (Jackson Rathbone) and Cheryl (Hanne Steen) have a much closer relationship this time. It isn't Stephen, but a young boy named Joshua (Jonathan Readwin) who fears to be the prisoner of deafness once more insofar as he had temporarily lost his sense of hearing after an accident when he was young. Another interesting link to be made with *The Midnight Meat Train* movie can be seen in Cheryl's filmed interview (0:19:21) where she explains that her dad, who molested her, was working at a meat-packing plant; a plant that might not be so different from the one where Mahogany is going to work.

As I have mentioned earlier, the two movies are also connected through their reflexivity; they indeed point to themselves. In *Dread*, Quaid no longer takes pictures as he does in the short story. He lures Stephen and Cheryl to do a fear study as a school project and to capture the interviews on video. The images of *Dread* therefore switch once in a while to the video captures or film-within-the-film recordings. In the scenes staging the interviews, the viewer finds himself or herself in the same position as Cheryl, Stephen, and Quaid: they are looking at people, trying to find their dread as well. Interestingly, in *The Midnight Meat Train*, Leon is no longer an accountant but a photographer. After the prologue of the movie, the first shot (0:02:51) is a close-up of Leon walking into the frame of an urban street, looking directly into the camera and taking a picture of nobody else other than the viewer; no reverse-shot reveals what or who he was shooting. During the subjective point of views of Leon taking pictures, the frame guide of his diegetic camera's viewfinder appears on the screen, recalling the one of the actual film camera of the director of photography Jonathan Sela shooting the movie. When Leon meets the gallery owner for the first time, she finds his photographs empty and gives him advice (0:08:05): 'The next time you find yourself at the heart of the city, stay put, be brave, keep shooting'. Since to shoot is to look (through the lens of a camera, and to view the image via a projector),[17] this line of dialogue is as much addressed to the viewer as it is to Leon. The viewer of a horror film has to stay put as well, to be brave, and keep looking at the screen. The audience certainly does so since they know this is a film. In the same way, Leon stays put, is brave, and keeps shooting the three men harassing the Asian girl in the subway (0:11:11) because he knows that he is being filmed by the surveillance camera. He points out the closed circuit television monitoring the event to the leader of the pack, preventing him from being assaulted by the gang.

We can easily underline an obsession for the act of looking in *The Midnight Meat Train*. The slaughter scenes stage attacks against the gaze. The first shot of the first murder of the Asian girl shows her in the train, sitting on the left side and facing the camera (0:13:39). She doesn't see, as the viewer does, the out of focus silhouette sitting in the background on the right side, nor does she see it walking toward her with a meat hammer in hand. When the girl is hit on the cheek, her head quickly turns to the side, a movement that is undoubtedly mimicking the one a viewer will be making in order to look away from the horror. During the second murder (0:20:51), the eyeball of a man – the husband in the scene – comes out of its socket under the impact of a hammer stroke to the head and is projected at the viewer. The wife slips on the eyeball. Her head is then detached from her body by yet another blow with a club. This fatal blow is filmed through the wife's subjective point of view. An ingenious camera movement tracks back from the blurred vision of Mahogany near the corpse and passes through the eye in order to reveal the head mere feet away from the decapitated body.[18] The third murder (0:31:31) is not that easy for Mahogany who, feeling faint, is assaulted by the tough black man. Coming to save Mahogany the butcher, the train driver shoots the opponent. Another special camera movement trails the bullet going through the head and straight out of the right eye. Two more eyeballs are taken out of their sockets in the fourth murder scene and are put in a plastic container (0:55:14). In the end, it is noteworthy to emphasise that the first and last images of *The Midnight Meat Train* are of eyes, responding to each other in a nice mirror effect. The first image is an extreme close-up of the last victim waking up in the train and facing toward the right of the frame (0:00:48).[19] The last image concludes with Leon, now the new butcher, turning back to look once again directly into the camera and at the viewer (1:35:28).

The above study heightens the viewer's awareness of the medium of cinema, and reflects what is most enriching in the process of adaptation. Beyond the subtractions, additions, and other narrative changes made to the original short stories of the *Books of Blood*, it is what the process of adaptation reveals that is worth analysing. Sarah Cardwell emphasises and supports this interest in 'Adaptation Studies Revisited: Purposes, Perspectives, and Inspiration':

> Through comparisons of texts in different media, we can move to comparison of the media themselves, which can lead us to a fuller and more complex understanding of the specificity of the media involved. That is, the study of adaptation is uniquely able to advance the study of medium specificity. This is a vital and underdeveloped area of aesthetics: the study of the unique features of different art forms, those features that distinguish them from one another and constitute their artistic potential.[20]

In such a practice, it becomes significant to consider the freedom allowed by the comic drawing toward the representation of reality (as opposed to the recording of real people and things on film). Making pictures with a pen can more easily create images of what is imagined. For instance, the beast Quaid is talking about in *Dread* comes into sight in a few panels which are cleverly associated with him, the antagonist. The beast appears in three panels on the bottom strip of pages 8 and 9.[21] In the last panel, Quaid's and the wolf-like beast's faces melt to create a single visage (Fig. 8).

The beast's teeth are placed on Quaid's head as a crown in the last panel of page 37. The face of the beast is used as the backdrop of page 10 while dealing with Quaid's unknown past. Its red eyes are seen in the background of the last panel of page 15 when Quaid talks about touching the beast. The wolf's profile with its menacing jaws wide open is shown over Stephen's worried face when he realises that his friend knows about his dread (page 20 – Fig. 9).

Finally, in the last panel and page of the book, the beast, now looking like a supernatural monster, is bent over Quaid when his 'dreams come true'. Characteristic to comics, these visualisations are not found in the short stories or in the film. The distinction of style is also more peculiar to the comics, called the ninth art by the Francophones.[22] Michael Davis' use of pastels and the blurrier pictures he has created for *The Midnight Meat Train* are really different from Dan Brereton's use of watercolours and the sharper pictures of *Dread*.

To study the specificities of the medium better while still bringing to light Clive Barker's influence on the comics and films, I'll concentrate on an emblematic moment in Barker's work and on one of its important aspects. For the author of the *Books of Blood*, 'Most horror, whether it's real or fictitious, literary or cinematic, deals with the eruption of chaos into human existence (or else the revelation of its constant, unseen presence).'[23]

This observation explains his preference:

> My favorite [sic] moments in horror movies and books are the 'unmasking' scenes, the key moment when the realities collide; the moment when the bourgeois assumptions

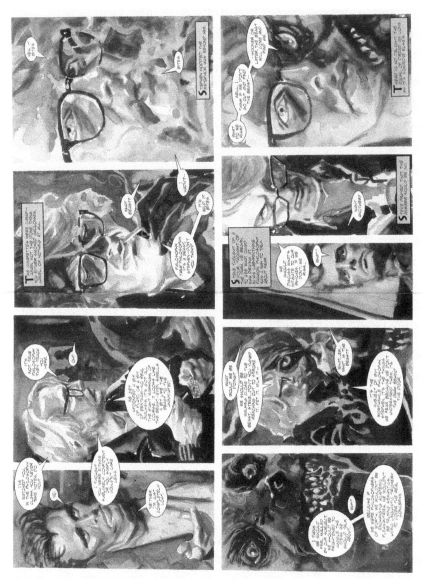

9 *Dread*, p. 20.

of the characters – who have muddled through so far unaware that an unspeakable 'thing' is hovering over their heads – finally look up and see the truth.[24]

Actually, Barker has written powerful 'unmasking' scenes. I'll consequently analyse the ways these make the most of the act of framing, of arranging a subject within a film image or a comic panel so that it is 'framed' in a specific way. As literature describes in words the act of making someone look, the comic book does it by arranging panels in the space of a page, and cinema by changing the scale of the object shown on the screen. The moment Kaufman comes out of his dreams – of his mother in her kitchen chopping turnips and smiling sweetly as she chopped[25] – to discover what is happening in the next car,[26] constitutes the key 'eruption of chaos' in *The Midnight Meat Train*. Barker writes:

> The window between the cars was completely curtained off, but *he stared at it*, frowning, as though he might suddenly discover X-ray vision. The car rocked and rolled again. It was really travelling again.
>
> Another ripping sound.
>
> Was it rape?
>
> With no more than a mild *voyeuristic urge* he moved down the see-sawing car towards the intersecting door, hoping there might be a chink in the curtain. *His eyes were still fixed on the window*, and he failed to notice the splatters of blood he was treading in. Until –
>
> – his heel slipped. […]
>
> His head was saying: blood. Nothing would make the word go away.
>
> There was no more than a yard or two between him and the door now. *He had to look*. There was blood on his shoe, and a thin trail to the next car, but *he still had to look*.
>
> He had to.
>
> He took two more steps to the door and scanned the curtain looking for a flaw in the blind: a pulled thread in the weave would be sufficient. There was a tiny hole. *He glued his eye to it*.
>
> His mind refused to accept *what his eyes were seeing* beyond the door. It rejected the spectacle as preposterous, as a dream sight. His reason said it couldn't be real, but his flesh knew it was. His body became rigid with terror. *His eyes, unblinking, could not close off* the appalling scene through the curtain. […]
>
> Then he fainted.
>
> He was unconscious when the train reached Jay Street. […] He would have asked what kind of train this could be. Except that he already knew. The truth was hanging in the next car. It was smiling contentedly to itself from behind a bloody chain-mail apron.
>
> This was the Midnight Meat Train.[27]

This passage is unquestionably very strong. Instead of focusing on the character's emotional state, Barker carefully expresses Kaufman's fear and horror through repetitive references to his gaze. The discovery remains truly visual, as is the finding of the creatures later on.[28] Hence, it has led to great comic page layouts.

The adapted scene is on pages 14–15 of the comic book (Fig. 10).[29]

10   *The Midnight Meat Train*, pp. 14–15.

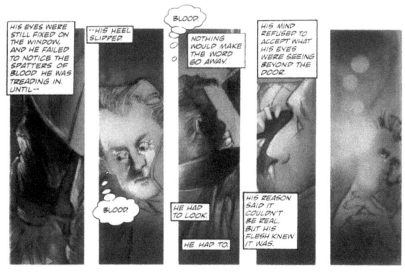

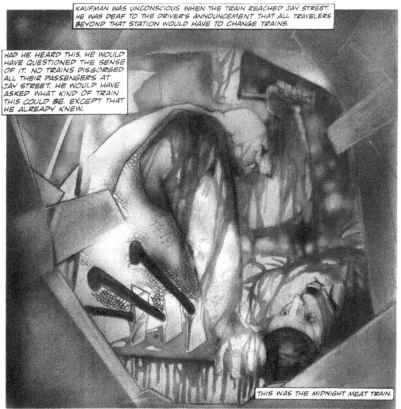

10   (Continued)

Excerpts of Barker's words are presented in descriptive boxes. Only two small speech balloons are used for Kaufman's thoughts about the 'blood'. The double page is well punctuated insofar as the number of vertical panels in the three strips leading to the climax increases. The two strips on page 14 have three and four panels respectively, and the one on page 15 has five. The bottom strip on page 14 creates a nice line toward the next page; it goes from a close-up of Kaufman's profile to a wide image of him: 'With no more than a mild voyeuristic urge, he moved down the see-sawing car towards the intersecting door, hoping he might get a peek'. The first panel on the top strip of page 15 starts by telling the reader that his eyes failed to notice the blood on the floor, blood that the drawing exposes. The next four panels stay on Kaufman's face. A significant flair effect in the last panel conveys the upshot of the gaze in the previous one. At last, the two penultimate sentences of the above quoted section are illustrated ('The truth was hanging in the next car. It was smiling contentedly to itself from behind a bloody chain-mail apron'). Denys Cowan exploits the full potential of the comic art, which, in addition to allowing the layout of various panels on a page (a spatial montage), permits change to the picture size as well. He uses a large panel, taking more than half of page 15, in order to reveal Mahogany bloodily chopping up the young boy. The shocking image is seen through the hole in the curtain, doubly affecting the reader's perception. Even if readers have seen the image when they turn the page, they still have to read it; the vision has to be reconstructed. The eyes need to examine the octagonal frame within the frame, find the balance, and understand the lines and colours in order to finally put together the hatchets and the characters.

The comic's structural layout is also emphasised when Kaufman finally gets in the next car while Mahogany talks to the driver. In Barker's words:

Kaufman *opened his eyes*, steeling himself for the slaughter-pen in front of him.
There was no avoiding it.
It filled every one of his senses: the smell of opened entrails, the sight of the bodies, the feel of the fluid on the floor under his fingers, the sound of the straps creaking beneath the weight of the corpses, even the air, tasting salty with blood. He was with death absolutely in that cubby-hole, hurtling through the dark.
But there was no nausea now. There was no feeling left but a casual revulsion. He even found himself *peering at the body with some curiosity*.[30]

This eruption of chaos is adapted on page 18, on the left and first panel seen when the reader turns the page (Fig. 11).

There is a vertical strip that constitutes three small panels, symmetrically portraying Kaufman crouched in the first and last ones, and Mahogany leaving the car in the middle one. Then, 'no avoidance' is possible. The horrible slaughter is shown in a full-size oblong vertical panel taking more than half of the page. This enables the sight of the three suspended bodies on the right side. Commencing under Kaufman sitting on the floor, the red of the blood fills the

11 *The Midnight Meat Train*, p. 18.

bottom of the image harshly. The containers under each one of the bodies create a fine line with Kaufman's gaze; a gaze that mirrors the one of the reader.

The film adaptation of the scene makes use of camera movements and dynamic montages, which are specific features of cinema. However, with its doors, windows, and support poles, the train is a place full of frames. As a result, the widescreen shots frequently resemble the layouts of a comic page in some instances. It starts right away (0:52:59), from the door Mahogany just walked up to with his meat hammer, while a pull-back shot reveals Leon hiding behind a half wall out of sight of the killer he has been tailing for a little while (Fig.12, Screenshot A). The shot ends with Leon on the left frame, still in a

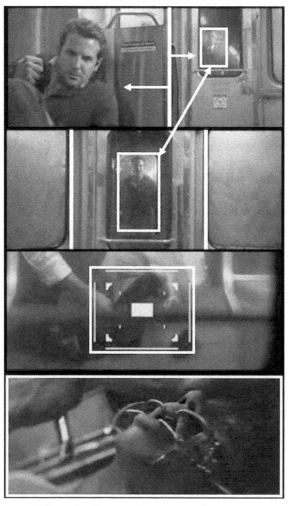

12   *The Midnight Meat Train*, screenshots A-B-C-D.

secure place,[31] and Mahogany framed in the window of the cars' doors, standing immobile for a few seconds and turning around to hit his victims. Leon dares to gaze (shot) at the window through which the butcher is spurting blood (reverse-shot), and he looks away (a close shot of his eyes). In the next car, as Mahogany drags a body on the floor, the camera moves toward the door where Leon now stands. In turn, he is framed in the window, in the middle of a layout of three 'panels' (Fig. 12, Screenshot B). The viewer is looking not so much at a window as he is gazing at a mirror. Leon is located on the other side of the looking glass. Since he has already been destined to replace the butcher (via his dreams and because Mahogany has spared him), he'll become Mahogany when he crosses to the other side, to the other car. For now, Leon overcomes his fear and takes photographs. In the first shot, the viewer sees the viewfinder's frame guide of Leon's diegetic camera on the screen and a black-and-white still is taken (Fig. 12, Screenshot C). Yet, all the subsequent images are shown directly on the screen from angles that are not seen from Leon's point of view (Fig. 12, Screenshot D). Contrary to the large panel of the comic book, many closes-up are edited together to describe Mahogany's methodical labour: pulling out teeth and nails, removing the eyes from their sockets (and placing them in a plastic container as I have previously noted), shaving the heads, planting hooks in the back of the feet and hanging the human carcasses. Therefore, if the act of seeing is motivated by the gaze of the character in the universe of the fiction (only two other reverse-shots of Leon photographing the butchery are edited; Leon is seen by Mahogany in the last one), it is the viewer who is finally made to look directly and closely at the horrific images.

Such tricky transitions from diegetic images to the ones of the film itself are at the heart of the three 'unmasking' scenes of *Dread*. The first one happens when Cheryl sits in front of the camera (0:19:07). The initial shot of the interview is of her face seen through the small LCD of the camcorder at the centre of the screen (Fig. 13, Screenshot A). The camera tilts up to show her visage. She starts to talk, looking straight at the camera, during which time the scene cuts to a quick shot of the bluish video recording (Fig. 13, Screenshot B). Most of the time, the rest of the interview models the frame of this first image, with Cheryl even glancing again at the camera (Fig. 13, Screenshot D). But it does not go back to the camcorder (until the end when Cheryl questions Quaid in turn about his own dread). The viewer listens to Cheryl as Quaid and Stephen do. The two boys, seen in reverse-shots, remain the diegetic viewers. A great shot frames the interview in a square in the middle of the widescreen (Fig. 13, Screenshot C). Quaid, on the left, and Stephen, on the right, are positioned in front of Cheryl. They are somehow placed in the first row, since their position copies the one viewers finds themselves in the movie theatre sitting behind other people.

The second important revelation is also only present in the movie: Stephen is going to listen to Abby. It begins with the image of the camcorder's lens filming (0:34:04 – Fig. 14, Screenshot A). It is followed by a focus pull; the focus changes during the shot from behind the left shoulder of Stephen to the

13 *Dread*, screenshots A-B-C-D.

face of Abby (Fig. 14, Screenshot B). When the camera cuts back to Stephen paying attention, we find the camcorder not on his left side, but rather on his right side (certainly to ease the shot and reverse-shot – Fig. 14, Screenshot C,). The focus pull was consequently made by DiBlasi's camera and everything is filmed by his camera (not Stephen's). It is only when Abby asks Stephen if she can show him something as she stands up to undress to expose her port-wine stain that the camcorder is filmed at the right side of Stephen, although much lower than at the beginning of the interview. Similar to the first shot of Cheryl's recording, the viewer sees Abby via the LCD viewfinder (Fig. 14, Screenshot D). Only one quick shot of the black-and-white footage is used, right at the moment Stephen stands up to gently reject her advances.

14 *Dread*, screenshots A-B-C-D.

The scene ends with Abby framed in the camcorder screen. Later on, with new material viciously added by Quaid, the tape is broadcast on a school TV (1:02:49), another screen within the screen of the movie theatre (or another TV into a TV during home viewing).

The third scene comes from Barker's work. In the short story, Quaid invites Steve to his place with the purpose of exhibiting 'some wonderful photographs'.

> Quaid pulled out a box from behind a pile of philosophy books. In it was a sheaf of black and white photographs, blown up to a twice postcard size. He passed the first one of the series over to Steve.

'I locked her away you see, Steve.' Quaid was unemotional as a newsreader. 'To see if I could needle her into showing her dread a little bit'.

[…]

Photograph One was a small, featureless room. A little plain furniture.

[…]

Photograph Four. On the table, on an unpatterned plate, a slab of meat. A bone sticks out of it.

'Beef', said Quaid.

'But she's a vegetarian'.

[…]

Fifteen: she touches the meat.

'This is where the cracks begin to show', said Quaid, with quiet triumph. 'This is where the dread begins'.

Steve studied the photograph closely. The grain of the print blurred the detail, but the cool mama was in pain, that was for sure. Her face knotted up, half in desire, half in repulsion, as she touched the food.

[…]

Thirty-seven: she eats the rancid meat.

[…]

Steve stared at the photograph.[32]

There are 39 photographs of Cheryl's captivity in the room. Her descent into hell is to be looked at. As Barker writes about Quaid a few pages later:

> To the limits. Death was at the limits. And wouldn't that be the ultimate experience for Quaid? Watching a man die: watching the fear of death, the motherlode of dread, approach. Sartre had written that no man could ever know his own death. But to know the deaths of others, intimately – to watch the acrobatics that the mind would surely perform to avoid the bitter truth – that was a clue to death's nature, wasn't it? That might, in some small way, prepare a man for his own death. To live another's dread vicariously was the safest, cleverest way to touch the beast.[33]

The last sentence is in fact a great definition of horror fiction. And as far as Quaid's solution to get access to the knowledge of dread rests on a visual device, this is even more germane for a comparative study.

In the comic book adaptation, Steve and Quaid look at the photographs of Cheryl over the course of six pages. The first one overlaps two panels at the bottom of page 25. This is not a *fotonovela*, but the drawn printed images fit perfectly in the comic arranged as graphics and texts. They suit the sequential art even more since they remain truly fixed images of the scene, and the gutters between the panels express, by their nature, the temporal ellipses between them. It is only through their black-and-white tonalities and the way they are slightly unframed in order to show their edges (in the fourth panel of page 26, the second, fourth, and sixth of page 28, the second of pages 29 and 30) that the photographs are distinguished from the images of the two men in the present time.[34] Following the example of Cheryl's interview in the movie, the first panel on page 30 is reflexive; it presents the two men holding a photograph in the foreground (number thirty-three of Barker's short story) examining it in the same manner as the reader is doing in front of the comic book. But if the reader is not really looking at a picture, in that this is a drawing of a picture, it is also because Dan Brereton makes the best of the artistic potential of the comic medium as Denys Cowan did for *The Midnight Meat Train*. He doesn't limit himself to the regular format of, as described in the short story, 'photographs, blown up to a twice postcard size'.[35] Instead, he uses the variable and elastic possibilities of the 'putting in panel' to work on the tabular configuration of his plates. The layout of pages 26–27 is, for instance, balanced by the two vertical oblong panels at the bottom of each page, one a photograph of Cheryl and the other of Steve and Quaid (Fig. 15).

The image subsequent to Cheryl vomiting is also presented in a vertical oblong panel at the bottom of page 29 (photographs twenty-nine and thirty of Barker's story), a position and format more likely to translate Cheryl's hopelessness. Brereton also focuses the attention on what is important. Although, as we can envision, Quaid was shooting from one point of view, the days of captivity are always seen from a certain distance. The action is reframed to follow Cheryl's physical and emotional movements in the room. When she breaks down and 'eats the rancid meat' (photograph thirty-seven), Brereton repeats the action in the last two images of page 30; the second one is a horizontal panel closing in on the face of Cheryl biting her 'fear' (Fig. 16). Furthermore, pointing to the act of looking, the first panel frames a photograph in the frame with Steve and Quaid looking at it just as the reader does.

Akin to the sequence written by Barker in his short story, and contrary to Cheryl's pictures, the 'infra-red photographs' of Steve's own captivity are not numbered or delineated as clearly (except for one overlapping another on page 41) in the comic book adaptation. Between pages 35 and 43, there are only five panels of the forty-three that let the reader see Quaid, four of which where he is pointing his camera. Inasmuch as almost all of the drawings share the same tonalities, the photographs of the action and the action itself are hard to differentiate.

From the perspective of analysing medium specificity, the switch to a camcorder in the movie is an obvious and appropriate one. It allows the same kind of image juxtapositions that the comic book displayed. DiBlasi starts the scene as he did with Abby's interview (1:16:13). This time, however, it is the lens of a video projector that is turned on (Fig. 17, Screenshot A). Quaid wakes Stephen up, tied to a chair in front of a screen. The latter is forced to witness what happened to his sweetheart. Once again, such a shot reminds viewers of their position as spectator (Fig. 17, Screenshot B). This shot might be a bit more interesting since, as in a film theatre, it is a projector and not a camera that is found behind the characters; the film projector is projecting the image of a video projector on a screen, displaying, in its turn, an image on a screen. The same strategy is used

Drawing (to) fear and horror   103

15   *Dread*, pp. 26–7.

15   (Continued)

16 *Dread*, p. 30.

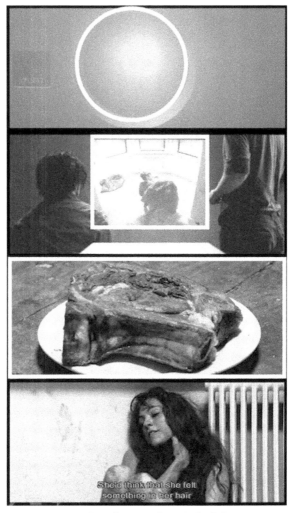

17   *Dread*, screenshots A-B-C-D.

yet again. Despite the fact that we only see the set-up of one camcorder in the scene where Quaid is preparing the room to lock Cheryl up, the video footage is taken from three different angles: one frontal (the point of view we have seen Quaid verify), one from the ceiling, and one from the side showing the door. Albeit we can presume that Quaid could have controlled his camcorder(s) in order to pan, tilt, and zoom in and out, the images at floor level are problematic as the many variations of frames and scales suppose that the amateur cineaste would have been behind his camera all the time to watch Cheryl's behaviour closely. In actual fact, Quaid's diegetic video footage is edited in the same way as DiBlasi's film footage and produces the same effects. Some cuts shift from a video to a film shot. The first one is the shocking close-up and slight zoom in on the beef in the middle of the room (1:18:02 – Fig. 17, Screenshot C). Specifically, after the moment Cheryl starts to break and hallucinate, the images are not mediated through the camcorder (Fig. 17, Screenshot D). The viewer catches sight of her vomiting into the bucket on video and next sees her in a state of fury on film. The climactic moment during which 'she eats the rancid meat' is entirely witnessed directly on film. Compared to the two scenes previously scrutinised, the tricky transition from diegetic images to the ones of the film itself is even more complex here in regard to time. Quaid's study is not watched at the same time as it happens. The video footage is from the past. As the images of Cheryl are not marked as something that has already happened, they are subsequently perceived as occurring at the same time as those of Quaid and Stephen. Or, read differently, the viewer is brought back to the past during the film footage to experience the sick experiment with Cheryl. The spectacle of the poor woman eating the rotten beef is so sickening in part because the viewer loses the distance of the video image. The viewer therefore faces the horror alongside Cheryl; drawn to her fear.

I have tried with this chapter to show how the comic books and cinema were able to exploit the full potential of their own features in order to render Barker's powerful writing style and strong imagery. The main goal was to put forward forms that might not have been visible at first, but have a great impact on the experience of each adaptation: the lines and colours of the drawings and the co-existing frames in tabular configurations for the comic books, as well as the *mise en abîme* of the act of looking through the lens of a camera and the montage of various shots within each film. In the end, what my narrative and formal comparative analysis demonstrates is summed up by the French philosopher Éric Dufour. Writing about cinema, Dufour notes:

> it is true that the horror film can be described as adolescent in that it shows the freedom, the lack of concern and the disrespect that is precisely the characteristic of youth. If the horror film is a teen cinema, it is because it fears nothing, that for it there is nothing forbidden, taboo, and that it dares to question what we later on learn we should not be touching [...]. In this sense, the horror film is an examination of the powers of the image.[36]

Through the way they frame content and point the reader and the viewer to their own position as a spectator, the two stories of the *Books of Blood* and their adaptations are eloquent examinations of the power of the image. They show how much Clive Barker is a visually clever dark imaginer. He knows that: 'There is no delight the equal of dread. As long as it's someone else's.'[37]

Notes

1 Cherrington said this during the introduction to the first *In Conversation* with Clive Barker panel which the participants had the pleasure to share at the *Dark Imaginer* Conference (Dublin, 13 July 2011).

2 Dick Hansom, 'To Hell and Back' [1989], in Stephen Jones (ed.), *Clive Barker's Shadows in Eden* (Lancaster, PA: Underwood-Miller, 1991), p. 359.

3 Clive Barker, *Books of Blood, Omnibus Edition*, Volumes 1–3 (London: Sphere, 1988).

4 The short story is in Volume 3 of *Clive Barker's Tapping the Vein*. The five volumes were edited into a single collection by Checker Book Publishing Group in 2002.

5 I will not be referring to the theatrical release of the film, but to the Unrated Director's Cut available on DVD and Blu-ray. *The Midnight Meat Train*, Dir. Ryûhei Kitamura, Lionsgate Home Entertainment, 2009, DVD/Blu-ray.

6 Ryan Turek, 'Facing the Beast: On the Set of Clive Barker's Dread' (October 2008), Shocktillyoudrop.com. 24 November 2009, http://shocktillyoudrop.com/news/topnews.php?id=12919. Date accessed: 8 June 2011.

7 See for instance 'News – Clive Wants To Save Midnight Meat Train!', *Revelations: The Official Clive Barker Website*, www.clivebarker.info/newssavemmt.html. Date accessed: 8 June 2011.

8 Stanley Wiater, 'Horror in Print: Clive Barker', in Jones (ed.), *Clive Barker's Shadows in Eden*, p. 193.

9 'The Book of Blood' (first story of Volume 1) and 'On Jerusalem Street' (postscript of Volume 6) were adapted to film as *Book of Blood*. Dir. John Harrison. Matador Pictures, Midnight Picture Show, 2009.

10 Frédéric Sabouraud, *L'Adaptation: Le Cinema a tant besoin d'histoires* (Paris: Cahiers du cinéma/Scérén-CNDP, coll. Les Petits Cahiers, 2006).

11 The short story was also adapted into a comic book by Steve Niles and illustrated by Les Edwards in 1993 (Eclipse Books). It is a much better adaptation in my opinion.

12 This is another pinpoint on the cover of Sabouraud's book.

13 Those lines of the first page of the story do not appear in the descriptive boxes of the comic: 'Was it really only a season since he stepped out of Port Authority Bus Station and looked up 42nd Street towards the Broadway intersection? [...] He was embarrassed now even to think of his naivety. It made him wince to remember how he had stood and announced aloud: "New York, I love you." Love? Never. It had been at best an infatuation.'

14 For example, these sentences of the short story have been cut out: 'Steve was beginning to feel like Quaid's straight-man. Except that Quaid wasn't in a joking mood. His face was set: his pinprick irises had closed down to tiny dots'; 'Quaid's loquaciousness deserted him suddenly'; and 'Steve could see the punchline coming' (p. 4).

15 This was the goal of the two screenwriters. See their comments: 'Clive on the Midnight Meat Train', *Revelations: The Official Clive Barker Website*, www.clivebarker.info/mmt.html. Date accessed: 10 June 2011; and *Revelations: The Official Clive Barker Website*, www.clivebarker.info/dreadmovie.html. Date accessed: 10 June 2011.

16 And not 'Steve' as is in the short story and comic adaptation.

17 If I were to push my reading further, the few shots showing the flickering light of the train movement through the tunnel can easily be seen as a meta-reference to the flickering of the celluloid going through the projector.

18 In the audio commentary of the bonus features of the Blu-ray, Barker and Kitamura explain this shot by talking about the consciousness of the eye, the thirty seconds of consciousness before death.

19 The prologue is actually the end of the film.

20 Sarah Cardwell, 'Adaptation Studies Revisited: Purposes, Perspectives, and Inspiration,' in James M. Welsh and Peter Lev (eds), *The Literature/Film Reader: Issues of Adaptations* (Lanham, MA: The Scarecrow Press, 2007), p. 59.

21 *Dread*, Fred Burke (adapt.) and Dan Brerton (art), graphic novel [1992], Eclipse publishing, Rpt. (London: HarperCollins, 1993). The pages are not numbered. I'm taking the first title page as page one. The first drawing is on page 3.

22 In France, the 'bande dessinée' (comics) is considered the ninth art since the beginning of the 1960s.

23 Clive Barker, *Clive Barker's A-Z of Horror* (London: BBC Books, 1997), p. 15.

24 John Brosnan, 'Terror Tactics,' in Jones (ed.), *Clive Barker's Shadows in Eden*, p. 91.

25 Clive Barker, 'The Midnight Meat Train,' *Books of Blood*, Volume 1. (London: Sphere, 1988), p. 21.

26 The opening of the film is somehow catching up with this scene.

27 Barker, 'The Midnight Meat Train,' pp. 22–3. Italics added.

28 *Ibid*. 'He could not look away. Not that terror froze him as it had at the window. He simply wanted to watch' (p. 31). 'That was all Kaufman could see, and it was more that he wanted to see. There was much more in the darkness, flickering and flapping. But he could look no longer' (p. 34).

29 'The Midnight Meat Train,' graphic novel, *Tapping the Vein*, Chuck Wagner, Fred Burke (adaptation) and Denys Cowan, Michael Davis (art), Eclipse Publishing, Issue 3 (1989–92). The pages are not numbered. I'm taking the first title page (*Tapping the Vein*) as page 1. The first drawing is on page 5. The double page is illustrating more than the passage I have been quoting.

30 Barker, 'The Midnight Meat Train,' p. 26. Italics added.

31 In the comic book, following the short story, Kaufman hides under a bench. In three long horizontal panels in the last half of page 16, the reader see Mahogany's feet passing by.

32 Clive Barker, 'Dread,' *Books of Blood*, Volume 2, pp. 14–18.

33 Barker, 'Dread,' pp. 22–3.

34 *Dread*, graphic novel, p. 33 includes a panel consisting of Steve literally looking down at a picture depicting a close-up of Cheryl. In the next panel, he is looking at it while the reader only sees the back corner of it. A descriptive box overlaps the two panels: 'It was the moment when Cheryl first picked up the rotting meat that fascinated him most. Her face wore an expression completely uncharacteristic of the woman he had known. Doubt was written there, and confusion, and deep – Dread'. The last word appears at the top of the second panel.

35 Barker, 'Dread,' p. 14.

36 Éric Dufour, *Le Cinéma d'horreur et ses figures* (Paris: Presses universitaires de France, 2006), p. 45. My translation.

37 This is indeed one of the most famous assertions of 'Dread' (Volume 2, p. 4).

6

Beauty, pain, and desire: gothic aesthetics and feminine identification in the filmic adaptations of Clive Barker

Brigid Cherry

Be my victim. (*Candyman*, 1992)[1]

With these words, the Candyman seduces Helen into his dark realm, but they might also apply to the viewer, who is similarly seduced into the fictional worlds created by Clive Barker. In relation to horror film spectatorship, the viewers could be seen as positioning themselves as willing victims of the visual and narrative horrors unfolding on screen. In relation to the horror genre as a whole, this is not an unproblematic position and many horror film theorists have debated this at length. For example, Linda Williams' account of female horror film spectatorship suggests that female spectators are punished through being forced to look on the monstrous body whilst also othered by being aligned with the monster,[2] whilst Noel Carroll's philosophical approach argues that horror film viewers must suffer fear and disgust in order to have their narrative curiosity satisfied.[3] Cynthia Freeland, on the other hand, maintains that audiences have a direct interest in the horrific and take pleasure in horror films' presentations of evil.[4] However, what is clear from even a cursory study of horror film fandom, is that 'victimhood' in this sense is complex and multilayered. Horror film viewers thoroughly enjoy being scared,[5] and furthermore the pleasures of horror film viewing are wide and varied. Barker's work, and in this context the filmic adaptations of his fiction, are uniquely interesting in terms of their horrifying and yet pleasurable affects.

In the field of horror film and literature, Barker's name epitomises, even more so perhaps than many other horror auteurs, the diverse pleasures of horror, and not least those horrors organised around monstrosity, sexuality, and the representation of pleasure and pain. This is primarily because Barker's vision offers a complex interplay of aesthetics and modes of emotional affect, and more importantly for the female horror film audience, his sensibility invites a strong sense of identification and desire around the concept of highly ambiguous and desirable figures of monstrosity. Barker's work (in both film and fiction) is in fact extremely popular amongst female horror fans and holds strong appeals for women.[6] The filmic adaptations of his work are a specific pleasure for these female horror fans, with *Hellraiser*, *Candyman*, and *Nightbreed* being well-loved and highly regarded films amongst this group. In the discussion that follows, I will interrogate the ways in which these films offer specific sets of pleasures (both visual and narrative) in light of the views expressed by female fans. (Whilst *Lord of Illusions* is also significant in terms of its representations of pleasure and pain, it is less highly regarded or discussed, and will not for the most part be specifically included.) With a particular focus on feminine spectatorship and identification, I analyse responses to the forms of cinematic horror depicted in these films and how the representations of monstrosity parallel and exceed those on offer in the gothic mode. This chapter is informed by responses to the chosen films by female viewers, and I primarily consider these responses in relation to the aesthetic qualities of the films.

Feminine aesthetics in horror

Certainly a taste for horror can be strong in some viewers, but putting aside the question of why viewers enjoy horrific material ostensibly designed to trigger negative emotions (not least since fans of horror clearly do enjoy it), it remains a useful avenue of exploration to ask why certain fans enjoy certain kinds or aspects of horror. General questions of aesthetics do arise, but in the context of Barker's status within the fan canon, and especially amongst female fans, how might responses in the chosen audience to his films aid our understanding of the aesthetic pleasures of horror cinema? Furthermore, in considering the female audience specifically, what is it about films adapted from his work in particular that hold such strong appeal?

Key points in this respect may emerge from the different weightings the male and female fans give to different aesthetic styles of cinematic horror, with male fans more likely to consider themselves hardcore horror fans and privilege the gore and explicit effects in body horror and splatterpunk, whilst female fans may be more likely to privilege the suggestive styles of the supernatural and gothic horror (though these may be no less graphic). But this cannot explain the pleasures female viewers look for and experience in their entirety. Even if, in general, male fans are more likely and female fans somewhat less likely to profess a taste for explicit horror films, as my previous research suggests, this is by no means universal. Furthermore, even where fans do express a preference, this does not mean they never watch other styles. Whilst it is true that many male horror fans do privilege gore, this is not all by any means and the additional preferences and pleasures gained by male viewers may also be varied and complex. Equally female fans do not straightforwardly enjoy the subtler supernatural and uncanny forms of cinematic horror alone. Certainly, many female fans of gothic horror still chose to view examples of body horror and find pleasure in them. Lastly in this respect, many films include different sets of styles, sometimes in the same scene, and subgenres frequently merge into one another.

Noel Carroll's model of the emotional affects of horror in *The Philosophy of Horror* (1990) has already been widely discussed, but the empirical studies of horror film fans in particular suggest the audience cannot easily be divided into the clear and distinct subgroupings of average and specialist viewers he assumes. Although some fans differentiate between the gore film as a subcategory of horror that Carroll's specialist connoisseurs of graphic horror might prefer[7] – and such a category might include so-called video nasties, torture porn, and splatterpunk – and other, less graphic, forms of horror (which Carroll suggests appeal to the average mainstream viewer), this is not in practice easily observed. Many fans do enjoy both forms, and even where they profess a preference for one this does not lead to outright rejection of all films in the other category. Fans might 'feel like' one form of horror on one occasion and a different form at other times, when in a different mood. Or it might depend on availability and accessibility of films they have not yet seen or fancy seeing again. And while some fans do actively select or prefer one style in preference to others, they are not necessarily uncomfortable with different aesthetics at different points in the film or in the same sequence. Any number of factors may therefore apply, and this is potentially one of the main reasons why Barker's films have wide and long lasting appeal, offering a range of varied affects at the same time as having a unique vision of monstrosity (as in *Nightbreed* where the typical dichotomy of human/good and monster/evil is reversed, or *Hellraiser*'s borrowings of S&M-styling in the Cenobites and ornate designs of the Lament Configuration).

Furthermore, particular patterns of taste are often acquired or adapted when fans become immersed in specific fan cultures and where fans hold particular films up as 'superior' examples of horror. Fan communities thus privilege particular kinds of cinematic horror. Thus, Barker's films might be held up as great examples of splatterpunk in fan communities that are interested in gory and explicit imagery (despite Barker himself objecting to the splatterpunk classification on the grounds that it oversimplifies his work[8]), but this does not exclude other readings or responses. *Hellraiser*, for example, is easily categorised as a 'splatterpunk' or gore film containing several graphic 'numbers,'[9] but it also contains many elements of cinematic horror that can be classified as gothic and fairytale. As Freeland acknowledges, gore can be as integral a part of the uncanny as suggestive horror, and atmospheric horror can be found in the graphic forms.[10] In any case, as Matt Hills argues, the 'suggestive' and 'creepy' versus the 'gross' and 'gore-splattered' aesthetics are ideologically loaded terms that can, and should, be contested.[11] As a case in point, Barker's films are not easily classified or distinguished by one set of aesthetics over another.

Closer analysis of the findings of my audience study further fractures the apparent binary – particularly since the female viewers themselves are in fact, despite their stated preferences for one form over the other, inveterate boundary crossers. Whilst the aesthetics of horror are not strictly gendered, Barker's work does have particular appeals to female viewers.[12] Saying this, however, is not to fall into the convenient stereotypes of male and female taste patterns that have marked horror as a masculine film genre for some time. There is no intention in referring to a feminine aesthetic of horror to imply that only female fans are interested in these styles. In fact, it may be that the appeal of this aesthetic is universal, or a factor in patterns of consumption and canonisation amongst horror connoisseurs (as opposed to more casual viewers) of both sexes. Nevertheless, the conjunction of aesthetic elements in Barker's films is one that that the female fans consider imaginative or has a lasting impact after the film has ended. These elements include complex relationships between multi-dimensional characters, the foregrounding of aesthetically or erotically appealing monsters, and Barker's status as a horror auteur. These key factors in the pleasures of horror for female fans are considered further in this chapter.

A Barkerian cinema

Before discussing the films themselves in relation to the affects and pleasures experienced by the viewers, it is useful to position Barker's work within horror fan culture. Although he is primarily known as a horror novelist, he has also worked in comic books, video games, and illustration. However, amongst horror film fans, Barker is regarded as a significant figure in horror filmmaking, alongside George Romero, David Cronenberg, John Carpenter, Wes Craven, Sam Raimi, and other more established horror film directors. Although he has directed only three films and two early shorts, many other productions have been based on his characters and stories – including several sequels in the *Hellraiser* and *Candyman* series, film productions based on several short stories (for example, *The Midnight Meat Train* and *Book of Blood*), *Saint Sinner* for the Sci-Fi Channel (now SyFy), and two episodes of *Masters of Horror* for Showtime ('Valerie on the Stairs' and 'Haeckel's Tale'). Subsequently, the name Clive Barker has become a brand identity used to market films adapted from his writing and sensibility. As a case in point, *Candyman* may have been written and directed by Bernard Rose, but it is adapted from Barker's short story 'The Forbidden' and he is credited as an executive producer. The poster tagline plays this up, selling the film as 'From the chilling imagination of Clive Barker'. In fact, for some of the fans the fascination with Barker and his work overrides other considerations; for these fans *Candyman* is Barker's film and they do not overtly acknowledge Rose as either director or scriptwriter. Fans also acknowledge that even where Barker has no scriptwriting or directing input into the early sequels for *Hellraiser*, he did have final approval of the films and the projects were assigned to individuals he trusted creatively.[13] Since fans, in their discussion and consideration of his work, often fail to explicitly distinguish between Barker as an author and Barker as a filmmaker, or to separate his own work from that of others drawing on his oeuvre, it is useful to consider the work as a whole. Certainly, for the fans, *Candyman* (as well as other productions) is most definitely a 'Barkerian' film. Moreover, the presence that Barker has achieved within horror fan culture through this branding has facilitated his inclusion in the horror fan canon. More importantly, fans' tastes and preferences should be considered significant, and a Barkerian sensibility is also key to the canonical position he and his films, together with films based on his work, are held in, not least for the female audience.

My previous accounts of the horror film fan audience have discussed fan tastes in different demographic groupings, but particularly within the female horror film audience. In my earlier study of the tastes of the female horror film audience, *Hellraiser* was the most frequently named favourite film amongst the respondents,[14] whilst *Candyman* and *Nightbreed* were also highly popular. Barker is mentioned frequently by female fans both during discussion of their overall attraction to horror and also in reference to the specific films that they enjoy, many naming Barker's films as particular favourites. *Hellraiser*, adapted and directed by Barker from his novella *The Hellbound Heart*, is the most frequently mentioned film, named by 33 participants. *Nightbreed* (again adapted and directed by Barker from his novel *Cabal*) is named by 13 participants and appears in 13th place on the list. In addition, two *Hellraiser* sequels – *Hellbound* and *Hellraiser 3* (both written by Barker's friend and collaborator Pete Atkins and directed by Tony Randel and Anthony Hickox respectively) and *Candyman* (adapted and directed by Bernard Rose) are also on the list at 14th, 25th, and 32nd place, with 13, 12, and 6 mentions respectively.

In the wider contexts of this research, I have also sought to identify a fan canon of horror cinema that reflects ongoing debates between and amongst various groupings of fans,[15] and Barker's position in this canon is significant. Any attempt to develop a definitive canonical list of key films is fraught with difficulties, not least since there is a tendency for individual fans to give precedence to films which reflect their own familiarity with the genre as opposed to a set of films that are held up as great examples of the genre across a wide spread of horror fandom.[16] Nevertheless, *Hellraiser*, *Nightbreed*, and *Lord of Illusions*, as well as *Candyman*, are notably included in fans' lists of films they consider important works in the history of the genre. *Hellraiser* is positioned as the eighth most mentioned film when fans (both male and female) were asked what they regarded as the greatest examples of horror cinema, or would recommend to others. *Candyman* is 33rd on the list, and *Nightbreed* and *Lord of Illusions* both appear in the lower reaches between 50 and 88. To give some idea of the relative significance of this positioning, three John Carpenter films (*Halloween*, *The Thing* and *Prince of Darkness*), two George Romero films (*Night of the Living Dead*, *Dawn of the Dead*), the first two *Evil Dead* films directed by Sam Raimi, Dario Argento's *Suspiria* and *Opera*, and David Cronenberg's *The Fly* appear high on the list (in the top 30), whilst two other Romero films (*Day of the Dead* and *Martin*), Raimi's third *Evil Dead* film *Army of Darkness*, another Cronenberg (*The Dead Zone*), and Wes Craven's *Scream* are also listed. Barkerian films are therefore prominent in the horror fan canon, and this is important because they indicate a feminine interest in horror, representing the tastes of female fans (who select them most often).

One of the problems inherent in any account of taste or discussion of a fan canon is that, over time, tastes change (reflected in evolutionary changes in the genre) and films lose their affective power, so might fade into insignificance if other compensating factors are not present. As Schneider suggests, there might be only a few films that can retain their affective qualities in terms of the constructions of cinematic horror they contain and thereby achieve longevity.[17] In addition, when horror film viewers are asked to name their favourite horror films they frequently include films they have seen recently (this is especially true of the intended teen horror film audience).[18] *Hellraiser*, *Candyman*, and *Nightbreed* might well have a high profile in my original research due to the time at which it was carried out. However, this point may be refuted by the finding that these films continue to find a place in fan discourses and canons of horror cinema. Though the Barkerian films under consideration are 20 years old or more, they continue to be held in high esteem. In the updated research findings I draw on here, online horror film communities still discuss these films. Examples of these include the Barker-specific community The Hellbound (www.cenobite.com), the general horror film fan sites Horror.com (www.horror.com), the Horror Movie Fans forum (www.horrormoviefans.com), and the Horror Knits group on the handicrafting site Ravelry (www.ravelry.com).[19]

A further factor in the canonical status of Barkerian films is the development of a franchise that keeps fans returning to them – *Hellraiser* has three film sequels, plus a number of straight-to-video sequels, and *Candyman* has two. On the Horror Movie Fans forum, members voted 28:1 declaring themselves fans of the *Hellraiser* series and discuss which in the series of films they either enjoy the most or think are the best. In doing so, they establish a discourse that gives recognition to straight-to-video instalments not highly regarded for their quality, but enjoyed nonetheless. Such discourses help to establish *Hellraiser* the series as having a cult-like status (where films are acknowledged for being 'so bad they are good'). Films which fans also regard as worthy of repeat viewing also contribute to a cult status, at least in the individual fan's view; for example, VK from the Horror Knits group says 'I have to watch that every Halloween!' In the establishment of a cult status amongst horror fans, and in terms of Barker's work having the qualities of authorial vision, the original cut and re-release of

Nightbreed is also the subject of much discussion. This is supported by posts on the Occupy Midian website and petition (www.occupymidian.com) and of screenings at horror film conventions and festivals of the composite 'Cabal Cut'. This does raise interesting points regarding the gendering of cult film,[20] and whether it is the male-dominated forum discussion that privileges cult status and works (at least in part) to exclude female fans. One female Barker fan, CSD, says for example that, '*Hellraiser* is one most people know that are into horror movies and a lot of the general public as well, but *Nightbreed* seems to be more of a cultish thing. Too bad as it is one of my favorite [sic] movies.' The 'too bad' here seems to suggest that cult status is not something she entirely welcomes, positioning herself closer to mainstream horror film reception and further away from a 'hardcore' masculine fandom. This, however, should not diminish either the fan status of female horror film viewers or the pleasures they gain from Barker's work. Given that Barkerian films not only retain a central position in the horror fan canon, but have enduring attractions for female fans, the main question that arises is what the specific pleasures of the films are for the female fans.

Imagination

In terms of Schneider's account of cinematic horror,[21] *Candyman* in particular attains longevity for many of the female fans in Horror Knits because they consider the mirror sequences as some of the scariest. These scenes have stuck in their minds, and thus retain their affective horror, to the extent that even the thought of saying Candyman five times continues to give them the chills. This may have a nostalgic component, these fans continuing to hold the film in high regard because it scared them when younger at a time when they first began to watch horror films or consider themselves horror fans. TG says that she 'grew up loving movies like that', and ML recalls it as a pivotal film in her developing taste for horror: 'The scariest thing I've ever seen was definitely *Candyman*. Just thinking about it gives me shivers, and I saw it when I was 9, I think.' More importantly, however, the film also attains longevity because – in common with the films Schneider discusses – fans viewing it for the first time two decades after its first release still find it affective. DM says 'Who couldn't like *Candyman*? I only just saw it for the first time last year and I thought how could I have possibly let that one slip?' and JG says 'I only saw *Candyman* for the first time a couple years ago, and I was actually impressed with how good and scary it was.' *Hellraiser* also continues to work as affective horror. JB watched it for the first time in 2012 and says, 'I absolutely love it.' Illustrative of the impact that it had on her, she goes on to explain that it 'made me read "Hellbound Heart" and it is [now] one of my favourite books. He writes with so much detail, but doesn't explain too much. I don't know how to explain it, but it is amazing.' In this way, the film does not stand on its own merits but becomes part of the much wider appreciation of Barker as a horror auteur.

These comments relate to one of the key factors most frequently mentioned by fans in discussing the appeals of Barkerian cinema, namely the imaginative qualities at work in the films and the lasting impacts they have in the mind of the viewer. This taps into the finding in my previous research that female fans prefer thought-provoking horror, regardless of its stylistic approaches (it is gore and graphic effects for their own sake that some reject, rather than a dislike for graphic horror *per se*).[22] Barkerian films are significant in this respect due to the literary merits accorded to Barker's fiction by these fans. Adaptation of source material is therefore important. EE, who thinks that '*Candyman* is awesome', discusses the film in terms of it being 'Another movie based on a short story, and although it's not quite the same as the story, it manages to make a creepy, fun movie. That's how adaptations should be done!' The obvious connections with Barker's writing are not always unproblematic, however, and the films can be diminished in light of the status Barker fans place on the fiction (a common problem with responses to book-to-film adaptations). As JG states 'I'd been reluctant to see *Candyman*, since I was such a fan of the short story by Clive Barker that the movie is based on.' AB, for example, finds the differences between the short story and the film a barrier to enjoyment of the film: '"The Forbidden" […] terrified me when I read it some years back. Quite remarkable since I read and watch a great deal of horror but this one just set me on edge. I'd love to see it more accurately portrayed in film.' Such a nostalgic component to horror fan responses is widespread, with memories of films or fiction that particularly scared the fan when they were younger – and especially when they were forming a taste for horror – remaining strong and potentially influencing their responses to more recent viewing. For AB, the film is just too far removed from the short story (she describes it as 'very loosely based') to recreate those earlier emotional responses.

Nevertheless, for many of the fans, narrative style, characters, and world-building satisfy the desire for films that play on the imagination of the viewer. This can work through both storylines and visual style. Some of the fans focus on the cinematic and technical qualities of the films, privileging the effects and make-up as typical male fandom does, but often focusing on how the visual qualities of the film are different from the usual generic styles of American horror cinema. A, for example, says 'I do like *Hellraiser* best, mostly because while the production budget is not what one would have today (as it was miniscule), it's visually interesting and super-ambitious.' CSD says of *Nightbreed* that 'The make up alone is worth watching the movie for', but also adds 'not to mention the story!', suggesting narrative qualities are also extremely significant in conjunction with filmic style. For MB, this comes down to elements of the film that are psychologically or emotionally scary, as opposed to the appreciation of any visual components for their own sake: 'I have watched a million and a half horror movies. I love scary movies. The only one that has actually creeped me out was *Candyman*. I am not 100% sure what about the movie freaked me out, I think the mirrors aspect. I hate mirrors.' This suggests that it is not necessarily a horrific image that is most affective in a horror film, but any element of the *mise-en-scène* that triggers something in the mind of the viewer, and this can be a very personal trigger. These fans frequently use terms such as 'freaked out' and 'creeped out', making the horror very much a mental process. GL (who places *Candyman* in her list of the scariest films of all time) has a similar response, and furthermore her comments suggest that Barkerian films work in this way because they play with the emotional responses of the viewer: 'I can take gore and screaming and killing and not even flinch, but the mindfuck ones are the truly scary ones.' The idea of a 'mindfuck' is one that permeates the discourse. SW says that *Hellraiser* is 'gory in places but more of a mindfuck than anything', supporting the finding that these female fans do not seek out graphic horror for its own sake, but do not object to it as an adjunct to the modes of emotional affect they prefer. AG, who says that she 'love[s] *Candyman*', states that the film 'mindfucked me. I didn't sleep all night after watching *Candyman*, I was convinced the branches moving in the window were him, and after a night of no sleep, I went to get up and brush my teeth after getting dressed, and we had new neighbours, and I could hear noises in the bathroom and I was convinced he was coming to get me, I dropped my toothbrush and ran outside and to my car and went to work.' For fans like her, it is the longer lasting affects that remain significant, not just the physical responses and the feelings or emotions experienced during viewing. Another comment by SB puts forward the idea that this comes down to a qualitative difference between these types of responses and those normally elicited by horror films. She says that, 'Some [films] that disturb me, but don't really frighten me, are the *Hellraiser* movies. Clive Barker is a very twisted man.' This fan thus engages with a difference between horror cinema more widely and Barkerian films, clearly attributing this to Barker's own sensibility (even where he does not write or direct the series of films beyond the first). Another fan, A, suggests that these films can emulate a hallucinogenic or drug-like state: 'I sat and watched *Hellraiser* and *Hellraiser 2*: Even more Hellraiser-y. *Hellraiser 2* is trippy. I mean, [the first] is weird and all, but 2 is just plain triptastic – right to the very end.'

These reported affects and responses suggest a particular set of qualities that can be observed in the films. These include vivid depictions of fantastical worlds, frequently juxtaposed with the real mundane world, depth, and complexity of characterisation, ambiguous and often sympathetic monsters, and complex relationships. Narratives are often more focused on the monsters than on human characters, but the positions of both are frequently reversed such that human characters are monstrous and the monsters are not just humanised but often heroic or moral in some way. The key factor in this is the depiction of othering that takes place (as it frequently does in the horror genre), foregrounding questions of difference. In Barkerian cinema, monsters are configured in ways that allow identification (especially for viewers who have experience of difference or being othered themselves)[23] and depict individuals or groups who have been oppressed by the dominant hegemony and ghettoised (as with the poor black community in *Candyman*) or driven underground (as in *Nightbreed*). It is notable in this respect that this worldview can be linked to Barkerian films as queer cinema,[24] and this dimension of his work is one of the key factors in its appeal for female fans. The fans, whose social situations and domestic arrangements may well be heteronormative, nonetheless find such representations to be appealing as sexually escapist fantasies, and to be thought-provoking in terms of their interests in horror generally and in monstrous characters specifically. This certainly explains the interest in *Nightbreed*, a film that allows these fans to invest strongly in the eponymous community – the group of monsters who are forced to live outside of normal (that is, human) culture. The female fans who find points of identification or sympathy with the Nightbreed are not themselves monstrous of course, but they often feel that they do not fit into acceptable mainstream categories of femininity – they are fans, nerds, bookish, non-sporty, and so on. The Nightbreed are seen as reflecting the sense of apparent difference on the outside but at the same time are felt to have inner beauty or positive qualities. KB describes them as 'all manner of crazy and monsterously [sic] bulbous headed but otherwise fairly well formed creatures'. Furthering this idea, the opposite of this – a perfect outer appearance harbouring evil or unlikeable qualities – is also seen as one of the factors of viewing pleasure. GK – who describes *Nightbreed* as 'my absolute fave', says: 'I am so glad it is not just me that can see how arrogant and selfish the human race is. And Peloquin is very tasty. Freaks of the world unite!' This suggests an affinity with specific monstrous characters (in this case Peloquin – she can see beneath his appearance and he is not just admirable but attractive too), with freaks in general, and also with Barker, with whom she imagines a shared view of human nature.

Gothic and fairytale characters

Barker's films, or films associated with his name, are thus seen as qualitatively different from much of the rest of the horror genre. One way in which this can be seen narratively is in the way female characters are positioned, in contrast to the common portrayal as victims, even in the role of the final girl, in the horror film. Films in which the stalking, torture, and murder of female characters is foregrounded and exaggerated for spectatorial pleasure (assuming a male spectator who is placed in the position of male killer or monster, supported by the narrative and stylistic point of view of the killer) are often cited in support of the argument that female spectators are punished and othered by the horror film.[25] In Williams' account, this is a reason why women are not (and should not be) eager viewers of horror films, but nonetheless such an assumption is contradicted by the enjoyment many women gain from watching horror films. This does not mean, however, that female fans blindly accept such representations. It could be argued, for example, that in *Candyman*, Helen is portrayed as a victim. But the Candyman's words can be read as an invitation rather than a threat, he also invites her to 'Come with me and be immortal' – a status she eventually achieves through her own agency at the end of the film when she takes the Candyman's position and slays Trevor (which can also be read as an act of female revenge). Female fans seem particularly responsive to this, SB saying 'I love how it ends' for example.

It must be noted however, that it is not the female characters in their own right who are the predominant interest, but their narrative journeys (as here, with a potentially feminist reading of the ending) and the way in which they are positioned with respect to an appealing monster (which I discuss further in the next section). In terms of the appeal of Barkerian films, certainly in respect of Barker's imaginative stories and themes, this goes back to their predominantly negative feelings about the formulaic aspects of much of the horror genre.[26] Barker's themes are located within an exploration of gender and sexual politics that can be considered decidedly queer, and certainly contains the additional potential for straight queer readings. Certainly, some fans do find the juxtapositions noteworthy, A saying: 'I really like the juxtaposition of the very humdrum bourgeois suburban home with the German bondage disco thing happening in the attic.' This comment lends itself to an interpretation of the film as an interesting variant on the gothic mad-woman-in the-attic trope. Non-bourgeois sexuality (as represented by Julia and Frank as passionate lovers) is an escape from the stifling constraints of marriage and feminine domesticity (as represented by Larry and Julia as boring suburban couple). Passionate feminine sexuality is positioned as monstrous in the narrative, but this is never quite that narratively straightforward in Barker's work. As with examples of the woman's film, non-hegemonic femininity can be read as liberating, and audiences, female audiences in particular, might well read against the grain. At the very least, they enjoy the rejection of patriarchal values and conformism, as A does here. In this way, viewers might not, or might not only, invest themselves solely in the main character of the drama, but alongside this they may well take away from the film a series of memorable moments which are orientated around the monstrous characters, as well as the scenes of cinematic horror around which the genre is orientated. Pleasure is therefore not as straightforward as enjoying these films for the unfolding narratives and the disclosure and final destruction of the monster by the female hero.

Certainly in films such as *Hellraiser*, the narrative development is organised around a sequence of horrific scenes involving Frank's search for pleasures of the flesh: his passionate liaison with Julia, his original destruction by the Cenobites, his accidental resurrection in the attic, and Julia's predatory snaring of unwary men in order to feed him and make him whole. These scenes (around which Kirsty's growing wariness of her stepmother and what is going on in the attic is only at first tangentially woven) are foregrounded and dominate the first 53 minutes of the film. At least in the feminine aesthetic epitomised by *Hellraiser*,[27] the representations of strong femininity and female sexuality are shared between Kirsty as a strong female hero and Julia as a monstrous femme fatale, and in Julia are given an aberrant flavour. It is also important to note that since she is not one of a group of teenagers and is not stalked by a killer, Kirsty is somewhat different from a typical 'final girl'. She might share some aspects of the final girl profile, being resourceful for example, but overall she exceeds the confines of such a character in key ways. She does not react passively – running from imminent danger even though her boyfriend Steve urges her to, or taking up household implements to defend herself against the monstrous entities in the film, the Cenobites. Rather, she faces the monster down, using her intellect to bargain with lead Cenobite Pinhead and defying the inevitable consequences of opening the Box. In fact, she is never quite a passive victim of the monster, it being her own curiosity and ingenuity that land her in danger in the first place. This is not necessarily an untroubling position; in some respects the character could be read as a signifying process for feminine weakness and stupidity – walking into danger just as some of the teen victims of the slasher do. However, it is also family circumstance that places her in that position in the first place and she bears many points of overlap with the heroine of the fairytale. She is the victim of a wicked stepmother (and in *Hellraiser II* of the evil queen Julia becomes).[28] But in this respect, she also possesses and owns female agency, and is thus a strikingly active character with many appeals for the female viewer alongside their enjoyment of the monsters and the scenes of explicit horror. This is not, however, the factor that stands out in the fans' discussion of the film. In light of A's response about the contrasts between domesticity and BDSM-style sexuality in the attic, it is the appeal of monstrosity and its link with aberrant sexuality that represents an area of Barkerian cinema that is of rather more interest to the female fans.

The erotic appeal of monstrosity

Many female horror fans have a tendency to react to certain kinds of monsters with sympathy,[29] even where this is mixed with horror or revulsion, and – in certain cases, especially when monsters are attractive, as they frequently are with vampires for example – to find them erotically appealing. Such desire for the monster may seem on the surface to be aberrant, but it does illustrate the attraction of the genre for many female fans. They take pleasure in viewing physically appealing monstrous characters, and even desire them. This seems to be related, at least in part, to the attraction of dark, dangerous, Byronic heroes. Given the attraction of a queer sensibility in Barkerian cinema, such desire is a major factor in the status they accord Barkerian films and it explains in a large part their enjoyment of them. Pinhead from *Hellraiser* and the eponymous Candyman are key figures in this respect.

Both these characters are tall, imposing figures, with a great deal of presence that dominates the screen. These monsters do not lurk in the shadows, but reveal themselves in a narrative that depicts them enticing, if not seducing, their female victims. The Candyman invites Helen to be not just his victim, but his bride. Kirsty too is positioned as Pinhead's victim when she opens the box, but he also promises her entry into his world – 'we have such sights to show you' – and is willing to bargain with her when he learns she has knowledge that can lead him back to Frank. Helen and Kirsty might both be frightened at the sight of their monsters, as the viewer may be, but they (characters and viewers alike) never shy away from interacting with them. As also observed in other fan communities, the actor plays a large part in the eroticisation of the role they play.[30] Casting is important in this respect: the actors Tony Todd and Doug Bradley both have the physical and screen presence for these roles and this permits the female fans to find the combination of actor and monster appealing and sexually attractive. Pleasurable fan responses are not just associated with actors playing normal-looking characters, but macabre, grotesque, or horrific looking ones too.

When these fans talk about this aspect of the film, they do not always distinguish between actor and character. In some cases it is the character that is cited as the appealing factor of the film, in others it is the actor, and sometimes both are conflated. LKV, for example, discusses various aesthetic elements of the film, positioning the character as one more pleasurable element: 'Love that movie! The music freaks me out, the 80s over-saturation freaks me out, the fact that Candyman is somewhat compellingly hawt [sic] freaks me out.' OU, on the other hand, lists *Candyman* as one of her favourite movies of all time, not just horror, placing it alongside classics such as *Rear Window*, *Some Like It Hot*, *Mildred Pierce*, *The Godfather*, and *Goodfellas*. *Candyman*, she states, is 'my all time favourite' because 'I just love Tony Todd.' CT describes *Hellraiser* as 'my favourite' because 'I lurve [sic] Pinhead!' KB says 'Oh yes, yes and *yes* to Pinhead/Doug Bradley!', also acknowledging the role of Barker as the creator of such appealing monstrosity when she adds: 'Also Clive Barker who made him come to life.' Fans do not always conflate role and performer in this way; EE notes that 'I met [Doug Bradley] a few years ago and he is lovely, but so soft-spoken in person it's hard to believe he is Pinhead.' On the whole, though, for these fans desire for the star and desire for the monster often overlap. Monstrosity itself is complicated and problematised by such fan behaviour, because it may have a strong influence over the fan's responses to the text, conceivably also dampening the horror.

This further acknowledges the importance of Barker's sensibility to these fans, not least in relation to monstrosity as a form of queered, non-normative feminine sexuality. The fans themselves recognise that such fan worship of male stars is complicated by the fact that they are playing monsters in horror films. KB, for example, finds it difficult to articulate: 'I have always thought of this but could never voice it, people would think I'm weird … well, I am but you know what I'm saying.' The fact that she ends this remark with a giggle suggests a wry, knowing and teasing response, as well as the embarrassment she admits to. Similarly, KT asks: 'How hot is the actor who played Candyman?' and answers her own question by describing him as 'completely awesome'. She goes on to describe the response she has to him in any role, even when he is playing a monster as in *Candyman*: 'I always get naughty tingles every time he plays any character, any time in any show, ever. Way better actor than he gets credit for, too. And he's on my Freebie Five[31] – with or without the hook.' In one sense, this seems to elide monstrosity at the same time as it embraces it. However, these fans do not always just 'see through' the monstrosity to the actor, the monstrosity can be essential to their pleasure. As DDW puts it: 'The Candyman. Nom [sic]. I like 'em creepy. I like him more when his eyes are all slitted and he's in evil mode. He has a nice dark voice, too.' As DDW's final remark also illustrates, in the context of *Hellraiser* and *Candyman*, dialogue and delivery are an essential part of these feminine responses. SB echoes DDW's thought: 'Tony Todd's voice does funny things to me', and EE states: 'Doug Bradley's voice is fantastic.' Vocal qualities are paramount, and this is narratively significant as the voice works as a tool of seduction on Helen in the car park and Kirsty in the hospital room. As with Anderson's music fans,[32] excessive sexual desire for the monster and the actor playing the monster creates a sense of 'euphoric empowerment' for the fan. Moreover, there is a clear sense in which sexuality and desire permeate the monstrous figure in Barkerian films.

Conclusion

Whilst I would not wish to argue that Barkerian film is distinctly feminine, a significant proportion of the female viewers both quoted here and contributing to my research over the years are drawn to the particular combinations of aesthetic features in Barker's work. In labelling this set of features – imaginative world-building, horror that plays on the imagination long after the film is over, a queer sensibility that foregrounds aberrant femininity and sexuality, and erotic constructions of monstrosity – a feminine aesthetic is to ascribe to it the appeals to female fans. It is undeniable that such gendered distinctions are integral to these fans' taste for these films. The aesthetic elements explored in their discourses are a major factor in the continuing appeal of Barker's work. Most importantly, the depictions of pleasure, pain, and monstrosity in *Hellraiser*, *Candyman*, and *Nightbreed* are, for these female fans, a means to explore the pleasures and pains of sexual desire and excess, rather than simply the destruction of the human body and the self frequently depicted in horror cinema.

Notes

1 *Candyman.* Dir. Bernard Rose, Polygram, 1992.
2 Linda Williams, 'When the Woman Looks,' in Mark Jancovich (ed.), *Horror: The Film Reader* (London: Routledge, 2002).
3 Noel Carroll, *The Philosophy of Horror or Paradoxes of the Heart* (London: Routledge, 1990).
4 Cynthia Freeland, *The Naked and the Undead: Evil and the Appeal of Horror* (Boulder: Westview Press, 2000).
5 See Daniel Shaw, 'A Humean Definition of Horror,' *Film-Philosophy*, Vol. 1:4 (1997), www.film-philosophy.com/vol1-1997/n4shaw), for example.
6 See Brigid Cherry, 'Broken Homes, Tortured Flesh: *Hellraiser* and the Feminine Aesthetic of Horror Cinema,' *Film International*, Vol. 3:17 (2005), pp. 10–21; and 'Gothics and Grand Guignols: Violence and the Gendered Aesthetics of Cinematic Horror,' *Participations: International Journal of Audience Research*, Vol 5:1 (May 2008), www.participations.org/Volume%205/Issue%201%20-%20special/5_01_cherry.htm.), where I have explored this in respect of *Hellraiser* specifically.
7 Carroll, *The Philosophy of Horror*, p. 193.
8 See Gary Hoppenstand, *Clive Barker's Short Stories: Imagination as Metaphor in the* Books of Blood *and Other Works* (Jefferson, NC: McFarland, 1994), pp. 41–2.
9 Freeland, *The Naked and the Undead*, p. 256.
10 *Ibid.* pp. 215–72.
11 Matt Hills, 'An Event-Based Definition of Art-Horror,' in Steven Jay Schneider and Daniel Shaw (eds), *Dark Thoughts: Philosophic Reflections on Cinematic Horror* (Lanham, MD: Scarecrow Press, 2003), p. 141.
12 Brigid Cherry, 'Subcultural Tastes, Genre Boundaries and Fan Canons,' in Mark Jancovich and Lincoln Geraghty (eds), *The Shifting Definitions of Genre: Essays on Labelling Films, Television Shows and Media* (Jefferson, NC: McFarland, 2007), pp. 201–15.
13 Douglas E. Winter, *Clive Barker: The Dark Fantastic* (London: Harper Collins, 2001).
14 Brigid Cherry, 'Refusing to Refuse to Look: Female Viewers of the Horror Film,' in Richard Maltby and Mervyn Stokes (eds), *Identifying Hollywood Audiences* (London: BFI, 1999), p. 194.
15 See Brigid Cherry, 'Beyond "Suspiria": The Place of European Cinema in the Fan Canon,' in Patricia Allmer, Emily Brick, and David Huxley (eds), *European Nightmares: European Horror Cinema Since 1945* (London: Wallflower Press, 2012), pp. 25–34; and Cherry, 'Subcultural Tastes,' pp. 201–15.

16 See Cherry, 'Subcultural Tastes', pp. 204–5 for details.
17 Steven Jay Schneider, 'Toward an Aesthetics of Cinematic Horror', in Stephen Prince (ed.), *The Horror Film* (Piscataway, NJ: Rutgers University Press, 2004), pp. 131–49.
18 See Cherry, 'Subcultural Tastes'.
19 The latter group is particularly significant in researching female fans' responses to horror, since its members are predominantly female, and this may mean that they feel more able to discuss horror on their own terms (as opposed to potentially exposing themselves to male fan opinion). As Penny (2013) argues, gender power relations on the Internet can be problematical for women.
20 See also Joanne Hollows, 'The Masculinity of Cult', in Mark Jancovich (ed.), *Defining Cult Movies: The Cultural Politics of Oppositional Taste* (Manchester: Manchester University Press, 2003), pp. 35–53.
21 See Steven Jay Schneider, 'Towards an Aesthetics'.
22 See Cherry, 'Refusing to Refuse to Look'.
23 *Ibid.*
24 Harry M. Benshoff, '"Way Too Gay To Be Ignored": The Production and Reception of Queer Horror Cinema in the Twenty-First Century', in Caroline Joan S. Picart and John Edgar Browning (eds), *Speaking of Monsters: A Teratological Anthology* (Basingstoke: Palgrave Macmillan, 2012), p. 132. See also, Harry M. Benshoff and Sean Griffin, *Queer Images: A History of Gay and Lesbian Film in America* (Oxford: Rowman & Littlefield, 2006), p. 77.
25 Williams, 'When the Woman Looks'.
26 See Cherry, 'Refusing to Refuse to Look'.
27 See Cherry, 'Broken Homes' for a fuller engagement with this.
28 Peter Atkins, in an interview with (Brigid Cherry and Brian Robb (1989).
29 Cherry, 'Refusing to Refuse to Look'.
30 Female forms of fandom have long involved sexual and romantic desire for male stars across music, cinema, TV, sport, and celebrity (see, for example Tonya Anderson, 'Still Kissing Their Posters Goodnight: Female Fandom and Politics of Popular Music', *Participations: Journal of Audience and Reception Studies*, Vol. 9:2 (2012)). This response can be widely observed in female fan cultures, for example to David Tennant playing the Doctor in Doctor Who or Alexander Skarsgård as Eric Northman in *True Blood*.
31 The Freebie Five is a concept that derives from the TV show *Friends*. It is a list of five actors, stars, or celebrities with whom one is allowed to have sex without it being regarded as cheating on one's significant other.
32 Anderson, 'Still Kissing Their Posters Goodnight, p. 261.

Part III

Labyrinths of desire

18 Clive Barker, 'Saint Sinner', 1993.

7

Clive Barker's queer monsters: exploring transgression, sexuality, and the other

Mark Richard Adams

> I think of sexuality as being this incredibly malleable, protean, changeable, wonderful, flowery thing. I don't think that it is fixed. I don't think that it is about saying I am this and I will always be this. I think that it is about being aroused by the world and finding the world sexy. (Clive Barker)[1]

Inspired by the failure of two previous adaptations of his work,[2] Clive Barker endeavoured to direct his own interpretation of his novella *The Hellbound Heart*. Adapted as *Hellraiser* (1987), Barker's debut featured images of sadomasochism, deconstructed bodies, and conflicted collisions between sexuality and horror. Following *Hellraiser*, Barker would direct just two other feature films, *Nightbreed* (1990) and *Lord of Illusions* (1995), both of which continued the engagement with themes of transgression, sexuality, and the body. This chapter will examine how each of Barker's directorial efforts deals with these issues in relation to notions of the monstrous 'Other', and more specifically, in relation to its portrayal of homosexuality and alternative sexualities. It will position this textual analysis within the context of 'queering' the horror genre, and through an analytical approach to the narratives and characters of the three films.

Whilst there is no doubt that each individual film could sustain an analysis in its own right,[3] this chapter is preoccupied with drawing links across Barker's cinematic works, to highlight the reoccurring commitment to both transgressive and positive queer representations within a genre usually defined by its conservatism. The three films directed by Barker are wildly different in tone, themes, and arguably even genre, but still constitute a trilogy connected by a distinct attempt to negotiate not *what*, but *who* monsters are, and what they can represent. Barker's authorial voice is prominent across all three films although this is not a claim for any auteurist veneration, but rather an understanding of how his own queer identity and politics has informed the creation and representation of the monstrous in the films he both directed *and* scripted. This analysis will demonstrate how Barker constructs his 'queer monsters' and how they are often more complex, sympathetic and/or heroic than the heteronormative characters within his narratives. In turn, by queering horror, it will demonstrate how the genre can be utilised for more progressive and inclusive ideologies and modes of representation.

Queering the horror genre

As a genre, horror is traditionally associated with conservative ideology, the monstrous 'othering' of difference and the brutal punishment of transgression. Whilst more diverse work is now available on the genre, the wider cultural perception of the genre as a whole has barely shifted from the rhetoric of patriarchal punishment, and certainly the possibility of an overtly progressive approach to difference is one less often entertained. Robin Wood first established how the figure of the 'Other' was utilised in the horror genre, drawing connections between various cultural 'Others', such as foreign ethnicities, homosexuals, or alternative political systems and their counterparts within cinema.[4] Wood suggests that 'the release of sexuality in the horror film is always presented as perverted, monstrous and excessive',[5] and later laments that 'it is the reactionary horror film that dominates the genre'[6] at that time. However, the potential for impossible imageries and bodily deconstructions, coupled with other-worldly narratives, entities, and philosophies makes horror the ideal genre for an exploration of the fantastic (phantastic?) and it is from this perspective that Barker's films should be approached. In the decades since Wood considered the reactionary nature of horror, the genre and its academic study have both expanded greatly, although many of the most common mainstream criticisms of the genre remain trapped in the rhetoric of morality and punishment. In interview with Paul Wells, Barker's perspective on the genre is evident;

> Horror fiction is reaching for high cultural status in the scale of its potential content. You are talking about death, obsession, insanity – the conventional subjects of horror fiction; these are *not* and *should not* be light subjects. It is unfortunately very easy when you are using this rich visual material and very rich sub-text to make a laugh out of it. I'm not terribly interested in going the easy way; I want to create a kind of undertow in a movie that may never leave your mind.[7]

Barker is interested in exploring ideas through horror that resist the clichéd perception of horror as being represented by the slasher-genre format of 'adolescent sexual curiosity deserving immediate, violent retribution'.[8] Harry Benshoff asserts that there can be queer authorship and that a 'homo-horror film is one written, produced, and/or directed by a gay man or lesbian, even if it does not contain visibly homosexual characters'.[9] Barker's trilogy is infused with his queer approach, not only to character and narrative, but also a queering of the horror genre – an approach to the material which conflicts with conventional mainstream understandings of the genre and expands on existing theoretical approaches.

It is in the figure of the 'Other' that the horror genre finds its most prominent queer representative. Through their difference, the Other 'reciprocally bolsters the image of "normality", a contrast of binaries often including deformed versus attractive, savagery versus civilisation, soft bodies versus hard bodies and, of course, queer sexuality versus heteronormality'.[10] Annamarie Jagose suggests that there exists in Western society, 'a culture that commonly understands homosexuality to be a derivative or less evolved form of heterosexuality' and thus assumes straightness as 'the more self-evident, natural or stable construction'.[11] The unstable body of the monstrous Other is one of the first distinctive signs visible to the viewer of the queerness of these creations, while arguably advocating a queering of the horror genre is a struggle in itself. Alexander Doty argues that 'any text is always already potentially queer' and that queerness should not be seen as something that is 'read into' a film or something 'alternative' but rather as something as inherent within the film itself as straightness is perceived to be.[12] He further suggests there is often a strong resistance to making these 'queer readings', and that those opposed to the idea may believe 'you need to be pressured or patronised into feeling that you have made the wrong or the "less common and therefore easy to undermine or put in its place" choice'.[13] This resistance is certainly understandable since queer theory 'opposes the binary definitions and proscriptions of a patriarchal heterosexism', effectively freeing any given text from any preconceived ideologies or assumptions.[14] On Barker, Benshoff perhaps notes the defining feature of the imaginer's approach to queer politics, characters, and worlds, suggesting that his 'voice is in celebration of change – infinite, endless, exquisite change … the joy of ambiguity, the possibility that things are not fixed'.[15] Thus both the horror genre and, more precisely, Barker's trilogy open up and embrace the queer potential of film, with Barker's work specifically foregrounding the queer monsters so they cannot be easily dismissed as incorrect or alternative readings.

There has, however, been criticism of Barker's films, and it is perhaps best addressed up front, so as not to cast a shadow over the following discussions. Christopher Sharett is one notable example, claiming that it is in some of Barker's works that the 'close association of dread and disease with unbridled eros and alternative community is no better evidenced'.[16] This is a restrictive reading, limited in its failure to presuppose an alternative approach to such material. Barker himself expresses his distaste for horror fiction that celebrates the values of bourgeois society and reinforces the status quo; he tells Wells 'I don't want to buy into what I see as "escapist" fiction and the myth of bourgeois perfection'.[17] Rob Latham claims Sharrett underestimates the texts and has 'an approach which views films as mere social allegories, insufficiently perceives their complexly mediated nature, and drastically oversimplifies the interpretative exchange between them and their sometimes fractious audiences'.[18] Latham's views correspond with Benshoff's assertions that 'Barker's best work challenges the genre's implicit demonization of queer sexuality, in so doing not only exposing the institutions which carry on such oppressive practices, but the processes of static binary thinking which support them'.[19] Sharrett is certainly guilty of this 'static binary thinking' in his analysis of the texts, only reading literal meanings into what are far more complicated texts. His assessment of monstrous beings as merely negative, 'grotesque (and worse, ludicrous)'[20] creations fails to identify not only with Barker's own ideas of 'repulsive glamour' but with the possibility of a queer perspective within the text.[21]

Hellraiser – transgressive bodies

Hellraiser opens with Frank Cotton (Sean Chapman with skin, Oliver Smith without) purchasing and then solving a puzzle box that summons the Cenobites – androgynous, sadomasochistic demons, who tear Frank apart and transport him to their world to partake in experiments in pleasure and pain. When the blood of Larry, his brother, is spilt on the site of his departure, Frank is resurrected as a skeletal husk and solicits the help of his sister-in-law and lover, Julia (Claire Higgins), in bringing him victims whose blood he needs to heal himself. Throughout the narrative there is an evolution of Frank's body, which appears to begin as heteronormative but transforms into a displaced 'Otherness' as his body and gender become conflicted. This evolution begins when Frank is first introduced, his body coded as hyper masculine. He dresses in tight denim trousers and a clinging white vest, accentuating his body, and his unshaven face completes the image of a sexualised 1980s male. The nature of this 'hard body' later contrasts with his 'soft body' once he encounters the Cenobites. Anna Powell describes the opening sequence in which Frank summons the Cenobites thusly; 'his glowing, warm-looking skin, slick with the sheen of sweat, is shown in close-up. The tactile smoothness of his naked flesh increases the visceral impact of its coming torture.'[22] As well as contrasting with the subsequent horror, Frank's body is also displayed as spectacle in both this sequence, and later when Julia remembers her first encounter with him. Frank frames himself in the doorway, actively displaying his body as the door swings open, whilst the younger Julia is kept hidden, focusing the audience's gaze entirely on the spectacle of Frank. The lingering emphasis of Frank as spectacle foreshadows the queer sexual identity that is revealed as his body is literally deconstructed and then re-structured later in the film. The opening scene described by Powell is representative of the film's central themes, contrasting Frank's masculine outer body with his revealed inner 'soft body' and showcasing the sadomasochistic world of the Cenobites, who Frank summons in the expectation of sexual gratification. The Cenobites have not merely tortured and mutilated Frank, nor have they transformed him into a monstrous state; Frank's skin concealed his already existing 'Otherness', revealed through the Cenobites' flaying. Powell suggests the visions of his scattered form 'are designed to haptically induce physical agony, and possibly masochistic pleasure, in the spectator'.[23] The audience are again invited to gaze upon Frank, but this time upon his interior form, mirroring the earlier encouraged pleasure in his outer physicality. Frank's first reappearance after escaping the Cenobites is as a decayed corpse. There are no visible signs of his past gender or strength, instead he must rely on Julia to act as a 'mother' to him following this re-birth, as he is rendered effectively helpless. It is in this form that we see an exploration of Frank's gender and identity play out as, at each stage of his reconstruction, the spectator is invited to gaze upon the image of his deconstructed form and witness the new colours and designs of the layers of his body. As his physical form develops he becomes a shining, red figure whose flesh glistens and drips with moisture. Alongside these overt sexual connotations, this body is also physically penetrated by Kirsty (Ashley Lawrence), the film's heroine, who thrusts her hand inside his stomach as she attempts to escape the attic later in the film. The fear of castration, of being feminised, is somewhat embodied by Frank, who desperately seeks to regain his masculinity. Kirsty's penetration of Frank with her fingers also echoes the method by which he extracts the vital blood he needs to revive himself, an element reminiscent of the vampire genre.

Though *Hellraiser* does not feature much of the traditional iconography of the vampire film, it does display the prominent anxieties associated with the genre, particularly those of penetration, transgressive sexuality, and the exchange of bodily fluids. The fact that Frank and Julia's primary victims are male also has certain queer connotations. Richard Dyer discusses how the vampire's bite is a sexual act that is 'analogous to other forms of oral sex acts, all of which importantly involve contact not only with orifices but with bodily fluids as well'.[24] He further suggests it takes place 'archetypally in a bedroom, that is, the same place as our society accords the sex act'.[25] Frank represents a crude form of vampire, instead of the seductive (romantic?) subtlety of the 'kiss', Frank violently penetrates his victims using his fingers and sucks their bodies dry, leaving a shrivelled husk. 'This isn't the bedroom', states the first victim as Julia lures him into the room where Frank is waiting and she reassures him that she has 'always preferred the floor'. This appropriates the space as one of sexual activity whilst removing the comforts associated with a bedroom and replacing them with the damp wooden boards of the attic. If vampirism is equivalent to a sex act, then surely Frank's brutal penetration in inhospitable surroundings can be read as a rape and the fact that all the victims are male then relates these assaults to further implications of queerness and Frank's

sexual ambiguity. The irony is that this is part of a process of physical reconstruction where Frank is actually attempting to rebuild his masculine identity and
yet his vampirism positions him closer to being understood as a 'queer monster',
thus creating further confusion within his own sexual identity. Dyer suggests
'vampires are driven on by the absolute necessity for blood to stay "alive", they
can't help themselves',[26] which echoes Clive Barker's comment that Frank 'can't
help himself' in this scene.[27] Julia aside, his victims consist entirely of men,
including his own brother in one of two potential acts of incest within the
film, suggesting a repressed queer desire on Frank's part. His relationship with
the Cenobites has served to illustrate Frank's desire for something other than
heteronormative interactions, and the incestuous overtones in the film are one
example of the extremes of sexuality that he negotiates in his search for
fulfilment.

'It's never enough' Frank states after first having sex with Julia, establishing
his constant search for new, fulfilling, sensations which eventually leads him to
seek out the Cenobites, who are self-proclaimed 'explorers in the further regions
of experience'. Sharett claims the Cenobites 'are demons representative both of
repression (their priestly garb and emphasis on "discipline") and of "desire" … the
Cenobites, with their tired conflation of sadomasochism with sexuality in general,
associate erotic transgression with self-destruction', which arguably suggests a
failure to look beyond a conservative and heteronormative reading of the text.[28]
Paul Wells' suggestion that 'Barker's bodies are concerned with perspectives
outside social orthodoxy, and "horror" comes out of the fear of a perverse yet
partially desired experience of a marginalised or unknown Otherness'[29] is closer
to describing the relationship Frank has with the Cenobites, whose pleasures
he both fears and desires. The Cenobites are not the monsters of the film – a
role instead taken by Frank – and with their obvious sadomasochistic imagery,
by invoking the cultural groups such as 'modern primitives', and androgynous
appearances, it is easy to see that they represent queerness within *Hellraiser*.
Carl Holmberg discusses the idea of 'taboo', which 'prohibits but also tantalises
people about what is forbidden'[30] and creates borders, which thus 'suggests a
place individuals, pairs, and groups can teeter before going over the edge, and
transgressing that border, if indeed they ever go over the edge'.[31] The Cenobites
have gone over an 'edge' with no form of punishment or repercussions, and are
presented as an alternative community contained within their own world or
sub-culture. Barker discusses how the horror genre is 'usually about a return
to the status quo – the monster is the outsider who must be banished from
the sanctum … I've created monsters who come from the outside and who
call out to somebody to join *them* in the sanctum'.[32] It is this notion of the
monster seeking to bring others to their communities that forms the basis for
the portrayal of the Cenobites. However, in this case it is Frank who actively
seeks *them* having failed to find fulfilment in 'normal' sexuality. He summons
the Cenobites whose desires are laid out simply, 'you solved the Box, we came,

now you must come with us, taste our pleasures'. Thus the Cenobites do not seek to invade, nor do they seek to force themselves upon anyone beyond those who have called out to them. It should also be made clear that, despite Sharett's claims, the Cenobites do not simply offer destruction but, instead, a form of transformation, a fluidity of identity. Frank desires what the Cenobites offer, however now instead of it being 'never enough' it is a case of being 'too much'; he cannot gain satisfaction from 'normative' heterosexuality but fears to embrace a transgressive, queer sexuality.

The confusion of sexual identity experienced by Frank is central to the character. He is displaced, and while he appears to seek to return to his previous masculine identity, it is clear that this would still not satisfy him. The closest Frank gets to restoring himself is stealing and wearing the skin of his brother, after which he finally has sex with Julia. This act attempts to reaffirm his heterosexuality, but he soon dispatches her and attempts an incestuous rape of his niece, unable to be satisfied with a stabilised sexuality. His displacement comes from being unable to come to terms with his queer identity, fleeing the Cenobites despite his obvious enjoyment of their 'pleasure' (illustrated by his smile and licked lips in the finale where they tear him apart), and being unsatisfied with heteronormative practices. Frank is not a demonised monstrous-bi either, since bisexuality still suggests a specific identity, whereas Frank is permanently displaced. Ultimately Frank cannot accept the Cenobites' alternative life-style as it denounces the physical hetero-masculinity he strives to keep hold of. The trajectory of Frank's character is an inevitable one, his masculinity is frail at best, barely concealing the queer identity beneath, and his body is an area of contradiction and debate, constantly being altered and changed from one form to another. Frank cannot define himself as either straight or queer and neither can he hold on to his desired masculine identity. Thus his monstrosity does not stem from the act of sexual transgression but from the inability to be able to locate himself within any community.

Through Frank's constantly changing body, Clive Barker explores various issues relating to sexuality whilst avoiding overtly demonising specific orientations and submitting to tired, conventional notions of transgressive behaviour deserving punishment and retribution. *Hellraiser* follows Frank from his initial masculine identity, through his transformation and feminisation, through his conflicting desire to reconstruct his straight identity and the exploration of his homosexuality, and culminating in his displacement between the 'normative' heterosexual world and the queer culture of the Cenobites. The Cenobites are not destructive, they are creators who attempt to unlock Frank's potential and it is Frank's own reluctance and resulting displacement which causes the film's narrative conflicts. The other occasions where the two worlds collide, the meeting between Kirsty and the Cenobites, is a direct result of Frank's own disrupting influence causing conflict between the two communities which otherwise would not harm the other. Frank is rendered monstrous by the repression of his 'queerness' and the inability to obtain any specific identity, whether it is straight, gay, bisexual, or any other of the myriad human sexualities.

Nightbreed – queer community

Nightbreed was Barker's second feature film and built on a number of the themes dealt with in *Hellraiser*, chiefly those of alternative communities and queer identity. *Nightbreed* fully embraces the concept of the monstrous 'Other' as not being a force for evil but simply an alternative to 'normality' and demonstrates this through the creation of a potentially utopian queer society. Barker clearly stated his aims in making *Nightbreed*, claiming he 'was trying to invert the conventional morality of horror movies; again making the monstrous persuasive and romantic, while making the forces of law and order, which in a conventional horror narrative, are also the forces for "good", the subject of unacceptable villainy and troubling morality'.[33] The film follows the journey of Aaron Boone (Craig Sheffer), who suffers dreams of monsters (the titular 'Nightbreed') living in an underground city called Midian. His psychiatrist, Phillip Decker (David Cronenberg), frames Boone for murders he has committed and Boone flees to Midian where he becomes a member of the Nightbreed, the last remnants of ancient tribes of creatures driven underground by persecution. Lori (Anne Bobby), Boone's girlfriend, inadvertently leads Decker to Midian and he discovers the Nightbreed. Believing them monsters, Decker then brings an army of locals to Midian, intent on wiping out the peaceful Nightbreed whose only hope is to fight back against their oppressors.

   Nightbreed allows the audience to step into the world of the 'Other' in order to sympathise and understand an alternative perspective. The Nightbreed are representative of any form of alternative community, symbolising any minority group that has suffered from persecution and oppression, though the queer connotations are the most apparent in both the novella and the film. Benshoff picks up on the queer iconography, observing that 'the monsters sport leather, tattoos, body-piercings, shaved heads and/or pony-tails, Doc Marten boots, vests upon bare chests, and van dykes, a look that was concurrently being made fashionable by Queer Nationalists, members of Act Up, and the visual stylisations of queer theatre pieces'.[34] They are a literal underground community consisting of those who have been driven into hiding through persecution from 'normal' society, which hates and fears them due to their 'Otherness'. At the same time, the film is also careful to emphasise the differences between the individual Nightbreed, who are said to be 'the last survivors of the great tribes' and 'remains of races your species have almost driven to extinction'. Thus, whilst they are part of one community, the Nightbreed come from various different origins, echoing the reality of queer communities. Midian is thus a utopian queer community where Nightbreed of different races and backgrounds are brought together by their common 'Otherness'.

In *Nightbreed* the slasher villain is present in the form of Decker, whose victimisation of Boone, and the other monsters, stems from his own repressed sexuality, much like Frank in *Hellraiser*. In reference to slasher films, Barker has stated he believes that 'stalk 'n' slash is a very uninteresting sub-genre ... I wanted to kind of collide that with a much older tradition, which is this kind of fantastical tradition of monsters'.[35] In contrast to the slasher then, the Nightbreed are an open community of 'Others' who are accepting of their identities, as seen in the characters of Devil Lude (Vincent Keene) and Leroy Gomm (Tony Bluto), who are represented as an obvious queer couple, seen living together in Midian. Lude lovingly places an arm on Leroy's back, who himself has an effeminate voice and soft body, and they are rarely seen apart. Benshoff summarises this sufficiently in saying 'the film also sets up a dialect between the slasher film villain and the "traditional" monster: the former is unmistakably a human being who has gone mad for various reasons, while the latter is a separate but "natural" species'.[36] Barker thus contrasts the repressive monster of Decker with the persecuted, yet accepting community of the Nightbreed. The character of Boone helps negotiate the audience between the two ideologies as he uncovers his own 'queerness' throughout the film.

Benshoff claims that '*Nightbreed*'s story itself dramatizes a coming-out narrative', where the protagonist Aaron Boone learns that he is 'not a normal heterosexual human being but a normal queer monster'.[37] Boone's journey into the world of the Nightbreed is a demonstration of the difficulties faced in negotiating sexual identity. In the beginning, he seeks psychiatric help in his attempts to discover what is 'wrong' with him, only to eventually realise that his perceived problem is something perfectly 'normal' (in that he is queer). The notion of homosexuality as a medical illness was once prolific, with debates centred on 'the need to discover a "cause" of homosexuality', presenting it as a problem that science and culture had to overcome.[38] Boone's sessions with Decker are about discovering the reason for his dreams of 'monsters' and of Midian, a place where all sins can be forgiven. Decker works to convince Boone that these are just fantasies, yet not only are they ultimately shown to be true but they are also beneficial rather than destructive. Homosexuality is not a fantasy and for Boone it is a positive attribute in opposition to the more repressed sexuality of Decker. Boone's situation is further complicated by Lori, his girlfriend, who attempts to help him forget his 'bad dreams' of queer community, thus acting to further heterosexualise him. Benshoff suggests that 'queer couples spent their cinematic lives torturing one another, triangulating their desires through the heterosexualized normal couple'.[39] Decker and Boone can be read as one such queer couple, with Lori as the heterosexualising agent, thus following the traditional trajectory of horror. However, the inclusion of the

Nightbreed allows the film to present an alternative path for its closeted queers. *Nightbreed* identifies and criticises the idea of homosexuality as a 'nightmare fantasy' and/or illness, and it is only when Boone begins to realise this that he can begin his journey out of the closet and into the queer world of Midian and the community it represents. Despite attempts at 'normalisation', the event that galvanises Boone into finally accepting his 'Otherness' is Decker framing him for the murders of several families that he, himself had perpetrated. Thus, whilst Boone now accepts that he may be queer, this is far from a positive development from his perspective, having been conditioned by society to believe in the inherent monstrousness of the 'Other'. Warren Blumenfeld points out that 'members of a sexual minority often live in a psychological closet', fearing the reactions and repercussions of their coming-out and believing themselves to be in some way 'wrong'.[40] Decker showing Boone the photographs of his alleged victims was the catalyst that convinced him to accept a queer identity, but it is the assertion of his innocence by Peloquin (a member of the Nightbreed) that allows Boone to disavow any negative perceptions of himself. Accepting that his queerness is not inherently demonic, that he can be queer but also innocent, allows him to not only step out of the closet, but to literally be reborn with a new identity after he is gunned down by the police (representing forces of conservatism). The coming-out metaphor of *Nightbreed* is so thinly veiled that it adds a bemusing twist to the otherwise inappropriate tag-line given to the film; 'Lori thought she knew everything about her boyfriend … Lori was wrong'. Boone eventually lets go of the trappings of his 'false' heterosexual life to embrace the queer community of the Nightbreed, who offer him a far more welcoming alternative to the oppressive forces of the supposedly 'normal' society.

There are three key figures of authority within *Nightbreed*: Decker the psychiatrist, representing science, Eigerman the red-neck sheriff, representing the law; and Ashberry, a drunken, faithless priest, representing religion. Benshoff suggests 'traditional forces of "good" are represented by white men in business suits, priestly vestments, and police uniforms, all of which mark them out as fascists out to destroy the relatively peaceful Nightbreed'.[41] Each of these institutions can be connected to the oppression of homosexuality. Both science and psychiatry were used to treat homosexuality as a disease or illness whilst religious oppression of alternative sexuality remains an increasingly politically sensitive issue. Jeffrey Levi has suggested that 'the most explicit form [of oppression] is the criminalisation of our sexuality by the government' and mentions the example of 'sodomy laws' which made 'certain forms of consensual adult sexual behaviour illegal'.[42] Ordinary people were essentially made criminals in the eyes of the law, based entirely on their sexual orientation. Whilst *Nightbreed* may be fantasy, the issues it deals with are very real. It seems clear that Barker is deliberately criticising these 'authorities' as the primary areas in need of reformation.

need to fight for its independence and rights. The traditiona
d' represented by various authorities are shown to be homophobic
ve compared to the Nightbreed's openly queer community. However,
also suggests the queer community needs to fight for its voice to
ewhere and not be content to stay settled 'underground'. The ultimate
also be equality and the removal of oppressive forces. Of all his
htbreed best represents Barker's progressive approach to horror and
ates how he uses the themes and trappings of the genre to explore
sexuality and queer society.

Lord of Illusions – queer romance

ackson suggests 'it is in heterosexual relationships that romantic love
een institutionalised as the basis of marriage, and it is heterosexual love
h dominates cultural representations of romance'.[46] In *Lord of Illusions*
er challenges these representations and explores both homosexual and
rosexual romances, using contrasting ideas and differences in how they
portrayed to examine and negotiate queer romance. *Lord of Illusions* opens
h Swann (Kevin J. O'Connor) returning to a desolate house where his former
aster, Nix (Daniel von Bargen), leads a cult which has kidnapped a young
ild. Swann resists his feelings for Nix, allowing him to help kill and then
ind Nix with an iron mask. Thirteen years later, New York detective Harry
D'Amour (Scott Bakula) investigates the supposed murder of Swann and learns
that one of Nix's cultists, Butterfield (Barry Del Sherman), is trying to resurrect
his dead master. Harry teams up with Dorothea (Famke Janssen), Swann's wife,
who is also the girl he saved, and they discover Swann has faked his death to
escape Nix. Butterfield resurrects Nix who sacrifices the rest of his cult, deciding
'only Swann is worthy'. Nix wants Swann by his side as he destroys the world
but then kills him out of jealousy towards Dorothea. Nix himself is then destroyed
by Dorothea and Harry.

Lord of Illusions thus deals with a number of relationships, both straight
and queer, but the central couple of the film is undoubtedly Nix and Swann,
and it is around their romance that the central plot is structured. Nix is a
supernatural creature who, in his own words, 'was born to murder the world'
and yet Barker's script places this apocalyptic threat secondary to Nix's desire
to have Swann at his side. Both characters are coded as 'Other', Swann less
obviously so in order to establish him as a character who, like Boone in
Nightbreed, moves between queer and straight relationships, in an attempt to
negotiate his identity. Swann is presented as effeminate and confused, and
despite taking the central role for the opening sequence, he is markedly inef-
fectual, distancing the audience from the character. Nix has a distinctly non-
masculine 'soft body' whilst his dirty, unkempt appearance is suggestive of

Religious oppression is shown
around a long time, as demonstra
nightmarish vision of the past whe
executed by a religious inquisition. I,
past the church all but wiped out the
temporary religion, Ashberry, is the lea
Midian. Commenting upon religion in ,
Barker has said:

> There is large, sweeping religious imagery in
> horror ... I think it's always been there in the ₤
> being true – because people don't believe in the
> we have a lot of movies where the vampire can r₍
> not be burned by it ... I think that reflects a new ₐ
> religious matters.[43]

Ashberry is representative of the loss of faith an
modern society, though this does not in any way l₌
persecuting force. If anything, Ashberry seems to
rallying cry, an enemy that will bring people togetheɪ
In contrast to this, Eigerman represents a more cleaɪ
whose only motivation for attacking the Nightbreed is th
Decker, there is an element of sexual repression inherent ͺ
having beaten Boone, lights a large cigar mirroring the steɪ₍
image. Benshoff suggests that Eigerman 'and his men takͼ
brutalising the monsters they capture, referring to one queͼ
"it" before they beat and kill him'.[44] The reference to a forɱ
homophobia is clear. In *Nightbreed*, Barker deconstructs an
prejudices in relation to religion, science, and the law and presentₛ
take on horror cinema where these institutions are the true monsteɪ
and oppressing the usually demonised 'Other'.

The explosive finale of the film sees Boone urge the Nightbre
back against the forces of oppression. 'If we want to survive we ₍
Brothers and Sisters it is time to fight', is Boone's impassioned rallyiɪ
the Nightbreed, but he could just as easily be calling for 'queer people ₍
out and fight back against the forces of society who would define difₜ
as monstrous', as Benshoff suggests.[45] In *Nightbreed* the queer commuɪ₎
fighting for its existence, its right to survive, just as in the real world q
individuals often have to struggle to achieve equality and the same rights ₐ
privileges as heterosexual people. Though the context is different, the messaₐ
is the same, and the climax of *Nightbreed* displays nothing more than a needlesₛ
waste of life for both of the two opposing groups, which have no genuine
reason for their conflict beyond society's inability to accept difference. The
conflict between the 'Breed' and the 'Naturals' is a metaphor for the queer

someone on society's fringes, he is introduced juggling fire and immediately marked out as different. Later, after his resurrection, Nix becomes more traditionally monstrous in appearance and gains the addition of a small, anal opening on his forehead.[47] However, the characters are not chiefly identified as queer by their appearances but by their actions and interactions. In the opening scenes Nix attempts to seduce Swann with promises of enlightenment which Swann only passively resists, desiring to learn from Nix despite his questionable actions. The master/apprentice relationship is a variation on a theme that has occurred often in classic horror cinema, that of a servant so devoted to his master that 'they are often under some kind of supernatural spell which keeps them in their masters' thrall'.[48] Whilst Nix may not literally have control over Swann he certainly has a powerful influence and, despite his attempts to distance himself, Swann is constantly drawn back to Nix. This is demonstrated in the opening sequence where Swann comes to Nix's summons and again at the conclusion of the film where he agrees to help him destroy the world moments after they embrace. The film suggests Swann is attracted to Nix's power and promises of 'the secrets of the universe', though it is also possible to understand this search for answers as Swann negotiating his own confused sexuality. Nix's offer to 'share the power' is a veiled metaphor for his desire to have a relationship; for all his abilities, he is ultimately lonely and in need of someone to love. The assertion that he and Swann were supposed to keep each other company after the destruction of the world is a darkly comic twist on the romantic notion of a couple being 'together forever'. Thus the film sets up a situation where they both need something from the other – Nix wishes for company and someone to share his life with, whilst Swann wishes to have someone to help him affirm his queer identity. It is a relationship based on mutual acceptance and need, forming a strong groundwork for their romantic entanglement, which is represented in ways that are comparable to Hollywood representations of romance.

Discussing the treatment of romance in Hollywood cinema, Virginia Wexman claims that 'Hollywood has positioned itself as a social institution', one that influences partnerships by 'modelling appropriate courtship behaviour' to the often young audience.[49] This is primarily heterosexual behaviour and thus Hollywood is influential in helping to form ideas of straight relationships and romance, a common central focus in society's youth. The inevitable conclusion of this romance would, of course, be marriage, which is the final signifier of heterosexual, patriarchal dominance. Despite its often-perceived conservative nature, romance is not a common central focus in the horror genre, usually secondary to the horrors of the Other, and the relationships are seldom developed. It seems important to emphasise at this point an admittedly basic distinction between sex and a romantic relationship; sex can be purely physical whilst romance encompasses emotional involvement as well as physical desire. Vito Russo claims 'it is an old stereotype, that homosexuality has to do only with sex while heterosexuality is multifaceted and embraces love and romance', and it is this point that *Lord of Illusions* addresses most effectively.[50] The key aspect of Nix and Swann's relationship is that it clearly is not based around sexual attraction but a strong, emotional need for each other, and it is this that marks it out as more overtly romantic. The romance cannot be read as a commercially motivated addition, nor can it be easily dismissed as being deliberately exploitative in shocking images of alternative sexuality, as it is emotionally based. *Lord of Illusions* explores different ideas of romance and how romance is used in Hollywood, applying them to a homosexual pairing whilst also negotiating the clichés associated with queer couples in film.

The film builds towards a climatic meeting between Swann and the resurrected Nix, returned from the grave by Butterfield. The enforced separation of the two characters has led to a build-up of tension which is brought out into the open in this sequence. Nix asks 'Where did I go wrong?', which acts as a somewhat comic statement in order to 'break the ice' between them. On one level it works as the reunion between master and apprentice but it also has connotations of a meeting of ex-lovers, with both characters not entirely sure how each other will react after the initial break-up/betrayal. The first thing Nix says is 'I've had a long time to think about you', which suggests that, despite the fact that Swann killed him, Nix has spent all his time thinking of how their relationship went wrong and how to best rectify that mistake. The fact of his death is immaterial, as this is about the characters' relationship, which once again pushes the horror narrative into the background in favour of their romance. Nix suggests he should have been honest with Swann from the start, the deceit in the relationship being of more importance than the fact that Nix is threatening the destruction of the world. *Lord of Illusions* consistently puts their relationship at the centre of proceedings and Clive Barker does not seem to have attempted to create much ambiguity as to the meaning of these scenes, the queer connotations are made readily apparent for the audience. Nix openly accepts his mistakes before embracing Swann in a loving gesture of reconciliation. However, Nix and Swann spend a large amount of the film separated and throughout this time Swann is constantly faced with challenges to their relationship, as well as challenges to his own feelings and sexuality, which ultimately their reunion cannot survive.

Romance in film is rarely straight forward, and couples inevitably find themselves confronted by an array of problems and obstacles to their relationship; circumstances serve to keep a romantic couple separate until the film's conclusion which is also the case in *Lord of Illusions*. Nix and Swann are separated by Swann's own fears of his sexuality, a situation complicated by Butterfield whose unrequited love for Nix puts him in opposition to Swann. This forms a complicated queer love triangle between the three characters; whilst Swann attempts to hide his homosexuality, Butterfield fully embraces it, though his devotion to Nix is single minded and his love is certainly unrequited. Barker discusses the relationship between Nix and Butterfield:

> When we see young Butterfield, we see this young, rather sexy lad who's obviously Nix's catamite, he's Nix's bumboy, he shares Nix's bed. Swann on other hand is this wild card, he has looked into the Abyss, the way Nix has looked into the Abyss. Whereas Butterfield is a very attractive lightweight, Swann has this dark undertow.[51]

What is interesting here is that Barker identifies Butterfield and Nix as having a purely sexual relationship, one based simply on sexual attraction and lacking in the depth that a relationship with Swann would offer. They form a 'love triangle' that would not be out of place within a romance narrative, where the love rival is often attractive but lacking in the emotional depth that the genuine romantic couple share. Butterfield is Nix's rejected lover whilst Swann is the reluctant object of his desire, torn between his own homosexuality and the desire to conform to society's expectations. Thus, Swann also spends much of the film resisting his emotional connection to Nix, mainly through constructing a relationship with Dorothea, about whom we are told 'didn't marry him for love'. Once she is revealed to be the young girl rescued by Swann the relationship can be understood to be based on Dorothea's 'hero worship' and his attempt at a straight romance, effectively using her to heterosexualise himself. However, where classic horror would support the heterosexualising of a queer character, *Lord of Illusions* suggests Swann is not content with married life, happy to fake his death, and effectively widow his wife at the first sign of Nix's coming resurrection. Heterosexual marriage may be what is accepted as normal and, though he may have some form of love for Dorothea, the union is not the romantic, emotional love that a queer relationship with Nix would offer. As a child, Dorothea may not have been aware of Swann's relationship with Nix but with his return she could discover his secret, and Swann would rather fake his own death (a more extreme alternative to divorce!) than come out to his wife, despite the effect it may have on her. However, what is most important about the characters of Dorothea and Butterfield is that they create conflict and obstacles that both Nix and Swann must overcome in order to be together. At the climax of the film Butterfield is disposed of and Dorothea enters into a more traditional heterosexual relationship with Harry, thus leaving Swann and Nix with only each other. When Swann suggests he still has some feelings for Dorothea, despite her relationship with Harry, Nix mortally wounds him in an attack which can only be read as being motivated by a jealous rage. This is further emphasised by Nix's dying act wherein he reclaims Swann's body, piece by piece, suggesting that they are bound together, even after death.

On the surface, *Lord of Illusions* appears to present homosexuality as far more monstrous than Barker's other works. However, the heterosexual relationships are barely developed and appear to be based purely on sexual gratification whilst homosexuality, in reversal of the norm, is shown as multi-layered and complex. Barker shows how homophobia, the pressures of society and stereotypes related to queer couples can all cause conflict. Nix and Swann share an emotional, romantic love that barely touches upon sex, whilst Butterfield's love is unrequited as he is seen by Nix only as sexually attractive. It also suggests how resisting and suppressing homosexuality, as Swann attempts, can only cause further suffering to everyone involved, something also explored in *Hellraiser*. *Lord of Illusions* is about appearances and deception and this theme is central to the relationships within the movie. Queer romance is not demonised in itself, rather, it is shown to be as equally loving and tender as heterosexual love is portrayed in other films, and it is in this aspect that *Lord of Illusions* best succeeds in creating positive ideas of queerness.

Queer monsters

The progressive potential for queer horror is rife within Barker's trilogy, often embodied in displaced, conflicted but not necessarily evil monsters whose personalities and characterisations often equal or even surpass characters more closely aligned to heteronormativity. In *Hellraiser* Frank brings about his own destruction through his displacement whilst in *Nightbreed* the forces of authority bring about their own destruction through attempting to oppress the queer community of Midian. *Nightbreed* is openly supportive of queer pride and, along with *Lord of Illusions*, presents homosexuality as multifaceted, involving romance and love, rather than being portrayed as purely sexual. The 'queer monsters' themselves are often heroic and complex characters whose interactions and relationships are every bit as, if not more, meaningful as the 'normal' characters in the narrative. There is the potential to further explore these texts, and more queer themes can be extrapolated from the trilogy, including the relationship of Boone and Decker, the queer transgressions of the Cenobites, or the queer identity of Butterfield. Their existence, however, highlights the limitless potential for exploring identity, character and alternative sexuality within Barker's work, and indeed, this goes beyond his cinematic endeavours to his novels, paintings, and photography.

This queer approach is not so much a deliberate politicisation of horror (although to some extent *Nightbreed* is the exception), but an extension of Barker's approach to narrative and character. Barker has addressed how he wishes to present both himself and his work;

> I want as many people as possible to know that these imaginings come from a gay man who's happy to be gay. One who's making work which will be read by straight readers and enjoyed by straight readers. I add nothing special for gays in my fiction, but they are part of the world I create and constructively so.[52]

Barker sees the importance of viewing homosexuality as equal and as valid as heterosexuality, not giving it any preference and not deliberately setting out to demonise or [in]validate either orientation. There is something of a paradox in Barker's work; whilst he embraces the monstrous and the Other, he also works to normalise the difference as part of a continuum of human sexuality. He both embraces and venerates Otherness whilst also rendering it *a* normality, as opposed to *the* normality. His queer monsters are thus both monstrous and normal in the same instance. Thus Barker's trilogy of films presents a menagerie of queer monsters that insist on a re-evaluation of the monstrous, and further open up the horror genre to the potential for progressive renditions of supposedly transgressive and queer themes, ideologies and characterisations.

Notes

1 Interview with Clive Barker,' *Loveline*, 21 August 1996. Radio programme. Transcript online: www.clivebarker.com/html/visions/confess/nonls/loveline/LoveLine8-12-96.htm.
2 The films in question were *Rawhead Rex*, based on his short story of the same name, and *Underworld* (aka *Transmutations*), based on an original concept. Clive's scripts were heavily re-worked, and his disappointment in their productions led to him directing *Hellraiser* himself.
3 And some examples of this can be found elsewhere in this collection.
4 Robin Wood, 'An Introduction to the American Horror Film,' in Barry Keith Grant (ed.), *Planks of Reason: Essays on the Horror Film* (Metuchen, NJ: Scarecrow Press, 2004), pp. 169–72.
5 *Ibid.* p. 189.
6 *Ibid.* p. 199.
7 Paul Wells, 'On the Side of the Demons: Clive Barker's Pleasures and Pains. Interviews with Clive Barker and Doug Bradley,' in Steve Chibnall and Julian Petley (eds), *British Horror Cinema* (London: Routledge, 2002), p. 176. Italics in original.
8 Christopher Sharrett, 'The Horror Film in Neoconservative Culture,' in Barry Keith Grant (ed.), *The Dread of Difference: Gender and the Horror Film* (Austin: University of Texas Press, 1996), p. 261.
9 Harry M. Benshoff, *Monsters in the Closet: Homosexuality and the Horror Film* (Manchester: Manchester University Press, 1997), p. 14.
10 *Ibid.* p. 8.
11 Annamarie Jaggose, *Queer Theory: An Introduction* (Melbourne: Melbourne University Press, 1996), p. 16.
12 Alexander Doty, *Flaming Classics: Queering the Horror Canon* (London: Routledge, 2000), p. 4.
13 *Ibid.* p. 4.
14 Benshoff, *Monsters in the Closet*, p. 4.
15 *Ibid.* p. 265.
16 Sharrett, 'The Horror Film in Neoconservative Culture,' p. 261.

17 Wells, 'On the Side of the Demons', pp. 177–8.
18 Rob Latham, 'Phallic Mothers and Monster Queers', *Science Fiction Studies*, Vol. 25:1 (1998), pp. 87–101, here p. 95.
19 Harry M. Benshoff, 'The Monster and the Homosexual', in Mark Jancovich (ed.), *Horror: The Film Reader* (London: Routledge, 2002), p. 265.
20 Sharrett, 'The Horror Film in Neoconservative Culture', p. 265.
21 Comment given by Barker to the costume designer on *Hellraiser* as mentioned on the Anchor Bay *Hellraiser* DVD documentary *Hellraiser: Resurrection*.
22 Anna Powell, *Deleuze and the Horror Film* (Edinburgh: Edinburgh University Press, 2005), p. 84.
23 *Ibid*. p. 84.
24 Richard Dyer, *Culture of Queers* (London: Routledge, 2001), pp. 75–6.
25 *Ibid*.
26 *Ibid*. p. 80.
27 *Hellraiser*, DVD commentary, 2004, Anchor Bay.
28 Sharrett, 'The Horror Film in Neoconservative Culture', pp. 261–2.
29 Paul Wells, *The Horror Genre: From Beelzebub to Blair Witch* (London: Wallflower, 2000), pp. 91–2.
30 Carl B. Holmberg, *Sexualities and Popular Culture* (Ohio: Bowling Green State University, 1998), p. 91.
31 *Ibid*. p. 93.
32 Barker quoted in Benshoff, *Monsters in the Closet*, p. 262. Italics in original.
33 Barker quoted in Wells, 'On the Side of the Demons', p. 179.
34 Benshoff, *Monsters in the Closet*, p. 260.
35 Barker, 'On Nightbreed', quoted on his official website at www.clivebarker.info/nightbreed.html.
36 Benshoff, *Monsters in the Closet*, p. 260.
37 *Ibid*. pp. 263–4.
38 Vito Russo, *The Celluloid Closet: Homosexuality in the Movies* (Revised Edition) (New York: Harper & Row, 1987), p. 298.
39 Benshoff, *Monsters in the Closet*, p. 69.
40 Warren J. Blumenfeld (ed.), *Homophobia: How We All Pay the Price* (Boston: Beacon Press, 1992), pp. 8–10.
41 Benshoff, *Monsters in the Closet*, p. 262.
42 Jeffrey Levi, 'Homophobia and the AIDS Public Policy', in Blumenfeld (ed.), *Homophobia*, p. 129.
43 Barker, quoted on his official website at www.clivebarker.info/ints90.html.
44 Benshoff, *Monsters in the Closet*, p. 263.
45 *Ibid*. p. 264.
46 Stevi Jackson, 'Women and Heterosexual Love: Complicity, Resistance and Change', in Tracey L. Steele (ed.), *Sex, Self and Society: The Social Context of Sexuality* (Belmont, CA: Wadsworth, 2005), p. 108.
47 Barker's own description as given on the *Lord of Illusions* DVD commentary.
48 Benshoff, *Monsters in the Closet*, p. 48.

49 Virginia Wright Wexman, *Creating the Couple: Love, Marriage, and Hollywood Performance* (Princeton: Princeton University Press, 1993), pp. 4–5.
50 Vito Russo, *The Celluloid Closet*, p. 132.
51 Barker, quoted on his official website at www.clivebarker.info/lordofillusions.html.
52 Wells, *The Horror Genre*, p. 177.

8

Breaking through the canvas: towards a definition of (meta)cultural blackness in the fantasies of Clive Barker

Tony M. Vinci

From *Weaveworld*'s Jerichau St Louis to *Everville*'s Joe Flicker to *Galilee*'s eponymous protagonist[1] to *Abarat*'s Finnegan Hobb, Clive Barker's black male characters slip into the interstitial realms between culture and metaphysics and return to the quotidian to share their stories with their respective tribes. Through their personal and collective histories of abuse, marginalisation, and discrimination, Barker's black males become shaman – spiritual healers and cultural revolutionaries who channel their traumatic experiences into transformative agency. By creating a context wherein the black male becomes acutely acclimated to this shamanistic calling, Barker's fiction upsets the prevalent inclination in some speculative narratives to code blackness as 'a representational space for repressed racial anxieties'[2] and instead constructs what might be termed a (meta)cultural blackness – a vision of blackness as a crossroads where the cultural and the historical meet and interact with the metaphysical and the marvellous. Developing Gary Hoppenstand's assertion that Barker's 'twin areas of artistic interest' are 'social progressivism and the transcendental',[3] I contend that, through Barker's experimentation with (meta)cultural blackness, progressive social ideals and metaphysics necessarily intersect to intimate an order of selfhood that is clearly culturally constructed but also operates beside, behind, or beyond the boundaries of cultural authority.[4] If, as Robert E. Fox argues, 'blackness is "a work," a project or process [...] that is also liberational',[5] then (meta)cultural blackness becomes a liberating project of ontological and social revolution, moving towards the creation of new modes of identity construction and counter-hegemonic force.

Barker explores (meta)cultural blackness and its transformative influence in many of his works, but it is perhaps never more fully and powerfully detailed than through the character of Pie 'oh' pah in *Imajica* (1991). In the language of the novel's storyworld, Pie is a Eurhetemec mystif, an extraordinarily rare being (he is in fact the only one in existence), marked by his unfixed flesh, which accommodates the gaze of others by reconfiguring itself to embody their worldviews and desires. Pie's protean body does more than comment on the ways in which the white gaze exploits and commoditises the contemporary black male body; it functions as an archive of historical narratives that embody a blackness defined through personal and cultural breaks, geographic dispersals, and historic projects of dehumanisation. Pie's exact age is never divulged, but it is made clear that he has lived for centuries, positioning him as a channel through which the reader encounters traces of the historical black experience pre and post the Middle Passage. His narrative arc both maps the ruptures caused by the slave trade, emancipation, modernisation, segregation, and disharmonious (re)integration, and explores the traumatised identities engendered by such ruptures. While Pie is not an allegorical figure (he is not meant, for example, to be read solely as slave or as an economically depressed victim of urbanisation and ghettoisation), his embodied history integrates fragmented, trans-generational traces of the diasporic black experience. Through a process of identification that Houston A. Baker Jr. terms the 'rites of the black (w)hole',[6] Pie channels his traumatic collection of narratives into a dynamic mode of (meta)cultural identification that offers possibilities for both personal and cultural change.

More than a project of cultural critique or personal empowerment, Barker's (meta)cultural blackness demonstrates the power of fantasy narratives to engage with and prefigure emergent forms of identity and agency – centreless, intersectional, multivalent, fluid, and porous identities that give form and voice to that which operates beyond the borders of the known and the accepted. Before I define how this (meta)cultural blackness functions in *Imajica* in detail, I offer a brief history of the politicisation of the fantasy genre and how this scholarship functions as a backdrop for Barker's work (and the small but significant body of criticism that endeavours to unpack it). Engaging Barker's fantasies as a prime test case, I argue that approaching fantasy narratives through critical race theory and other experimental frameworks of agency and identity can further mobilise the genre to participate in projects of cultural revolution.

Fantasy as revolution: Barker in critical contexts

Once the main body of fantasy theory moved beyond Tolkien's aesthetics and Campbell's myth criticism in the 1970s, scholars of the genre begin to view literary and popular fantasy 'as [a] system of orientations',[7] 'a way of perceiving human experience'.[8] The political and cultural applications of such perspectives remove the genre from the provincial, reductionist impressions that define it simply as a confluence of aesthetic conventions, a narrative repository of panhuman experience, or, even more limiting, a marketing category, and recontextualise it as a theoretical approach to reading narrative and culture. Illustratively, both W.R. Irwin and Kathryn Hume define fantasy as that which antagonises 'what is generally accepted as possibility'.[9] Hume develops this somewhat, discussing how fantasy also presents 'a reality fuller than our own', which reintroduces 'to our notice material which our consciousness normally filters out; by introducing us to outlooks we would not otherwise take.'[10] Read in this way, theorising fantasy becomes a project that seeks to interpret and decode the 'imaginary laws of the created world to postulate hidden principles on which our own might be organized'.[11]

Since the 1980s, fantasy scholarship has employed this type of analysis in order to position the genre in an overtly political context, arguing for its desire and ability to not simply decode or unveil the 'hidden principles' upon which our culture is constructed but to obliterate them, to alter them, to offer alternatives; failing that, to subvert and gain agency. Prefiguring Slavoj Žižek's notion that 'it seems easier to imagine "the end of the world" than a far more modest change in the mode of production, as if liberal capitalism is the "real" that will somehow survive even under conditions of global ecological catastrophe',[12] Christine Brooke-Rose states nakedly: 'never before, it is felt, has man been so squarely faced with the possible annihilation of mankind and all his works, his planet and perhaps more', but 'into a mere backdrop, apocalyptic no doubt, but a backdrop we cease to see'.[13] It is precisely this type of ideological blindness that fantasy upsets. As Ann Swinfen insists, fantasy is created from and expresses 'a desperate dissatisfaction with contemporary life' and, at its most engaged, it attempts revolution.[14] The revolutionary force of the genre gains its most powerful and eloquent expression in Rosemary Jackson's now seminal study, *Fantasy: The Literature of Subversion*. She argues that fantasy defines 'a culture's definitions of that which can be'[15] and subverts 'this unitary vision' by revealing 'reason and reality to be arbitrary, shifting constructs'[16] and 'introduc[ing] confusion and alternatives'.[17] It is within this revolutionary project of unveiling ideology and introducing real alternatives to gain agency and exert power, that much scholarship on Clive Barker situates his work.

Beyond Gary Hoppenstand's *Clive Barker's Short Stories: Imagination as Metaphor in the* Books of Blood *and Other Works* and Douglas Winter's critical biography, *Clive Barker: The Dark Fantastic*[18] (both of which characterise Barker as an exemplary literary author whose inventive content, complex voice and sophisticated thematic concerns earn him a place in the canon next to figures such as Marlow and Shelley), much critical work on Barker explores how his fiction functions in a post-industrial, new media-driven milieu engulfed in the nebulous workings of late capitalism. Some critics offer straightforward but thoughtful Feminist and Marxist interpretations.[19] Others deepen these analyses by moving Barker's work beyond cultural critique.[20] They argue that, through Barker's explicit challenging of genre fiction's heteronormative biases (especially in the arenas of 'deviant' sexuality, gender, and class), his work not only articulates an intense thirst for alterity and monstrosity, but engenders a subversive and transgressive cultural space that disassembles the hegemonic control capitalism holds over our imaginations and opens new sites for social resistance.[21]

Thus, there exists a schism between critics on Barker: some focus on the traditional humanism found in his tales, which privileges a romantic vision of self, soul, and imagination; others employ models of cultural criticism to analyse the political work that Barker's fiction performs. While this former criticism is significant for its disciplinary manoeuvring to code Barker as a serious artist, and this latter work is vital in its efforts to use Marx, Nietzsche, Delueze, Guattari, Baudrillard, Freud, Lacan, Barthes, Kristeva, and Foucault to unpack Barker's early fiction, each group tends to overlook the other. I contend that Barker writes about both metaphysics and cultural criticism with equal interest, constructing a sophisticated and subtle mode of fantasy fiction that depends upon a fruitful tension between these two realms.

What Barker achieves through engaging this tension is a type of Todorovian hesitation. In *The Fantastic: A Structural Approach to a Literary Genre*, Todorov defines the fantastic as the 'hesitation experienced by a person who knows only the laws of nature, confronting an apparently supernatural event'.[22] Instead of engaging the categories of the natural and the supernatural, Barker complicates Todorov's hesitation by engaging the tension between the metaphysical and the cultural as it is played out and rehearsed in the black male subject. Barker's fantasies dramatise Henry Louis Gates Jr.'s critique of the notion of the essentialised 'black subject, integral and whole'[23] by inviting the reader to experience a hesitation between the myth of the authentic black subject and the openness offered by exploding essentialist models of race and introducing alternatives.[24] Paul Gilroy clarifies the value of this type of hesitation, arguing that black identities 'are always unfinished, always being remade'[25] and, as such, necessitate 'a pluralistic position which affirms blackness as an open signifier'.[26] As 'a libertarian, strategic alternative', Gilroy's inclusive recasting of blackness as 'open' offers an opportunity to antagonise racist structures without reifying 'the concept of race';[27] it responds to ethnic absolutism by reading ethnicity 'as an infinite process of identity construction'.[28] Gilroy's 'infinite process' becomes the focus of Barker's depictions of blackness inscribed at the generative, hesitative moment between an essentialised notion of blackness un-ruptured by the history of the Middle Passage[29] and the limitless matrix of competing cultural discourses that inform notions of (racial) identity.

Painting the posthuman *flesh* 'against a brutal sky': cultural and metaphysical exile and (meta)cultural revolution in *Imajica*

Barker's *Imajica* is a novel haunted by the possibility of union, of singularity. Each of its primary characters is torn from people and places that, at least imaginarily, offer the promise of authentic personhood. Defined as exiles,

Barker's characters in *Imajica* endeavour to erase the interstices between self
and Other and heal the wounds that inhibit them from creating, finding, or
being capable of expressing a singular 'authentic' identity. This frustrated quest
to become whole is emblematised most powerfully in the narrative's cosmology:
the Imajica is a series of five dimensions (termed Dominions), four of which
stand connected while one, the fifth Dominion (Earth), is unreconciled and
cast into uncertainty about its own nature. Within this cosmology, Barker situates
blackness as an indication of exile from the possibility of wholeness, or, rather
from a type of ideologically constructed wholeness that cannot function within
the boundaries of (racial) difference. However, this is a fruitful exile that leads,
ultimately, to Houston A. Baker's theory of the *rites of the black (w)hole*.

   Through 'separation from a dominant, white society', 'a period of instruction
that is "betwixt and between" anything approximating a fixed social status',
and a reintegration 'with a new status', the black subject achieves 'what might
be termed an "ahistorical," "metaphorical" sense of the black self's historicity
or placement within a diachronic series of [events]', and ultimately 'ascends
to share his new knowledge'.[30] Barker stages the transformative potential of
exile through Pie 'oh' pah, the Eurhetemec mystif who has been exiled from
his Dominion, his city, his body, and, ultimately, his sense of stable subjectivity.
Even within his home city of Yzordderrex, Pie is part of a ghetto, a 'city within
the city',[31] termed a kesparate (evoking through homonymic resonance notions
of 'desperate' and 'separate'), a geographic location constructed for the isolation
of a particular cultural group. In this way, the novel negotiates 'the powerful
effects of even temporary experiences of exile, relocation, and displacement',
especially since Pie's flesh casts him into a type of permanent exile as eternal
Other.[32] As Paul Gilroy continues to argue, 'whether their experience of exile
is forced or chosen, temporary or permanent, [black spokespeople] repeatedly
articulate a desire to escape the restrictive binds of ethnicity, national identification, and sometimes even "race" itself'.[33] Thus, exile becomes central to Pie's
metaphysical and cultural existences, and it is this casting out and sense of
essentialised Otherness that marks his blackness as both cause of suffering
and shamanistic authority.

   Barker introduces Pie as an 'invisible' man who cannot be 'traced'.[34] This
allusion to Ellison's seminal novel aligns Pie clearly with Ellison's unnamed
narrator and his marginalised perspective; moreover, since Pie's identity is
linked to the black experience pre and post slavery, his invisibility comments
on the cultural subjugation of black history and its cultural effects. Pie is not
only invisible but also *untraceable*. This untraceability suggests a sort of non-
identity, a subject that is only allowed to exist in the cultural sphere as useful
object. It is significant then that Pie enters the novel through the vantage point
of Estabrook, Pie's white, affluent, would-be employer who finds Pie living in
an exotic London homeless park. Estabrook becomes a mediating force, initiating
the reader into Pie's world through a decidedly limited, racist, patriarchal

perspective, one that is quickly dismantled through Pie's physical presence(s). As Estabrook enters the trailer, 'A scent and sound met him, both sweet. Oranges had been peeled, and their dew was in the air. So was a lullaby, played on the guitar.'[35] Interestingly, it is the *effect* of Pie's labours that are detected, and they are surprisingly domestic, artistic, and peaceful.

Pie is first mentioned as part of a story, an almost mythical, untraceable assassin, then as an invisible man, then as a stunning sensual *effect*, illustrating a shockingly beautiful rite of passage for white subjectivity into the transformative world of (meta)cultural blackness.

When Pie is finally 'shown', it is as a distanced, marginalised figure, half-hidden but central: 'The player, a black man, sat in the farthest corner, in a shadowy place beside the sleeping child.'[36] Pie's blackness redefines blackness for Estabrook: it no longer denotes a useful, thuggish tool to perform what his white subjectivity cannot; it is gentle and sweet, nurturing and domestic, creative and haunting. Even more significantly, Estabrook finds in Pie's identity something with which to sympathise, something 'distressingly vulnerable'.[37] Pie's blackness does more than inform white subjectivity of the multivalent nature of blackness: it dismantles the very worldview of whiteness, thrusting its tragically limited egocentric perspective into a universe of complexity, flux, and possibility. Pie's final introductory signifier is, surprisingly, the one that usually dominates cultural representations of blackness – the embodiment of the black male, his skin and bone. However, after Estabrook transitions from a white subjective *perspective* to an indefinable sphere of black *actuality*, the black male body becomes something almost magical: he was

> perhaps only thirty, but wearied by some excess or other, the burnished sepia of his skin barely concealing a sickly iridescence, as though there were a mercurial taint in his cells. It made him difficult to fix … the merest motion of his head breaking subtle waves against his bones, their spume draining back into his skin trailing colours Estabrook had never seen in flesh before.[38]

This frenetic motion within the black male's most powerful cultural identifier – his skin – indicates a shifting not only of the perception of blackness in the novel but in its very definition and power.

Upon close inspection, the black male's skin and bone are revealed to be in flux; the interior and exterior slip into each other and result in an expression of (meta)cultural being. Pie's body resists classification by the white imagination and offers an inimitable sight that threatens Estabrook's racial (racist?) authority. As Badley contends, 'Barker uses the metaphor of the literalized body to express in flesh and blood that which Freud, Lacan, Barthes, Kristeva, and Foucault have merely discoursed of': a transgression of the symbolic order.[39] For Barker, the body is not an authentic sign but an opening or wound that defers simple signification. The movement of Pie's body defies attempts to 'fix' it, forcing the viewer (Estabrook and the reader) to give up all desire to locate Pie's blackness within the limited space of his or her own perceptions of the black body, and exist instead within this radical instant of rupture. Here, Pie's fluctuating body moves beyond clear definitions of base-line humanity and hints at being posthuman.

According to Jay McRoy, the power of the posthuman body lies in its ability to reveal 'an alternative economy of identity predicated upon thematics of multiplicity, hybridity, and alterity'.[40] McRoy argues for the posthuman body's 'potential for re-imagining monstrous (splattered/splattering) embodiments as oppositional and/or liberatory figures that, through their hybridity, challenge western capitalist master-narratives [...] by revealing a multiplicity of alternate subject positions'.[41] Pie's posthuman body becomes 'an intensive and hetero-geneous body, a perpetual contemporary and malleable physicality in the throes of continual self-construction. [...] a body that rejects the idea of "organism," fixed borders, and totalizing systems, embracing instead its own monstrous becoming.'[42] While McRoy's liberating vision for the posthuman body is engag-ingly argued and convincing, it does not take into account the potential commoditisation of the posthuman body. In order to accommodate this perspec-tive, I would like to revise subtly McRoy's topos by utilising Hortense Spiller's distinction between 'flesh' and 'body' to posit notions of the posthuman flesh and posthuman body.

Spiller negotiates a central difference between 'captive and liberated subject-positions' through differentiating between 'flesh' and 'body'.[43] Baker clarifies this distinction: 'The dissonance between *being* free and having freedom *bestowed* is, at least, the conflict between the flesh and the body'.[44] Pie's blackness is defined by both his liminal sexuality and intra-dimensionality, but it is the commoditisation of his posthuman *flesh* that transforms it into the posthuman *body*. This is demonstrated most profoundly in the fact of Pie's protean body, which changes its actuality and appearance in accordance with the desire of others. Remembering that Pie functions as sometimes slave and sometimes prostitute, the metaphor works perfectly to express the power the white gaze has held in regards to the black body: it has defined it, stolen it, limited it, and, by doing so, raped not only the commoditised body but (extending Spiller's flesh/body paradigm once again) what might be termed the *metaphysical body*, the usurpation and colonisation of the *metaphysical flesh*.

Working from these notions of the posthuman flesh and its translation into the commoditised posthuman body, Pie's blackness is defined as being marked profoundly by the experience of slavery and the identity-fragmenting horrors of the Middle Passage. While *Imajica* is not simply some fantasy coding of a nineteenth-century slave narrative, it does borrow some of its conventions: the historical rupture, the psychological damage, the physical torture, the notion of exile, and reconstitutions of love that may or may not be confused by the commoditisation of the body. Pie is torn from his Dominion into the interstice between the reconciled Dominions and Earth. Within this liminal space, Pie experiences indescribable physical and psychological horrors that torture him into an existential timelessness; he becomes 'nothing and no one'.[45] As Gates reminds us in his opening line to *The Signifying Monkey*, 'The black Africans who survived the dreaded "Middle Passage" from the west coast of Africa to the New World did not sail alone. Violently and radically abstracted from their civilizations, these Africans nevertheless carried with them to the Western hemisphere aspects of their cultures that were meaningful, that could not be obliterated, and they chose, by acts of will, not to forget'.[46] Likewise, when a white metaphysician from Earth conjures Pie from this inter-dimension, Pie participates 'willingly' as a slave, an experience that forces him to limit the scope of his identity, but he retains guarded within himself, a potentially (meta) cultural connection to his history, culture, and metaphysics. Bereft of any avenue through which to experience a material expression of his internal life or cultural past, Pie is forced to function externally as nothing more than a commoditised body; however, internally he retains imaginative and metaphysical bonds to his old culture and identity, fostering the hope of a return to the flesh. Like the African turned slave, Pie was compelled to 'maintain [his] cultural heritage at a *meta* (as opposed to material) level […] Primary to [his] survival was the work of *consciousness*, of nonmaterial counterintelligence'.[47] This counterintelligence, sustained through struggles of memory and spirit, is what empowers Pie to verify the existence of a trace of identity that operates beyond the body.

As Pie's flesh becomes embodied through commoditisation, he adapts a psychology of exile, which ultimately enables him to represent and create new possibilities for social and ontological transformation. Thus, the novel takes on the project of Pie's disembodiment and return to the flesh. As with his introduction in the novel, this disembodiment is mediated through a white gaze. More surprisingly, it is mediated by the white gaze of Pie's master, Gentle, John Furie Zacharias, the Maestro Sartori, who ultimately marries Pie. In a moment of narrative brilliance, Barker creates the master/slave dynamic as one of perpetual forgetfulness. Gentle, as the Maestro Sartori, willingly enslaves Pie, though, after failure and trauma, demands that Pie continually erase his memory every ten years so that he will never have to be or feel responsible for his sins. In this way, Barker imaginatively resolves the conflicts of black historical memory and the political and personal problematics of white power. Gentle is Pie's master; he just does not *remember* that he is. Therefore, he functions under the illusion that Pie has complete agency, while Pie continually functions as a slave for a Master that does not believe he expresses such influence. Crucially, it is Pie who must live with this oppressive and terrible knowledge, memory, and truth. Thus, the novel criticises the 'forgetfulness' of empowered whiteness (as manifested in institutional racism, a culture of white entitlement, and a psychological model of insistent racial hierarchy and difference). More significantly, Barker positions the (meta)cultural black shaman as liberator and saviour as one who can *remind* the white imagination of its transgressions and the power that those transgressions have garnered the white community, as well as the traumatic oppression it has caused the black community by becoming an echo of the African trickster figure Esu.

In his opening chapter to *The Signifying Monkey*, Gates delineates the ways in which Esu functions in African myth and culture: Esu is 'the guardian of the crossroads',[48] 'genderless, or of dual gender',[49] a 'sign of [sexual] liminality, but also of the penetration of thresholds, the exchange between discursive universes',[50] and the 'indeterminacy of interpretation'.[51] Similarly, Pie is a mediator between the cultural and the metaphysical, black and white, male and female, and as such, he confounds the rationalist and enforces a perspective of multivalency. Pie's *flesh*, especially its liminal sexual identities and functions, becomes an uninterpretable text; hence the significance of his limited, interpretable *body*. Very similar to the Esu myth in which Esu tricks two farmers into thinking that he wears both a white and black hat (while in fact he wears a hat that is half white and half black) Pie's body intimates the folly 'to insist [...] on one determinate meaning, itself determined by vantage point and the mode one employs to see'.[52] Pie is, in essence, the indefinable sign that resides at the (meta)cultural crossroads of infinite readings, and it is this position that empowers him to trick and to teach, to rupture the logic of the quotidian and introduce modes of identification based upon alterity and hybridity.

The first time Pie and Gentle have intercourse, Gentle exists as what Barker has termed a 'two-dimensional man', one trapped within the narrowly circumscribed arena of the cultural, and as such, his libidinous imagination is limited and provincial. He not only codes Pie reductively as a woman but as a woman with whom he is deeply familiar, and Pie, as slave/whore, goes along with the charade: 'Though he couldn't see her, the darkness was a black canvas, and he painted her there to perfection.'[53] Since desire transforms Pie's body, Pie becomes complete commodity, translated into desired object, owned and used; however, by the end of the encounter, Pie is revealed as himself, and this revelation inspires a revolution in Gentle's vision.

> His eyes had been feeding on darkness and projections for too long, and now, presented with solid reality, they were befuddled. Half concealed by shadow the woman was a mire of shifting *forms* – face blurred, body smeared, pulse of iridescence, slow now, passing from toes to head. [...] The roiling forms of her face resolved themselves like pieces of a multifaceted jigsaw, turning and turning as they found their place, concealing countless other configurations – rare, wretched, bestial, dazzling – behind the shell of a congruous reality.[54]

Gentle begins the encounter by projecting his perceptions and desires onto Pie's commoditised body, but as the liaison develops, his reading of Pie's body becomes 'befuddled', revealing the more complicated, multivalent reality of Pie's flesh. Borrowing from Eve Sedgwick's definition of 'queer' as a process by which dichotomies are destabilised,[55] I argue that Barker *queers* both Pie's body and Gentle's desire, unsettling them both as to reveal the multifaceted realities behind the convenient categories of racial identity and sexual orientation. As K.A. Laity suggests, despite the fear and anxiety such queering revelations may invoke, 'the new territory is the payoff; the adventure of the further realms of experience may be the reason to go on, to embrace the monster if only to achieve a moment of communion with something extraordinary'.[56] As Pie's flesh revolutionises Estabrook's vision and deconstructs the worldview of whiteness, it deconstructs Gentle's, though, in this case, it begins a transformative process that not only has the power to dismantle the prevalent ideologies of the present moment but reinscribes a new, unruptured history that constructs, in turn, a new, multivalent present.

Barker performs here what Fred Moten defines as the work of speculative fiction: the exploration of 'the total range of the possible, the implicit deconstruction of any singularist and set-theoretic conceptions of the total'.[57] Gentle's encounter with Pie fractures his two-dimensionality and engenders a new ontological framework in which to consider the limits of subjectivity and reality. While he cannot yet negotiate this newly opened space, he is driven to explore it. Lost and confused, Gentle attempts to construct an understanding of Pie's identity through painting, a particularly appropriate metaphor for this identity construction. The canvas functions in a few interesting ways. First, it is a mirror, suggesting that whatever Gentle paints will be little more than an aesthetic reflection of himself. Second, it is a representation of the flesh upon which the body is projected (that binary that Pie repeatedly confounds). Third, it is a tabula rasa, a clean slate upon which Gentle can authentically recreate a vision of the world. Considering these three possibilities – mirror, flesh, world – simultaneously enables us to unpack a bit more clearly the levels on which Barker's novel operates.

Gentle's imagistic attempt to make sense of his experience with alterity becomes emblematic of Barker's reworking of blackness in the historically amnesiatic white imagination. The painting itself does not become the sole focus of the scene; rather, Gentle's creative process, his activity of working through, his process of externalising his reactions, thoughts, and experiences, become Barker's centre: 'It was clear he'd worked on the canvas with no little ferocity. There were places where it had been punctured [...] other places where the paint was laid on with gluttonous abandon [...] All this to achieve the likeness of what? Two people, it seemed, standing face to face against a brutal sky'.[58] In order to 'capture' Pie's identity, Gentle must break through the very canvas – mirror, flesh, world – at some points and cover it completely at others. Barker's metaphor seems clear: in order to understand (meta)cultural blackness and its relationship to white culture, traditional conceptions of identity construction must be ripped through, ruptured, reconfigured. As Fox writes about the purpose of art after modernism, it 'struggles to re-collect the shards of our essential being.'[59] A simultaneous striving for the metaphysical (breaking through the canvas) and the experimental and interpretive attempts to describe ('paint laid on with gluttonous abandon') need to be conflated in an open-ended, eternally exploratory mode of world-building in order to 're-collect' fragments of self (or Other). Through this interpretive lens, the actual image that Gentle creates, two beings facing each other against a harsh but shifting background, suggests the necessity of plurality. Specifying an interpretation of the painting and its creation (does it depict varying versions of Gentle? Gentle and Pie? Varying versions of Pie?) is not as significant as noting the general process of uncovering, creating, discovering an unknown and porous topography that can negotiate (meta)cultural identity.

Gentle's new-found pluralist vision enables him to 'see' Pie as enfleshed, but it is not until they are married in the Cradle of Chzercemit within the walls of a psychiatric asylum turned prison that this flesh gains agency. Here, in a space removed from Earth by a Dominion, a pool of living water, and two institutions that alienate the couple from the heteronormative, racially limited paradigms of the contemporary West, Pie offers a hint of his 'authentic' blackness, and it comes at moment of sexual congress with a white male who was/is his master. This moment cannot be easily interpreted. While it is depicted as a progressive act of union, it includes a potentially Washingtonian perspective that espouses black assimilation into white normativity. I contend that this marriage, especially as it takes place in a metaphoric womb removed from the cultural, explodes the master/slave dynamic and constitutes the shamanistic power of Pie's (meta)cultural blackness to open up new modes of blackness and, in turn, deconstruct the physical and metaphysical centre of white patriarchy – the phallus as signifier and signified. As Baker argues convincingly, 'The PHALLUS, in a word, is the signifier that institutes a male-dominant cultural discourse and mandates a division of physiologically differentiated children into two, unequal sexes. To create a habitable space beyond the LAW of the PHALLUS, symbolic manipulation – an unveiling – is necessary.'[60] Pie instigates the 'unveiling' of phallic logic and power through his inter-racial, inter-species union with Gentle.

Before they consummate their nuptials, Gentle tells Pie, 'I don't want to dream you. […] How can I understand anything if all I look at is illusions?'[61] Gentle relinquishes his power (and desire) to translate the flesh and subjectivity of the black slave into an objectified body which he owns, upon which he can inscribe his desire, and with which he can perform experiences that might satiate his desire, and he does all of this to rewrite his worldview. When Pie reveals his genitals, Gentle responds as if experiencing a transcendental moment of the sublime. What he 'sees' necessitates a new vision in order to be comprehended; the law of the phallus is here undermined. The revelation that Pie can 'fuck or be fucked' with his sex, and that he can also give birth, motivates Gentle to re-imagine body, embodiment, and sexual congress.[62] He realises that there must be something beyond a penetrate-or-be-penetrated binary in regards to the understanding of sexual activity; there must be 'a third way'.[63] Pie tells him that there is, but that Gentle's phallus excludes him from participation in such an experience, to which Gentle responds by bemoaning the very existence of his sex. Ultimately, he expresses a desire to remove the phallus because it limits his sight and experience and questions its very power: 'I've used my dick every way I know how. Maybe it's redundant.'[64] Here, a black male inspires his white master to transform his phallus so that he may envision and engender a new way of seeing and being beyond limitations of race and gender. Their subsequent sexual act is one of mutual penetration, of flesh and imagination. For this reason, I read it as an act that resists acculturation and commoditisation; it is an act that Barker positions as a metaphor for a (meta) cultural interweaving, an open and multivalent model of identity construction that transcends body and creates flesh.

Fish within fish; worlds within worlds: the (meta)cultural apocalypse

Pie's revolutionary work throughout the novel does more than transform the ways in which the white imagination reads blackness; it does more than offer the black subject a way to return to the self-identifying agency of the flesh: it destabilises the hegemonic authority of the Unbeheld, the God of the first Dominion; burns away the ideological veil that has kept the Imajica in a paradigm of cosmological ignorance; and, ultimately, ushers in a strange and beautiful apocalypse that unifies the Earth with its sister dimensions, revealing the geometrical make-up of the Imajica to be a circle of worlds with an uncharted metaphysical geography at its heart. The previous world of stabilised cultural identities – defined by race, nationality, sexuality, and religion, etc – becomes outmoded and opens up into a new world of (meta)cultural *possibilities*. The patriarchal God Hapexamendios is killed by his own cleansing fire; waters defy gravity, rise and flood the city of Yzordderrex; humanoid fish climb to land and partner with human women; pathways between the Dominions are opened; the dead return to the living for a time and then search out the unexplored metaphysical territory of Nisi Nirvana: the unknown heart of the Imajica

Barker not only revises the physics and metaphysics of his imagined world, but reveals the foundations of cultural power in that world to be rooted in violence, oppression, rape, and total hegemonic control, thus signalling a deep cultural desire to reconstruct notions of identity free from clearly demarcated cultural factors. According to Hoppenstand, 'Barker sees his work as being anti-mechanistic'[65] in that it seeks to function on the other side of knowing. Its depictions of culture and metaphysics often eschew explanation, forcing the reader to function imaginarily within worlds that cannot be sewn together satisfactorily but invite an incessant interplay between imaginative and cultural forces. Like Pie's body (which seems to form a 'shell of a congruous reality'), the cultural and metaphysical structures of the Imajica neither hide nor offer complete access to truth. They become crossroads, interstices, places betwixt and between that facilitate new, destabilising modes of interacting with the world. In this way, *Imajica* (the collection of Dominions and the novel) becomes a staging ground for exploring radical cultural formulations. In the few glimpses Barker offers us of the Imajica's post-apocalyptic cultures (inter-species mating, the physical presence of multiple divine forces, a doorway to the afterlife within driving distance from a major city), he tests the limits of our most cherished cultural assumptions underwriting the ways in which we organise human life. As Winter states: *Imajica* is 'a singular pursuit of (im)possibilities;'[66] it is in edges, far-reaching imaginative territories that Barker posits a new space in which to conceive of who we are and who we may become.

Barker's theorisation of (meta)cultural identity is perhaps best illustrated in the Ugichee, Pie's favourite meal, a pregnant fish which lives in the belly of another fish (bloater), which resides within another fish (coliacic). This motif of worlds within worlds, identities within identities, is common for Barker, though with the Ugichee, he adds the notion that within the central fish is new life, accentuating the power and significance of the unending quest for a centre. Furthermore, considering the fact that this is a meal, the Ugichee might be read as the nurturing effect of paradox, and this is the true quiddity of Barker's (meta)cultural notion of identity – a powerful and trans-figurative force that works to mediate and rupture, reinscribe and recreate the boundaries of (racial) identity in an effort to obliterate, or recode as wildly inclusive and protean, such limiting categories of identification. Ultimately, through the shamanistic force of his (meta)cultural figures, Barker recodes Freud's famous definition of fantasy from the psychoanalytic – that impulse which causes one to retreat from the purely empirical into the dreamlike – to the ontological and socio-political. In Barker's work, fantasy becomes a revolutionary mode of cultural and subjective analysis that liberates by revealing the purely empirical to be radically dreamlike.

Notes

1 Perhaps even more than Pie 'oh' Pah, the major subject of this chapter, Galilee stands as Barker's most complete and probing characterisation of the relationship between blackness, trauma, and experimental subjectivities.

2 Adilifu Nama, *Black Space: Imagining Race in Science Fiction Film* (Austin: University of Texas Press, 2008), p. 95.

3 Gary Hoppenstand, *Clive Barker's Short Stories: Imagination as Metaphor in the* Books of Blood *and Other Works* (Jefferson, NC: McFarland, 1994), p. 186.

4 Considering Barker's inclination to label his novels and short stories as 'metaphysical fiction', I would like to revise Hoppenstand's use of 'transcendental' – a word

chosen to align Barker with the British Romantics – by replacing it with 'metaphysical', a term more amenable to open signification. 'Clive Barker', *The South Bank Show* (BBC, 1994, Videocassette).

5 Robert Elliot Fox, *Master of the Drum: Black Lit/oratures Across the Continuum* (Westport: Greenwood, 1995), p. 11.
6 Houston A. Baker Jr., *Blues, Ideology, and Afro-American Literature: A Vernacular Theory* (Chicago: University of Chicago Press, 1991), pp. 153–7.
7 John Fiske, *Television Culture* (London: Routledge, 1987), p. 11.
8 William Coyle, 'Introduction: The Nature of Fantasy', in William Coyle (ed.), *Aspects of Fantasy: Selected Essays From the Second International Conference on the Fantastic in Literature and Film* (Westport: Greenwood, 1986), p. 2.
9 William R. Irwin, *The Game of the Impossible: A Rhetoric of Fantasy* (Urbana: University of Illinois Press, 1976), p. 4.
10 Kathryn Hume, *Fantasy and Mimesis: Responses to Reality in Western Literature* (New York: Methuen, 1984), p. 84.
11 William R. Irwin, *The Game of the Impossible: A Rhetoric of Fantasy* (Urbana: University of Illinois Press, 1976), p. 36.
12 Slavoj Žižek, 'The Specter of Ideology', in Elizabeth Wright and Edmund Wright (eds), *The Žižek Reader* (Oxford: Blackwell, 1999), p. 55.
13 Christine Brook-Rose, *A Rhetoric of the Unreal: Studies in Narrative and Structure, Especially of the Fantastic* (Cambridge: Cambridge University Press, 1981), pp. 8–9.
14 Ann Swinfen, *In Defense of Fantasy: A Study of the Genre in English and American Literature Since 1945* (London: Routledge, 1984), p. 229.
15 Rosemary Jackson, *Fantasy: The Literature of Subversion* (London: Methuen, 1981), p. 23.
16 *Ibid.* p. 21.
17 *Ibid.* p. 35.
18 Douglas E. Winter, *Clive Barker: The Dark Fantastic* (London: HarperCollins, 2001).
19 See Craig William Burns, 'It's That Time of the Month: Representations of the Goddess in the Work of Clive Barker', *Journal of Popular Culture*, Vol. 27:3 (1993), pp. 35–40; Patricia Allmer, '"Breaking the Surface of the Real": The Discourses of Commodity in Clive Barker's *Hellraiser* Narratives', in Maria Holmgren Troy and Elisabeth Wennö (eds), *Space, Haunting, Discourse* (Newcastle: Cambridge Scholars Publishing, 2008), pp. 14–24; and Jay McRoy, 'There are No Limits: Splatterpunk, Clive Barker, and the Body *In-Extremis*', *Paradoxa*, No. 17 (2002), pp. 130–50.
20 See Linda Badley, *Writing Horror and the Body: The Fiction of Stephen King, Clive Barker, and Anne Rice* (Westport, CT: Greenwood Press, 1996), and K.A. Laity, 'Imagineer: Clive Barker's Queering of the Conservative Bent of Horror Literature', in Ruth Bienstock Anolik (ed.), *Horrifying Sex: Essays on Sexual Difference in Gothic Literature* (Jefferson, NC: McFarland, 2007), pp. 248–58.
21 The other trend in Barker criticism can be summarised as a scathing critique based upon highly subjective (and deeply limited) aesthetic standards. See S.T. Joshi, *The Modern Weird Tale* (Jefferson, NC: McFarland, 2001).

22 Tzvetan Todorov, *The Fantastic: A Structural Approach to a Literary Genre*, Trans. Richard Howard (London: Case Western Reserve University Press, 1973), p. 25.

23 Henry Louis Gates Jr., *The Signifying Monkey: A Theory of African-American Literary Criticism* (New York: Oxford University Press, 1988), p. 218.

24 Paul Gilroy, *The Black Atlantic: Modernity and Double Consciousness* (Cambridge, Mass: Harvard University Press, 1993), p. 7.

25 *Ibid.* p. xi.

26 *Ibid.* p. 32.

27 *Ibid.*

28 *Ibid.* p. 223.

29 The middle leg of the trans-Atlantic slave trade that transported slaves from West Africa to the New World.

30 Houston A. Baker Jr., *Blues, Ideology, and Afro-American Literature: A Vernacular Theory* (Chicago: University of Chicago Press, 1991), pp. 153–7.

31 Clive Barker, *Imajica* (NewYork: Harper, 1991), p. 152.

32 Gilroy, *The Black Atlantic*, p. 18.

33 *Ibid.* p. 19.

34 Barker, *Imajica*, p. 8.

35 *Ibid.* p. 9.

36 *Ibid.*

37 *Ibid.* p. 10.

38 *Ibid.*

39 Badley, *Writing Horror and the Body*, p. 75.

40 McRoy, 'There are No Limits,' p. 130.

41 *Ibid.* p. 134.

42 *Ibid.* p. 148.

43 Houston A. Baker Jr., *Workings of the Spirit: The Poetics of Afro-American Women's Writing* (Chicago: University of Chicago Press, 1984), p. 22.

44 *Ibid.* Italics in original.

45 Barker, *Imajica*, p. 57.

46 Gates, *The Signifying Monkey*, pp. 3–4.

47 Baker, *Workings of the Spirit*, p. 38. Italics in original.

48 Gates, *The Signifying Monkey*, p. 6.

49 *Ibid.* p. 29.

50 *Ibid.* p. 27.

51 *Ibid.* p. 35.

52 *Ibid.*

53 Barker, *Imajica*, p. 65.

54 *Ibid.* pp. 68–9.

55 Eve Sedgwick, *Epistemology of the Closet* (Los Angeles: University of California Press, 1990).

56 Laity, 'Imagineer: Clive Barker's Queering of the Conservative Bent,' p. 256.

57 Fred Moten, *In the Break: The Aesthetics of the Black Radical Tradition* (Minneapolis: University of Minnesota Press, 2003), p. 157.

58 Barker, *Imajica*, p. 103.

59 Fox, *Master of the Drum*, p. 83.
60 Baker, *Workings of the Spirit*, p. 146.
61 Barker, *Imajica*, p. 283.
62 *Ibid.*
63 *Ibid.*
64 *Ibid.*
65 Hoppenstand, *Clive Barker's Short Stories*, p. 185.
66 Winter, *Clive Barker: The Dark Fantastic*, p. 330.

9

'A far more physical experience than the cinema affords': Clive Barker's Halloween Horror Nights and brand authorship

Gareth James

We brought in the greatest mind in horror to create what will truly be the most interesting haunted experience ever. (Norm Kahn, Universal Studios, 1998)[1]

Strange creatures lunge out from smoke-filled rooms, whilst ominous music plays from the shadows. An audience is led by the leering figure of General Santiago through a maze, before being deposited back out onto the crowded lot of the Universal Studios theme park. The audience had just experienced Clive Barker's *Freakz*, a maze that was part of Universal Studios' Los Angeles Halloween Horror Nights in 1998. Over the following two years, visitors to Universal's annual Halloween celebration experienced new variations on Barker's particular brand of horror with *Hell* and *Harvest* mazes.[2] The three mazes were a success for Universal Studios and Barker, coming at a time when the author had already achieved iconic status within the horror community and popular culture for the films *Hellraiser* (1987) and *Candyman* (1992), and his prolific range of extreme horror and fantasy literature. The Barker-designed mazes formed part of Universal's 'family' of horror brands on the Los Angeles lot, joining attractions that included the studio's classic 1930s and 1940s monsters, and more contemporary horror icons like Chucky from the *Child's Play* (1988–) franchise, and *Tales from the Crypt*'s (1989–96) Cryptkeeper.

Barker's involvement in these theme park mazes has received no attention in scholarship on his relationship to the film and media industries, with most work focusing on his innovations as a director in early films like *Hellraiser*, and subsequent frustrations with studio interventions on titles like *Nightbreed* (1990) and *Lord of Illusions* (1995). By contrast, this chapter aims to move beyond discussions of Barker as a frustrated feature film auteur to consider his arguably greater and ongoing success as a brand-name auteur across media. Using the Halloween Horror Night mazes as a bridge between Barker's early film work from the late 1980s to the mid-1990s, and his later investment in different media forms in the 2000s, it is possible to suggest that the mazes offered Barker significant creative freedoms. Viewed in the context of industrial trends for branding, theme park design and negotiations over spectacle and narrative, the mazes offer insights into recurring themes and creative philosophies across Barker's career. Beginning with an overview of Barker's frustrations with the film industry, this chapter will then discuss the role of theme parks and Barker's mazes within broader industrial trends for branding, horror cinema and the aesthetics of his films. Finally, the article will identify how Barker's experimentation with theme park mazes informs ongoing trends for his success as a brand-name auteur and producer across different media forms through the 2000s and beyond.

'Something is always lost when words turn into celluloid': Clive Barker on screen

Film has always been a key medium for Clive Barker, but one that has been frequently problematic for him. As a young artist, Barker worked on the 8mm and 16mm shorts *Salomé* (1973) and *The Forbidden* (1978). Despite their low budgets, the shorts have a distinctive black-and-white style, and feature bodily transformations and magic in ways that foreshadow much of Barker's later work on *Hellraiser*. On re-watching the films in the 1990s, Barker reflected on how the 'images still carry a measure of raw power' that overshadows their technical crudity.[3] Barker returned to cinema in the mid-1980s, having moved from experimental theatre to breakout success as a horror writer with the *Books of Blood* (1984–85) and the novel *The Damnation Game* (1985).

In 1985 Barker wrote a screenplay for the low budget horror feature *Underworld* (1985), and also had his *Books of Blood* short story 'Rawhead Rex' (1986) adapted for the screen by the same producers. However, while *Underworld*'s original screenplay pitched gangsters against monsters in a lurid, violent world, the final filmed result was a low-budget mess. *Rawhead Rex* also suffered production problems, with the original short story twisted into a confused monster film that, like *Underworld*, Barker was quick to distance himself from.[4] The potential of Barker's screenplays, and his growing name value as a horror writer, was also demonstrated, though, by his contribution to the American television anthology *Tales from the Darkside* (1983–88). Frustrated by his early experiences in film adaptation and collaboration with producers and distributors, Barker obtained independent financing for *Hellraiser*, which he wrote and directed from his own novella *The Hellbound Heart* (1986).

Hellraiser remains Barker's most critically praised and well-known work. Stretching its budget to mix innovative SFX with a psychodrama that pitches a dysfunctional family against each other, the film has been widely discussed for its treatment of the body, its gothic horror influences, its gender politics, and for its importance to British horror trends and the wider history of the horror genre.[5] Barker's close involvement in multiple areas of the film's production also established his identity as a horror auteur with a unique vision and sensibility, setting up his role as a producer on *Hellbound: Hellraiser II* (1988), and a deal with 20th Century Fox to write and direct *Nightbreed* in 1990.

Having extended his shorter horror fiction into grander epic novels like *Weaveworld* (1987) and *The Great and Secret Show* (1989), Barker conceived *Nightbreed* as a visual expansion of his 1988 novella *Cabal*. Barker explained: 'I'm not interested in just telling a story. I want to explore the theme of mon- strousness, to create a mythos that goes beyond anything we've seen in this type of movie.'[6] *Nightbreed* was intended to provide a different kind of monster movie, one exploring a community of monsters and a protagonist that comes to realise the evil of a human enemy. However, with 20th Century Fox investing in tie-in video games, comics, and other merchandise, differences developed between the studio's idea of a horror-action film that could serve as the basis for a franchise, and Barker's personal vision for the project. Production difficulties led to the studio taking away the release cut from Barker, leading to a final film that was released to mixed reviews and low box office takings.[7]

Nightbreed was a pivotal experience for Barker, one that highlighted the difficulty of reconciling a personal vision with the demands and expectations of making a major studio film that could be marketed to broader audiences. The next few years did, though, see Barker experience success as a producer, both with Bernard Rose's low-budget urban fable *Candyman* and *Hellraiser III: Hell on Earth* (both 1992). In 1995 Barker directed another feature film, *Lord of Illusions*, which incorporates characters from his fantasy novels into a film merging film noir, dark comedy, and graphic horror. The final result, financed and released by MGM and United Artists, again suffered production and marketing difficulties.[8] By the late 1990s, Barker's negative experiences led him to take up a more consistent ongoing role as an executive producer and consultant on a number of films and other adaptations of his work. Success was found during this time with the award-winning *Gods and Monsters* (1998), a drama focusing on the life of James Whale and the *Frankenstein* films.

While this chapter will return to Barker's later experiments as a film and television producer and screenwriter in the 2000s, the decade or so spanning *Hellraiser* and *Lord of Illusions* represents the period most examined by scholars to date. The period also acts as a turning point in Barker's broader approach to horror cinema, which can be explored in more detail through the Halloween Horror Nights and his role as a brand-name producer, rather than auteur director of feature films. Before looking at these areas, it is important to briefly review some of the approaches taken to Barker's key films from the late 1980s to the mid-1990s, and to summarise some of the general observations made on his achievements as a horror auteur.

As previously noted, a significant amount of attention has been paid to the *Hellraiser* franchise. A number of approaches have also been taken to *Candyman* as an example of feminist and cultural critique, and in terms of the film's similarities and differences from Barker's original short story.[9] In terms of *Lord of Illusions*, Paul Meehan has used the film to discuss overlaps between the horror genre and film noir. More generally, Barker has been used as an example of a key director in contemporary British horror cinema, and as a producer of work that engages with postmodern representations of fragmented subjectivity, gender, and the body.[10]

Barker's greatest successes as a director and horror auteur have been linked to his literary skills for visceral representation or, as Paul Bamford notes, the visualisation of specific 'areas of horror and the grand fantastique'.[11] However, Bamford also points out that Barker's problems with major studios led to 'less impressive' returns after *Hellraiser*, and suggests that adaptations of Barker's work often struggle to reconcile striking images and epic worlds with commercial feature storytelling.[12] Barker is generally held up as having made a significant contribution to horror cinema, albeit with constraints imposed on his auteur vision by studio intervention that pushed him away from direct involvement in the medium by the end of the 1990s. Reflecting on the process of adapting his books and screenplays into feature films, Barker has noted that 'something is always lost when words turn into celluloid'.[13]

While not challenging the assumption that Barker lost patience with major studio filmmaking at an early stage of his career, it is possible to look beyond these directorial problems to his other media work, and particularly his involvement in the Halloween Horror Nights in the late 1990s. Viewing the mazes as part of wider industrial trends for film and broader media branding in the 1990s and 2000s, this chapter suggests they demonstrate how Barker has been more successful as a brand-name auteur across media, rather than as a feature film director. Moreover, it can be argued that the design of the mazes and the philosophy behind them reflect a broader sense of Barker as an artist and producer experimenting with the cinematic horror genre as an immersive form beyond standalone films. It is first necessary, however, to examine the Halloween Horror Nights, their relationship to the theme park industry, and their importance to film and media branding.

Branding and the Halloween Horror Nights

The Halloween Horror Nights launched at Universal Studios' Orlando theme park in 1992 as an extension of 'Fright Night' events at the same park in 1991. In 1997, the three-night annual event expanded to the Los Angeles branch of the Universal theme park. Over the past twenty or so years, the Halloween Horror Nights have become more elaborate in scale and execution, and have built from a few scattered events to represent a major branded event for Universal, which spans the September and Halloween period. A new version of the Halloween nights opened in Universal's theme park in Singapore in 2011. The

basic concept of the Halloween Horror Nights involves audiences moving
through a converted version of the Universal studio park, which predominantly
features rides from the studio's blockbuster and classic films. Divided into
different 'Scare Zones' and rides, actors participate in haunted house mazes
and interact with the park's crowds. Most of the annual events have been tied
together around a loose theme, as well as through an existing horror film icon
or an original creation as a host; these have included *Tales from the Crypt*'s
Cryptkeeper, and new characters such as Jack the Clown and Bloody Mary.
Each 'Scare Zone' features a mix of adapted and new rides and shows, and is
commonly focused on an existing property that is either horror-themed or
represents a Halloween-based version of a cult film.

In the early years of the Halloween Horror Nights, these events included
an animatronic Chucky doll from the *Child's Play* (1988–) franchise making
fun of passing guests, as well as live shows based on *Bill and Ted's Excellent
Adventure* (1989) and *The Rocky Horror Picture Show* (1975). As the Halloween
Horror Nights became more successful, Universal drew on other characters
and figures from their own studio archive, as well as hiring creators and filmmakers to work on producing their own rides for the park. Rob Zombie,
now known for films like *House of 1000 Corpses* (2003) and rebooting the
Halloween (1978–) franchise, has also contributed original rides to Universal.
Moreover, as well as finding a place for classic Universal monsters, in 2007
Universal partnered with New Line Cinema to use characters like Freddy
Krueger, Leatherface, and Jason Voorhees, and have more recently drawn on
the *Saw* (2004–) franchise for inspiration. The success of the Halloween Horror
Nights can be attributed to the more historic appeal of Halloween-themed
parks and haunted houses across the United States. Other Halloween-themed
studio variations also exist, including Disney's Halloween nights, while
theme park Knott's Berry Farm amusement park offers its own 'Scary Farm'
experiences.[14] The success of the Halloween Horror Nights can be linked to
corporate trends for intensified branding within the American film and media
industries.

Branding and media industries

Branding can be understood as the practice of attaching symbolic importance
to the packaging of a product or service, with the aim of establishing an identity
based on a set of values and a unified design that encourages affective loyalty
from consumers. While processes of product differentiation and the management
of brand identities between advertising agencies and manufacturers can be
traced to the late nineteenth and early twentieth centuries, Celia Lury suggests
that branding became an increasingly crucial cultural and economic process
from the 1970s onwards. Forming part of the consolidation of global markets

and corporate ownership of intellectual property, information economies driven by new technologies made it easier to promote products on a huge scale. Crucial in this regard is an intensification of marketing processes, whereby brand identities transcend single products to take on an iconic status for consumers that can be reinforced and extended over time.

This process of branding as a way of creating audience loyalty across products has gradually increased in importance for the film and related media industries. Again, while aggressive promotional and packaging strategies have existed throughout film and media history, the gradual integration of multiple media industries around global corporate ownership by the 1990s, and the growth of new distribution markets like cable television, video, and the Internet, helped to intensify branding as a practice. For Paul Grainge, studios and their conglomerate owners increasingly look to establish commercial consistency and cross-promotional opportunities by developing brands that can provide a set of values, logos, images, and characters capable of anchoring new entertainment products and services. At the same time, branding has become increasingly important as a way to differentiate entertainment products and services. Types of brands range from the marketing of mass market brands like major film franchises through to the courting of specialist audiences through television channels, music labels and film distribution brands tailored to niche tastes.[15] Notable examples include Lionsgate's marketing and distribution of horror and action franchises, as well as distributors specialising in art and 'indie' films, such as Miramax.

The studio theme park has developed within these trends as a key example of branding as an industrial practice, with parks bringing together a number of individual properties into a corporate space where audiences can strengthen their loyalties to products through interaction and consumption. Theme parks are particularly important to the process of branding as they represent an immersive audience experience that outstrips other forms of consumer interaction. From Disneyland and Disney World through to the Wizarding World of Harry Potter at Universal Studios in Orlando, the chance to engage audiences on a powerful immersive level demonstrates a corporate ideal for brand loyalty, and supports Grainge's argument that 'film and cinema have increasingly come to be understood as something environmental, a spectacular experience to enter and inhabit'.[16]

Theme park rides, immersive spectacle, and narrative design

The design of theme parks and rides can be viewed as a form of corporate or branded authorship, which can be tied to discussions of themed entertainment production, marketing, and transmedia storytelling. Constance Balides argues that the 1990s saw films like *Jurassic Park* (1993) increasingly blur the lines between what counted as a film and a theme park ride in terms of immersive spectacle. Other discussions have explored how theme parks form just one stage in an overall process of transmedia production and storytelling across different platforms. Different groups and authorial figures seek to standardise thematic, narrative, and stylistic continuity between various versions of the same property, providing multiple entry points and different representations of the same concepts.[17]

Discussions of contemporary Hollywood filmmaking, theme park design, and wider media practices touch on these creative and corporate negotiations as part of broader debates over the relationship between immersive spectacle and linear narrative storytelling. Andrew Nelson particularly identifies some issues within the argument that 'traditional rollercoasters have become more like the movies, and movies have become more like rollercoasters'.[18] Emphasising the importance of distinguishing between single amusement rides and theme park rides and mazes, Nelson argues that the attraction for audiences is 'not so much the sights, sounds and shocks, but something much larger: being made part of the thematically unified story world, with an unfolding line of action'.[19] Geoff King has similarly suggested that theme park attractions provide examples of coherent authorship across media, rather than examples of unstructured sensation, where the 'attractions are built around and extend the spectacular potential of the films', while playing on 'narrative resonances'.[20] Taken further, Angela Ndalianis identifies a contemporary negotiation of linear storytelling and the construction of immersive theme park and media worlds as sharing traits with sixteenth- to eighteenth-century baroque art, and its practitioners' fascination with 'complex, dynamic motion and multiple perspectives'.[21] Ndalianis' use of the term 'neo-baroque' refers to the creation of immersive fictional worlds and experiences balancing a central story with the non-linear pleasures of illusion, mazes, and puzzles.

In addition, Ndalianis suggests that horror cinema's traditional use of shocks and set pieces alongside goal-oriented narratives results in particularly effective examples of theme park adaptation. Linking the popularity of contemporary Halloween and horror-themed attractions to the amusement park history of the 'dark ride', Ndalianis notes how the genre lends itself well to producing narrative structures that act like episodic mazes, providing an 'affective assault on the participant'.[22] Ian Conrich has made similar links between the theatrical spectacle of nineteenth- and twentieth-century Grand Guignol theatre and the development of the horror genre, particularly in terms of their shared use of gory violence, audience immersion, and narrative structure. For Conrich, the horror film genre's fascination with the body and the uncomfortable immersion of the viewer within methods of torture and murder represent contemporary 'moments of grand guignol – interventions that allow for the graphic executions and the showcasing of the special effects',[23] both within and beyond the boundaries of a narrative.

Particular links between a theatrical tradition of haunted houses and gory theatre, and trends in gothic and contemporary horror and fantasy fiction, have been noted by Linda Badley. Suggesting that 'dark fantasy has always been a literature of extra-textual effects, their purpose to stimulate strong feeling',[24] Badley argues that trends in the horror film genre for turning away from psychological realism to shocks emulating rollercoaster rides and haunted house experiences was not a radical departure. Badley notes that 'horror did not "degenerate" into special effects; it returned to its theatrical roots – in the freak show, the phantasmagoria, the wax museum, the Théâtre du Grand Guignol of Paris, the Theater of Cruelty [sic]'.[25]

These contexts for the horror genre provide one example of how branded experiences such as theme park rides and mazes form part of wider immersive or transmedia narratives, with historical roots in live spectacle and baroque art. They can be used to inform the more general importance of looking at Barker's contribution as an auteur to the Halloween Horror Nights. Barker's involvement demonstrated the branding value of his name as something that could generate instant recognition and expectations for audiences. However, the theme park mazes also acted as an important medium where Barker could experiment with pushing the narrative and stylistic boundaries of his work into new areas, whilst retaining thematic consistency.

Brand Barker: designing the Halloween Horror Nights

Universal Studios' decision to commission *Freakz* from Barker in 1998 reflected their confidence in capitalising on his already established status as a brand name within the horror community to attract audiences. Andrew Higson has noted the extent to which Barker had achieved this auteur status by the mid-1990s, suggesting: 'such was his reputation among horror and fantasy fans that many of his films included his name in the title'.[26] The appeal of the Clive Barker brand for Universal can also be linked to Catherine Grant's assertion that auteurism carries a particular corporate appeal for tying together and legitimising different media forms, most notably in the case of the 'director's cut' and commentary tracks on DVDs. The branding value of an auteur extends beyond their single films to become the stamp providing a unique identity and a set of design and thematic cues to productions either directly produced by, or in association with, the filmmaker. The specific use of Barker as an overall creative figure for the mazes arguably extended his visibility as an authority on the horror genre by the late 1990s, which most notably included hosting the British documentary television series *Clive Barker's A-Z of Horror* (1997). It is also worth emphasising how Barker was already comfortable with exploring themes and visual interests across media, from theatre to artwork, live performance art, literature, illustrations, and comic book adaptations of his work.

However, as expensive flops like *Nightbreed* proved, trying to create a Barker-branded franchise spanning films and other forms of merchandise could be problematic. What is important to focus on, then, is that the rides were less about extending a specific Barker-written franchise like *Hellraiser*, but more about building value through Barker himself as the brand that could draw audiences to individual pieces of work displaying his style and sensibility. The strength of the associations made between Barker's work, from the use of visceral imagery to the revisiting of themes like Hell, sadomasochism, physical freaks, and magic seen in *Hellraiser*, *Nightbreed* and *Lord of Illusions*, could hold together the appeal of Clive Barker as a marketable auteur brand for Universal Studios.

Being hired to produce *Freakz* represented a new opportunity for Barker, already hamstrung by notable flops with his feature films, to exercise these themes and his visual style within a more self-contained experimental project. Barker had creative control over every aspect of the production of *Freakz*, which involved 12 rooms, 35 actors, and 1,200 people passing through the maze every hour on its release. The maze's caretaker, General Santiago, guided the audience through a warehouse, with each room featuring a specific attraction: examples included double-headed freaks and a wedding chapel featuring an alien creature.[27] The same attention to detail also went into Barker's subsequent exhibitions *Hell* (1999) and *Harvest* (2000). *Hell* involved a further variation on the multiple rooms and creatures approach of *Freakz*, with Universal promoting the night as Barker dousing the 'guests in the heat of Hades, engulfing them in the fiery flames of … his Hell!'[28] The maze was constructed within a tent, and designed by Barker as a four-minute looping piece of theatre, including an S&M-themed room that proved particularly popular with audiences.[29] Allegedly based on a nightmare of Barker's, *Harvest* took a similar approach, melding a cemetery of zombies with science fiction elements and S&M designs. The front of the maze included a mausoleum with a hole in the wall that worked as an entrance; the maze began in a rotting crypt, before passing into an underground lair including aliens harvesting bodies, an egg chamber, a sewer system, and a construction site where the aliens fed on workers. The finale involved a giant alien puppet emerging to attack the maze-goers.[30]

When interviewed about the creative process of designing the rides, Barker explained how they gave him greater license to explore the aesthetics of horror cinema and the broader themes of his literary, painting, and theatre work, which he had arguably been unable to express when directing feature films. Barker was keen to emphasise the potential of the mazes for immersive entertainment, representing a different form of cinematic spectacle than his feature films. Describing the production of *Freakz* as being like a 'living movie,'[31] Barker suggested that the experience of passing through a maze would be like 'what you thought horror movies would be like before you saw a horror movie.'[32] The mazes also brought Barker back to his roots in theatre and art exhibitions, and the creative potential of a visceral, immediate experience spread over multiple performances. Barker argued: 'my work in (theatre) has left me with an appreciation of things that can be done in a "live" medium that simply cannot be done in movies'.[33]

However, Barker did emphasise how he still wanted his mazes to have a narrative structure that could contain their 'crazy circus energy', suggesting: 'I think it's much scarier if it has a sense of story'.[34] This negotiation between creating a spectacle that could best demonstrate Barker's love of visceral horror, and telling self-contained stories, can be tied back to discussions of theme park rides as examples of neo-baroque spectacle combining the affective appeal of immersion with a narrative structure. Designing theme park mazes enabled Barker to extend his visions beyond the constraints of feature films as negotiations of spectacular excess and more conventional storylines. The self-contained bursts of the story-driven horror of the mazes could be similar to a short story or a theatrical production, but without the structural problems or tonal issues suffered by more ambitious films like *Nightbreed* or *Lord of Illusions*.

Barker's films before the Halloween Nights arguably demonstrate a fascination with cinema as a medium of sensation, and represent partial opportunities to create haunted house sequences that could intensify narrative experiences. Describing his interest in directing for the screen in 1987, Barker argued that he wanted to capture some of the 'immediate gratification' afforded by live theatre and the descriptive power of the written page through the bloody set-pieces of *Hellraiser*.[35] A similar interest in using his films to unsettle audiences is also expressed in a later interview with Paul Wells, where Barker notes his interest in exploring the 'undertow in a movie'.[36] Other approaches to Barker's films also identify tropes that act as precedent for the ideas explored in the theme park mazes. When analysing *Candyman*, Brigid Cherry emphasises the importance of the audience's positioning within a tenement building as an example of a 'maze-like – and thus Gothic – space'.[37]

The idea of Barker's earlier films containing experiments with mazes and other haunted house-like structures can be extended to the *Hellraiser* films and *Nightbreed*. In the *Hellraiser* series, the central labyrinth of the story's Hell acts as a vast maze of terrors for protagonist Kirsty (Ashley Laurence) in *Hellbound: Hellraiser II*. In *Nightbreed*, the character of Lori (Anne Bobby) descends into the underground world of Midian, and passes a series of rooms where members of the Nightbreed appear to her like attractions from a freak show or haunted house. Barker has also noted that, as a producer on *Hellraiser III: Hell on Earth*, 'I tried to make the thing work more like a rollercoaster ride'.[38] The same thinking can be found in *Lord of Illusions*, a film that contains many examples of characters entering into staged spaces for displaying magic. The Halloween Horror Night mazes therefore represent a seemingly marginal, but arguably crucially overlooked, example of how Barker could find an outlet for his ideas about cinema that could balance immersive spectacle and storytelling. The mazes can be used to demonstrate an example of corporate branding for Universal Studios, effectively exploiting Barker's name recognition for rides that were a focused embodiment of his design aesthetic and thematic interests, setting up Barker's success in the 2000s as a brand-name auteur linking multiple media.

Barker as a brand-name auteur in the 2000s

The 2000s saw Barker continue to lend his name to a number of different media projects, whilst maintaining a prolific output as an author. For the most part, Barker acted as a producer of projects for film and television. Notable examples included the cable television mini-series *Saint Sinner* (2002), as well as an involvement in film production that saw his name attached to low budget horror films like *The Plague* (2006). More recent productions have included adaptations from the *Books of Blood*, which have so far included *The Midnight Meat Train* (2008), *Book of Blood* (2009), and *Dread* (2009). These productions can be linked to the increased viability of niche markets for horror outside of theatrical release, from the ongoing consolidation of cable television and DVD distribution and exhibition, through to new forms of online distribution through services like Netflix. Barker admitted the freedom and flexibility to maintain oversight of a number of different projects connected by the marketable value of his name allows him to 'make smaller-priced pictures' for loyal horror and fantasy audiences.[39] This flexibility has also extended to short stories by Barker, providing the basis for episodes of the cable horror anthology *Masters of Horror* (2005–7). As noted by Heather Hendershot,[40] specialist gore-laden television series like *Masters of Horror* offered an outlet for horror auteurs who by the mid-2000s were less likely to receive widespread exposure in theatrical release. To return to Catherine Grant's discussion of the cult of the auteur receiving a boost through DVD promotion of brand-name labels, Barker's more prolific presence as a producer for film and television projects lent a branding consistency to multiple media forms.

The 2000s were also notable for Barker's experimentation with other forms of digital media and his ongoing interest in negotiating immersive spectacle and narrative. One key area that Barker moved into during the decade was video games, most notably the productions *Undying* (2001), and *Jericho* (2007). Both games offer links with Barker's fascination with mazes, immersion, and non-linear storytelling, and his branding role as a designer lending his touch to elaborate productions. *Undying* functions as a horror game that takes players through a haunted house structure; Barker has commented how the 'quests are clearly nonlinear narratives', with the game's 'circular structure' opening up possibilities for visceral effects.[41] The same logic for developing maze-like games that immerse their players is also found in *Jericho*: gamers navigate a walled city, and move through different mazes in a way that Barker has described as 'visceral as hell'.[42]

Barker's involvement in these games arguably provided a new variation on the creative freedoms enjoyed with the Halloween mazes. While video games could still allow him to develop a clear narrative, the overall experience of the game could be set against circular structures and labyrinths able to intensify horrific spectacle. This approach has also been evident in new projects focused on creating Barker-branded franchises, and opportunities to tie together epic book series in fresh ways. One example of this process has been the *Tortured Souls* series, a planned franchise taking in a toy line developed with Todd McFarlane, short stories, and a long in-development feature film. More notable, however, has been the development of children's fantasy series *Abarat* since 2002 as the basis for a transmedia franchise. The book series was initially licensed in collaboration with Disney Studios for potential adaptations into other media. Barker suggested that 'Disney will use the images as a jumping off place' for films,[43] theme park rides, and other merchandise. Although the deal eventually lapsed, one significant example of how *Abarat* could have expanded from the page to other media was the game *The Labyrinth of the Abarat*. The game was included on the HarperCollins website for *Abarat: Days of Magic, Nights of War* (2004), with users having to negotiate a boat around a maze and avoid pirate ships while looking for six magic books; the game offers additional evidence of how much of Barker's work and the worlds he creates lend themselves to this type of maze structure.[44]

This chapter has aimed to re-evaluate and significantly expand on discussions of Clive Barker's film career and the importance of his overall movement between media platforms. Rather than focus on Barker as a frustrated film auteur who has struggled to adapt his books and ideas to the screen, the article has emphasised the importance of viewing Barker's auteur identity as one increasingly embodied across different media. Moreover, it is possible to view Barker as finding particular creative success with more marginal branded projects that condense his thematic and stylistic interests into immersive worlds that retain continuity with his other media projects. The particular importance of the Halloween Horror Night mazes comes through their part in the industrial logic of the theme park as the epitome of contemporary branding trends, acting as a key embodiment of Barker's auteur appeal in balancing immersive worlds and narrative-led mazes. The Halloween Horror Nights offer a marginal, but crucial, insight into some of the broader themes and creative approaches operating across Barker's earlier experiments with feature films, and provide a useful bridge into similar work in video games and the design of potential franchises in the 2000s and beyond. To only view Barker's involvement in film as a process of studio frustration is therefore to overlook his long-term movement between media, and how Barker the brand-name auteur has enjoyed more success by lending his creative signature to varied projects like branded mazes or video games, which hold the potential to better represent his visual and thematic interests.

Notes

1 Norm Kahn quoted in Irene Garcia, 'The Horror!' *LA Times*, 15 October 1998. *Revelations: The Official Clive Barker Website.* www.clivebarker.info/halloweenhorror .html. Date accessed: 28 May 2012.

2 Significant credit for the research and writing of this chapter should be paid to *Revelations: The Official Clive Barker Website* at www.clivebarker.info, which inspired the original idea of looking at the Halloween Horror Nights. The site has also been an invaluable resource for quotations from Clive Barker, all sourced and archived by Phil and Sarah Stokes.

3 Clive Barker, 'Trance of Innocence', *Sight and Sound*, Vol. 5:12 (1995), *Revelations: The Official Clive Barker Website*, www.clivebarker.info/salomeforbidden.html. Date accessed: 4 June 2012.

4 Barker quoted in Michael Beeler, '*Lord of Illusions* – Filming the *Books of Blood*', *Cinefantastique*, Vol. 26:3 (1995). *Revelations: The Official Clive Barker Website*, www.clivebarker.info/ints95b.html. Date accessed: 4 June 2012.

5 For a recent collection of approaches to the *Hellraiser* franchise, see Paul Kane, *The Hellraiser Films and Their Legacy* (Jefferson, NC: McFarland, 2006).

6 Barker quoted in Philip Nutman, 'Birth of the Nightbreed', *Fangoria*, No. 86 (1989), *Revelations: The Official Clive Barker Website*, www.clivebarker.info/nightbreed.html. Date accessed: 4 June 2012.

7 For extensive accounts of Barker's problems with *Nightbreed*, see www.clivebarker.info/ nightbreed.html. A director's cut of *Nightbreed* was put together for specialist release in 2012, while a separate Blu-ray release appeared in 2014.

8 Barker, quoted in M. Beeler, '*Lord of Illusions*'.

9 Particularly see Brigid Cherry, 'Imperfect Geometry: Identity and Culture in Clive Barker's "The Forbidden" and Bernard Rose's *Candyman*', in Richard J. Hand and Jay McRoy (eds), *Monstrous Adaptations: Generic and Thematic Mutations in Horror Film* (Manchester: Manchester University Press, 2007), pp. 48–63.

10 See Paul Wells, 'On the Side of the Demons: Clive Barker's Pleasures and Pains. Interviews with Clive Barker and Doug Bradley', in Steve Chibnall and Julian Petley (eds), *British Horror Cinema* (London: Routledge, 2001), pp. 172–82; Barry Keith Grant (ed.), *The Dread of Difference: Gender and the Horror Film* (Austin: University of Texas Press, 1996), p. 261; and Anna Powell, *Deleuze and Horror Film* (Edinburgh: Edinburgh University Press, 2005), p. 83.

11 Paul Bamford, 'Clive Barker', in Yoram Allon, Del Cullen, and Hannah Patterson (eds), *Contemporary North American Film Directors: A Wallflower Critical Guide* (London and New York: Wallflower Press, 2002), p. 37.

12 *Ibid.* p. 37.

13 Barker quoted in Anon, 'Clive Barker: AOL Appearance', Transcript. AOL. 16 July 1996. *Revelations: The Official Clive Barker Website.* www.clivebarker.com/html/ visions/confess/nonls/cb71696.htm. Date accessed: 30 May 2012.

14 Knott's Berry Farm, for example, becomes Knott's Scary Farm for Halloween, and in 2014 provided mazes featuring Elvira, Mistress of the Dark, and a special event focused on a zombie apocalypse. See B. McDonald, 'Knott's Berry Farm Unveils Halloween Haunt 2014 Mazes', *LA Times*, 8 August 2014. www.latimes.com/travel/themeparks/la-trb-halloween-haunt-2014-knotts-berry-farm-20140807-story.html. Date accessed: 1 April 2015.

15 Paul Grainge, *Brand Hollywood: Selling Entertainment in a Global Media Age* (London: Routledge, 2007), pp. 3–17.

16 *Ibid*. p. 66.

17 For an overview of transmedia trends, see Henry Jenkins, *Convergence Culture: Where Old and New Media Collide* (New York: New York University Press, 2008), pp. 95–134.

18 Andrew Nelson, 'Cinema From Attractions: Story and Synergy in Disney's Theme Park Movies', *Cinephile: The University of British Columbia's Film Journal*, 4 (2008). www.cinephile.ca/archives/volume-4-post-genre/cinema-from-attractions-story-and-synergy-in-disney%E2%80%99s-theme-park-movies/. Date accessed: 2 April 2012.

19 *Ibid*.

20 Geoff King, *Spectacular Narratives: Hollywood in the Age of the Blockbuster* (London: IB Tauris, 2000), pp. 182–3.

21 Angela Ndalianis, 'Architectures of the Senses: Neo-Baroque Entertainment Spectacles' in David Thorburn and Henry Jenkins (eds), *Rethinking Media Change: The Aesthetics of Transition* (Cambridge, Mass: MIT Press, 2003), p. 360.

22 Angela Ndalianis, 'Dark Rides, Hybrid Machines and the Horror Experience', in Ian Conrich (ed.), *Horror Zone: The Cultural Experience of Contemporary Horror Cinema* (London: IB Tauris, 2010), p. 22.

23 Ian Conrich, 'The *Friday the 13th* Films and the Cultural Function of Modern Grand Guignol', in Conrich (ed.), *Horror Zone*, p. 177.

24 Linda Badley, *Writing Horror and the Body: The Fiction of Stephen King, Clive Barker, and Anne Rice* (Connecticut, Greenwood Press, 1996), p. 3.

25 *Ibid*. p. 3.

26 Andrew Higson, *Film England: Culturally English Filmmaking Since the 1990s* (London: IB Tauris, 2011), p. 107.

27 Garcia, 'The Horror!'

28 Anon, 'Halloween Horror Nights III', Universal Studios Press Release, 1999, *Revelations: The Official Clive Barker Website*. www.clivebarker.info/halloweenhorror.html. Date accessed: 2 June 2012.

29 Phil Stokes and Sarah Stokes, 'Universal's Halloween Horror Nights', *Revelations: The Official Clive Barker Website*. www.clivebarker.info/halloweenhorror.html. Date accessed: 12 April 2015.

30 Mike Murder, 'Clive Barker's Harvest'. *Horror Night Nightmares*, 31 July 2012. www.horrornightnightmares.com/forums/index.php/topic/2664-clive-barkers-harvest/. Date accessed: 12 April 2015.

31 Rob Lowman, 'Freakz Alive, Clive! His "Living Movie" an A-Maze-ing Experience', *Daily News*, 14 October 1998, *Revelations: The Official Clive Barker Website*. www.clivebarker.info/halloweenhorror.html. Date accessed: 2 June 2012.

32 Barker quoted in Dennis Cooper, 'Fuck the Canon', *LA Weekly*, 31 August–6 September 2001, Literary Supplement. *Revelations: The Official Clive Barker Website*. www.clivebarker.info/halloweenhorror.html. Date accessed: 2 June 2012.

33 Anon. 'Clive Barker's Freakz', Press Release, Universal Studios, October 1998, *Revelations: The Official Clive Barker Website*. www.clivebarker.info/halloweenhorror.html. Date accessed: 2 June 2012.

34 Clive Barker quoted in Garcia, 'The Horror!'

35 Clive Barker, 'Interview with Larry King', Larry King Live, CNN, 6 May 1987 (transcript), *Revelations: The Official Clive Barker Website*. www.clivebarker.info/ints87.html. Date accessed: 2 June 2012.

36 Barker quoted in Wells, 'On the Side of the Demons', p. 176.

37 Cherry, 'Imperfect Geometry', p. 62.

38 Barker quoted in Edwin Pouncey, 'Barker Psychosis', *New Musical Express*, 13 February 1993, *Revelations: The Official Clive Barker Website*. www.clivebarker.info/ints93.html. Date accessed: 2 June 2012.

39 Barker quoted in Smilin' Jack Ruby, 'Clive Barker's Busy, Busy, Busy Year', *13th Street*, 13 July 2001. *Revelations: The Official Clive Barker Website*. www.clivebarker.info/ints01b.html. Date accessed: 2 June 2012.

40 Heather Hendershot, 'Masters of Horror: TV Auteurism and the Progressive Potential of a Disreputable Genre', in Michael Kackman, Marie Binfield, Matthew Thomas Payne, Allison Perlman and Bryan Sebok (eds), *Flow TV: Television in the Age of Media Convergence* (New York: Routledge, 2011), p. 145.

41 Barker quoted in Eric Twelker, 'Crossing Over', Amazon, January 2001. *Revelations: The Official Clive Barker Website*. www.clivebarker.info/undying.html. Date accessed: 2 June 2012.

42 Barker quoted in P. Stokes and S. Stokes, 'Hellfire and the Demonation', 7 September 2007, *Revelations: The Official Clive Barker Website*, www.clivebarker.info/intsrevel19.html. Date accessed: 2 June 2012.

43 Barker quoted in Anderson Jones, 'Movie Scoop', Yahoo Entertainment, 11 October 2002, *Revelations: The Official Clive Barker Website*, www.clivebarker.info/ints02b.html. Date accessed: 2 June 2012.

44 See www.clivebarker.info/abaratgame.html for more information on the game.

Part IV

Legacy

19   Detail of cover from *Books of Blood*, Volume 1.

.

10

'What price wonderland?' Clive Barker and the spectre of realism

Daragh Downes

> And what do I do, surrounded by such wonders? I dream banalities.
> (Clive Barker)[1]

It is perhaps the defining conundrum of Clive Barker's career that his powers as a non-realist writer have been so overvalued and his powers as a realist one so correspondingly undervalued. For several decades now, Barker has been creating characters – and hailing readers – who, like Lewis Carroll's Alice, must get into the way of expecting nothing but out-of-the-way things to happen at every turn. His career-long rebellion against what one of his early narrators calls 'the tyranny of the real'[2] has been in truth a rebellion against the tyranny of realism itself – its limits, strictures, and demands. But also its possibilities: the opportunity cost incurred by Barker's policy of relentless 'fantastication' has been heavy indeed.[3]

Barker first came to international prominence with *Books of Blood* (1984–85), a collection of thirty stories of which only one (and arguably its best, the psychological thriller, 'Dread') might be said to adhere to basic protocols of bourgeois realism (if by that last term we understand, minimally, an absence of supernatural incident). A further four tales – 'In the Hills, the Cities', 'New Murders in the Rue Morgue', 'The Age of Desire', and 'Babel's Children' – offer scenarios that are fantastic without perhaps altogether breaching the limits of the realist-possible (being, as the Aristotelian critic might put it, improbable but not impossible). A sixth, 'The Life of Death', offers a supernatural horror scenario that gets rationalised back down to a realist horror premise at the end – before, at the *very* end, taking a gently supernatural turn again. All the other tales in the six-volume collection take strong and unequivocal recourse to supernatural machinery to secure their effects.

Long before these stories' appearance, Barker had already shown a marked preference for the non-realist mode. His immersion in the works of Edgar Allan Poe, Lewis Carroll, J.M. Barrie, H.P. Lovecraft, C.S. Lewis, and other non-realist greats was coupled with a long-standing dream of bringing Marvel

Comics-style action adventures to life in prose and drama. Barker's sense of mission was already well developed by the time he became an undergraduate at the University of Liverpool. On one occasion a generally supportive English lecturer there asked him when he was going to move beyond 'these fantastical worlds' – she meant his current Tolkien fixation – and 'get to the human drama'.[4] The question nettled Barker, who years later would explain why he found its sponsoring dichotomy so thoroughly bogus: 'Of course, if I'd had my wits about me, I'd have said, *Everything in Shakespeare is fantasy*. The only thing which isn't fantasy is its observations about human nature; and if any art is any good, then that's going to be there – it's going to be in *Reservoir Dogs*, it's going to be in *Peter Pan*, it's going to be there.'[5] Barker's credo was clear: the fantastical suspension of realist limits opens art up to a wider spectrum of experiences whose worth and reality are in no way diminished by their failure to meet some regulative realist standard. From the start, Barker wished to posit not just improbable possibilities in art but improbable impossibilities too.

The *Books of Blood* did not, then, come out of nowhere. There was backstory here, and a lot of it. Barker had already spent years, in his hometown of Liverpool and down in London, trying to get himself on the map as a writer, director, and performer of experimental plays and arthouse films. He had also written, though not published, a small amount of fantasy fiction for children and juvenile readers. It is tempting to regard these years as Barker's apprenticeship years, with *Books of Blood* representing the first great flowering of his maturity. I wish to press the contrary and no doubt heretical case that *Books of Blood* are themselves best seen as prentice works too. Barker, at the time he wrote these stories, was still finding his range as a writer and artist. The excitement of these texts lies precisely in their hit-and-miss experimentalism and fearlessness.

If *Books of Blood* were prentice works – bursting with potential but prentice works nonetheless – why were they not greeted as such? Why were they so widely fêted as ripe fruit? Thirteen words: 'I have seen the future of horror, and his name is Clive Barker.' Long after Barker had put distance between himself and the label 'horror writer', Stephen King's endorsement would continue to shadow his name. Rather less ballyhooed by the promotional machine, at any time, was the rather amusing circumstance behind King's comment. King had been attending the October 1984 World Fantasy Convention in Ottawa. Over lunch he was intrigued to hear his companions Peter Straub and Douglas E. Winter rhapsodise over a debut collection of short stories by a promising young English writer. After lunch, King found himself on a panel with Straub and used the occasion to make generous mention of Barker's name: 'Well, I haven't read this guy, but from what I understand it's like what Jann Wenner said – *I have seen the future of rock-and-roll, and his name is Bruce Springsteen.* Sounds like Clive Barker might be the future of horror.'[6] King's endorsement was as faith-based as it was throwaway. But it hardly seemed to matter. A small tweak to that last sentence (with permission duly sought and granted by the ever-gracious King),[7] and the subjunctive mood of the original remark was cleanly expunged. Barker's newly secured Stateside publishers Berkley suddenly had themselves an irresistibly potent soundbite with which to launch *Books of Blood* on a massive market: 'I have seen the future of horror, and his name is Clive Barker'.

In one sense, King's words still ring true, albeit not quite in the sense originally intended. For Barker never truly became anything other than a *future* horror writer, a horror writer full of *promise*. The stories in *Books of Blood* read now, some three decades on, like so many promissory notes from a young writer en route to possible horror greatness. Barker did revisit the out-and-out horror genre immediately after his *Books of Blood* success – *The Damnation Game*, a novel, came out in 1985, with the novellas *The Hellbound Heart* and *Cabal* following in 1986 and 1988 respectively – and he was to deploy horror themes and motifs on many occasions across his subsequent writing career. However, much of the latter half of the 1980s was spent working energetically to turn 'Clive Barker' into a byword for something more capacious than horror *tout court* – dark fantasy or *fantastique*. Barker saw the provocative and fearless medleying of body horror, noir thriller, splatterpunk, weird fiction, historical fiction, and epic fantasy as a way of moving beyond horror alone while still maintaining his standing as a writer who pushed boundaries (and 'taste') with matchless gusto.

In breaking out of what threatened to become a comfort zone marked 'Horror Fiction', Barker displayed rare courage and integrity. However, for the admirer of Barker (of whom I account myself one, albeit a troubled one), it is easy to miss the fact that one assumption went wholly unqueried, by Barker as by his audience, as he moved into the 1990s and beyond – the assumption that non-realism was and always would be the optimal arena for his talents. I believe that King's well-intentioned endorsement of Barker was a short-term triumph for the young Liverpudlian but a long-term misfortune. Put simply, King's words trapped Barker in a straightjacket of reader and industry expectations. More damagingly still, they seemed to reinforce Barker's own self-image as a writer whose grand vocation it was to excel in non-realist modes. Even as he became a dark imaginer, a practitioner of something wider than horror, Barker shut himself off more and more wilfully from other possibilities. Barker's obsession with transgressing limits at every turn ended up being the great limiting factor in his artistic development. His embrace of supernatural sensationalism turned him into the most conservative of storytellers. The critical, popular, and commercial success of *Books of Blood* flattered the non-realist in Barker, distorting his artistic development by over-promoting a certain side of his talent and luring him into a sustained misdirection of artistic energies. If there was a comfort zone he ought to have worried about as the 1980s progressed, it was not that of horror *per se* but that of non-realism. This, it seems to me, is the great interior secret of the *Books of Blood*: they are the production of a young writer en route to possible *realist* as well as non-realist greatness, a young writer whose confidence in his realist impulses is not yet as developed as his confidence in his non-realist impulses, a young writer who does not yet realise that he need not alienate and sabotage his realist impulses at every turn.

Informing my thesis here is not the least investment in genre snobbery. I make no claims whatsoever as to the respective merits of realist versus non-realist writing (or of 'literary' versus 'genre' fiction). It is a good thing indeed that *The Dead Zone* is a paranormal horror tale; it is a good thing indeed that Jane Austen did not jazz up *Northanger Abbey* with biometamorphic chase scenes. Why is it, then, that Barker has left unexplored what we might call the Stephen King mixed-economy option – the option, that is, of *not* always (or: not *always*) shackling his fictional scenarios to a supernatural machinery?

On many occasions in Barker one finds a strong, at times compellingly strong, realist premise rendered mediocre by a turn to the non-realist. A subway serial killer who can be glossed as 'a lunatic with a strong sense of tidiness' is intriguing;[8] a subway serial killer who turns out to have been doing his abattoir deeds at the bidding of man-eating City Fathers seems suddenly banal. A psychiatrist discussing 'dream-crimes' committed by his patient is interesting; a psychiatrist discussing real crimes committed by his patient is more interesting yet; a psychiatrist convincing his patient that he, the patient, has committed the psychiatrist's own crimes is most interesting of all; but a psychiatrist discussing his own crimes with a patient who then turns into a post-mortal monster and takes up squatting rights in an underground den of kindred beings … it is hard not to feel that a large loss of storytelling nerve has occurred here some-where. Likewise, a suburban housewife who picks up men in a bar and lures them back to her house for slaughter is disturbing. Said woman's being in *folie-à-deux* cahoots with her demented brother-in-law makes her all the more disturbing. Within these realist parameters, Barker shows himself well capable of serving up dark terror on a realist principle:

> 'What … in God's …?' he began. As he pointed into the darkness she was at him, and slicing his neck open with a butcher's efficiency. Blood jumped imme-diately, a fat spurt that hit the wall with a wet thud. She heard Frank's pleasure, and then the dying man's complaint; long and low. His hand went up to his neck to stem the pulse, but she was at him again, slicing his pleading hand, his face. He staggered, he sobbed. Finally, he collapsed, twitching.[9]

But in embedding this barbarity in an occult blood-sacrifice necrodrama, Barker leaves it nowhere much to go beyond the next slash of the knife, the next excruciation by the presiding Cenobites. It will take an inspired costuming choice at movie stage to immortalise the story.

This squandering of realist premise and promise becomes an especially acute problem in Barker's longer works, especially those that do not posit a full-blown secondary world. The rise of the Whitehead pharmaceutical empire (*The Damnation Game*) and the Kennedy-by-any-other-name Geary commercial empire (*Galilee*), with all the capitalist thuggery enforced along the way, could have given Barker a brace of gripping realist premises. The historical starting points of each empire – 1945 Warsaw, Charleston during the American Civil War – could have lent real depth to these premises. Instead Barker elects to present these instances of industrial and commercial will-to-power as modern Faustian pacts on a literally supernatural schema. The result is not a Thomas Mann-style intensification or deepening of the premise but its mere explaining away. In withdrawing realist limits from his stories, Barker's storytelling tends to become something of a free-for-all. Quality control gets lowered, focus and compression get lost, and an artistic challenge gets shirked. Barker, I submit, is simply too formidable a realist writer to justify this unfailing resort to non-realist plot premises.

The problem is at its most exquisite in the string of novel-length secondary-world fantasies: *Weaveworld*, *Imajica*, *The Great and Secret Show*, *Everville*, and *Abarat* (of which latter series three volumes have been published to date). In each of these books, the secondary world is a large disappointment, a mere simulacrum of transgressive imagination rather than the real thing. As was the case in one *Books of Blood* story after another, Barker in these longer works tries to muddle his way through to the startling, the memorable, and the cosmic by supercharging his story with supernatural incident and transmundane logic. From the Dominions of the Imajica, through to the Islands of the Abarat, Barker pluralises and elasticates his secondary worlds in a rather desperate effort to generate content and sustain narrative interest. In the last analysis, all this 'and then … and then' storytelling amounts to little more than a sterile over-elaboration of the slight but charming early children's fantasy work, *The Adventures of Mr. Maximillian Bacchus & His Traveling Circus* (written in 1974 but not published until 2011). In the later secondary-world novels, Barker seems badly *stuck*. What is lacking in these books is the kind of genuine idiosyncrasy of vision that would justify the entire enterprise. It all feels so irredeemably sub-Tolkien, so opportunistically post-Michael Ende. Even the at times startling linguistic brio Barker had displayed when he was on his game in *Books of Blood* deserts him as he takes his characters into the secondary world. Dialogue is standardised to clichéd functionality ('"Never turn your back on a dead man," Sartori said, finally showing his face'),[10] while character becomes flattened and fungible (Suzanna in *Weaveworld* is Judith in *Imajica* is Candy in *Abarat*). The more cosmic or outlandish a given incident, the less interesting or three-dimensional the psychology of the characters experiencing or instigating it. By the time of the *Abarat* books, the unhappy dialectic will have pressed its logic to a point that is almost unbearable, with Barker behaving not as an organic storyteller but as a designer of prefabricated video game characters whose sole task is to progress from one game level to the next.

Forfeited in these novels' signature turn to the fantastical is any existential interest that might have been sustained by a continuation of the basic realist premise. Randolph Jaffe, the thirty-seven-year-old balding employee in the Omaha Central Dead Letter Office at the start of *The Great and Secret Show*, could have formed the basis of a compelling study in suicidal-homicidal subaltern despair. He could have taken his place on a line of continuum going back to Melville's Bartleby or even Kierkegaard's soul sickening unto death. But when Barker exposes him to the Nuncio liquid and turns him into the terata-wielding 'Jaff' at war with his hallucigenia-wielding nemesis Fletcher, the novel suffers a devolution from concept to combat. The Jaffe who stabs his boss in the eye with a letter-opener is a more interesting fellow than the cardboard cut-out 'Jaff' waging cosmic war over the dream-sea Quiddity. A mundane, realist plot would have been more extraordinary than the supramundane, non-realist plot we end up getting. *The Great and Secret Show* is more enjoyable as a graphic novel than in its standard format, and there is a reason for that.[11] Much the same problem also bedevils *Everville*, its sequel. Near the start of that book, town lawyer Erwin Toothaker comes across some tantalising sentences by a local historian:

> The sad story of the death of Rebecca Jenkins is well known. She was a daughter of that fair city, much prized and adored, who was murdered in her eighth year, her body deposited in the reservoir. Her murderer was a man out of Sublimity who later died in prison while serving a life sentence. But the mystery surrounding the tragedy of poor Rebecca does not end there.[12]

This has all the makings of an unputdownable cold-case thriller. Yet it seems not to have even crossed Barker's mind to make a realist novel about Sublimity rather than a non-realist one about Quiddity.

In *Weaveworld*, *Imajica*, and the *Abarat* novels, by contrast, we are seeing not so much a failure to develop a strong realist premise but a failure to originate an interesting premise of any description. In this respect, these works give us the central problem of *Books of Blood* writ large. What protected that collection was the brevity of its short story form. It offered Barker a certain amount of cover for the thinness of so much of the material. So heady was its mix of stories, it was easy not to notice the flaws. 'The Book of Blood', the collection's opening frame narrative, is little more than an unconvincing (and, even on non-realist rules, pretty unworkable) footnote to Ray Bradbury's *The Illustrated Man* and Franz Kafka's 'In The Penal Colony'. 'Jacqueline Ess: Her Will and Testament' is a rather tired reiteration of Stephen King's *Carrie*. 'The Forbidden' (later adapted, and vastly improved, as the film *Candyman*) derives its big twist from *The Wicker Man*. Subsequent tales of out-and-out supernaturalism – we might name 'The Yattering and Jack', 'Hell's Event', 'Son of Celluloid', 'Rawhead Rex', 'Confessions of a Pornographer's Shroud', 'The Body Politic', 'Revelations', and 'Down, Satan!' – offer one weak-to-middling *Twilight Zone* scenario after another. On an uncomfortable number of occasions, Barker distracts from his dearth of ideas by fetching up tedious action sequences, facile bio-metamorphics, and 'edge'-lending violent and sexual content. As an example of this latter we might take the moment in 'Hell's Event' when the crowd sees the true character of the evil familiar that has been impersonating the runner Voight: 'The face dissolved. What had seemed to be flesh sprouted into a new resemblance, a devouring trap without eyes or nose, or ears, or hair [...] The mouth was huge, and lined with teeth like the maw of some deep-water fish, ridiculously large.'[13] We have here, in embryo, what will become the default programme for so much of Barker's later long-form output – endless riffs on Ovid's *Metamorphoses* that rely not on visceral terror, big idea, or compelling plotline but on the special effects department.

This problem of tactless supernaturalist inflation and overkill is broadcast in Barker, and it goes back to *Books of Blood*. In 'The Madonna', to take another example, the encounter of Jerry with the eponymous entity showcases the key Barker weaknesses of pseudo-visionary descriptive vagueness, facile multeity, and pointless effect:

> He knew indisputably that this creature was female, though it resembled no species or genus he knew of. As the ripples of luminescence moved through the creature's physique, it revealed with every fresh pulsation some new and phenomenal configuration. Watching her, Jerry thought of something slow and molten – glass, perhaps; or stone – its flesh extruded into elaborate forms and recalled again into the furnace to be remade. She had neither head nor limbs recognizable as such, but her contours were ripe with clusters of bright bubbles that might have been eyes, and she threw out here and there iridescent ribbons – slow, pastel flames – that seemed momentarily to ignite the very air.[14]

Barker gets away with this kind of thing in *Books of Blood*, at least for the most part, because of the briskness enforced by brevity of form. In the outsize fantasy epics, by contrast, the tendency will become fatal. A passage like the above, surely the artistic low point of 'The Madonna' and the moment the reader wonders whether Barker might not be running close to empty narratively, will become the fantasy novelist Barker's mainstay.

A further tell-tale sign that Barker is already in some trouble on the inventiveness front in *Books of Blood* is his penchant for the pretentious and ponderous send-off. His stories are being asked to carry more metaphysical or thematic weight than they can bear, and one ending after another seems to betray Barker's anxiety on this score. 'Jacqueline Ess: Her Will and Testament', for instance, ends with Vassi using an erection (his own) to kill the title character, while she returns the favour using nipples (her own): 'Her keen breasts pricked him like arrows; his erection, sharpened by her thought, killed her in return with his only thrust. Tangled in a wash of love they thought themselves extinguished, and were.'[15] It is a nice touch, but Barker cannot leave well alone. He must post an addendum: 'Outside, the hard world mourned on, the chatter of buyers and sellers continuing through the night. Eventually indifference and fatigue claimed even the most eager merchant. Inside and out there was a healing silence: an end to losses and to gains.'[16] *An end to losses and gains*: these last say-nothing words signal just how much Barker has lost his way, just how at a loss he finds himself with his story's telekinesis premise. Having pushed violence and sexual danger to the limits, and beyond, Barker now makes a terminal attempt to heal the abyss between 'normality' and supernaturalism with a dose of vacuous metaphysics. It just doesn't come off. But, again, the moving along of the reader to the *next* story and the *next* makes it easy to miss just how thin the gruel being served up is.

Reading *Books of Blood*, it is hard not to appreciate their variety, genre hybridity, and 'radical sexual openness' (as Barker's early champion Ramsey Campbell called it).[17] However it is not easy to shake the critical impression that they are written by a writer haunted by the fear that what he has to offer by way of story, character, and dénouement is never going to be quite *enough*. It all needs to be enlivened by a superaddition of sensation, a supplement or prosthesis that will somehow compensate for poverty of invention or inadequacy of execution. It is as though Barker does not trust himself to write directly to his premise and feels compelled instead to apply endless layers of sensationalism and meretricious non-realist 'effect' in order to (sometimes literally) sex up his texts.

This is not, of course, how Barker, or the many fans of his cultivation of bizarrity, will view the matter. Here is Barker himself:

> Because the living experience is also the dreaming experience, is also the fantasizing experience. And what I'm trying to represent on the page is not what it's like to get up in the morning and brush your teeth, but what it's like to get up in the morning and then dream of Never-Never Land for two minutes and then go take a crap. And what's missing in 'realistic' fiction is the visit to Never-Never Land.[18]

It is an odd line of defence. The scenario Barker evokes here – getting up, dreaming of a fantasy world, answering nature's call – is decidedly not the typical scenario the reader of a Barker story will find themselves confronted with. Standard Barker praxis will dictate something along less compartmentalised lines. The character may indeed 'take a crap', but there is every likelihood that the exercise will be interrupted by the emergence from the toilet bowl of a crap-monster with fangs or luminescent limbs. Should our hero manage, against all the odds, to gain entry to whichever secondary world is in play, that world will have none of the charm, nerve, or sheer imaginative anarchy of Barrie's Neverland. ('Wonderland' is, symptomatically, a much-loved and over-used signifier in Barker's fiction. So too is 'in extremis'.) The secondary world of Barker's post-*Books of Blood* epics – The Cosm in *Weaveworld*, the Quiddity/

Ephemeris realms in *The Great and Secret Show* and *Everville*, Dominions One to Four in *Imajica*, the Abarat in the three (to date) books in the *Abarat* series – is a flatland of mechanical imagination. Its fantasies are as tediously relentless as Emanuel Swedenborg's reports of his visions of the afterlife in *Heaven and Hell*. As soon as Judith and Dowd pass from the Fifth Dominion in *Imajica* and leave the familiar world behind them, the story actually *drops* in temperature, setting the reader up for the supreme longueurs of Gentle's second pilgrimage (this time with Monday) across the Dominions. Once Barker gets going with this sort of thing, he loses all feel for narrative economy. We long to go back to what the lawyer at Pie'oh'pah's trial refers to as the Fifth's 'mire of unmiraculous souls'.[19]

The greatness of works like *Peter Pan* or *A Song of Ice and Fire* is inextricable from their fantasticating character. Many a Barker work approaches greatness in spite of its fantasticating character. And many disintegrate because of it. The point in all this is not to dismiss Barker *tout court* or to read him purely on a deficit model. It is to cultivate an appreciation of his real strengths, which I believe to be prodigious. I submit that Barker's penchant for non-realist overkill has kept the realist Barker all but obscured from view. It is not for nothing that his most powerful evocations of horror have tended to be wholly realist in character. The Warsaw pages at the start of *The Damnation Game* are amongst the most harrowing he has ever written: 'A boy's brothel had been opened in the Zoliborz District. Here, in an underground salon hung with salvaged paintings, one could choose from chicks of six or seven up, all fetchingly slimmed by malnutrition and tight as any connoisseur could wish.'[20] Barker is bringing his reader into a heart of darkness here – a realist heart of darkness – far more shocking than anything to be found in *Books of Blood* or the later works of self-conscious bizarrity. Later in the novel we find Anthony Breer salivating over *Soviet Documents on Nazi Atrocities*:

> there were photographs of the dead. Some of them heaped in piles, others lying in bloody snow, frozen solid. Children with their skulls broken open, people lying in trenches, shot in the face, others with swastikas carved into their chests and buttocks. But to the Razor-Eater's greedy eyes, the best photographs were of people being hanged. There was one Breer looked at very often. It pictured a handsome young man being strung up from a makeshift gallows. The photographer had caught him in his last moments, staring directly at the camera, a wan and beatific smile on his face.[21]

Here again it is the much-disparaged real world that is supplying Barker's pen with an overplus of horror, a Grand Guignol of excess. It all makes the horrors of the Cenobites look positively kitsch. Yet here, as elsewhere, Barker loses the plot. *The Damnation Game* will go badly wrong, and just at the point where Mamoulian 'the magician' breaks into Whitehead's compound and starts shapeshifting ('Phantoms sprang from the flux of light', etc).[22] The switch to

Barkerian autopilot has been flicked. Balance and control are lost and a taut thriller starts to disintegrate into an over-extended *Books of Blood* out-take. The dead-not-dead (and skinned) Yvonne alone in the love-nest in Pimlico; the scummy tide of creatures coming out of the toilet to terrify Carys; the magical resuscitation of Bella the dog; the farcically overdone closing gorefest at the Pandemonium Hotel … so many stages in the non-realist botching of a brilliantly promising realist – or even semi-realist – novel. The more Barker ratchets up the supernatural bloodbath element, the more ordinary his characters become. The disastrously misjudged introduction of Chad Schuckman and Tom Loomis, two cartoon-like Memphis evangelists from the Church of the Resurrected Saints, will disclose just how far matters have slipped in the character development department. (Not until King Texas in *Everville* will Barker fall this low again.) Our heroes Marty and Carys will slowly deflate to an intrepid Enid Blyton double act. The more we get to eavesdrop on Mamoulian's inner thought processes, meanwhile, the less interesting *he* will become: 'He felt like a beaten dog: all he wanted to do was to lie down and die. It seemed today – especially since the girl's skilful rejection of him – that he felt every hour of his long, long life in his sinews.'[23] How dispiritingly easy it is to *relate* to the man's *pain*. Barker has allowed all mystique to evaporate from his novel's most sinister character. It is an error he will repeat again and again in later works, from Immacolata in *Weaveworld*, all the way to Katya Lupi in *Coldheart Canyon*.

The inverse proportion between supernatural-action inflation and character development in *The Damnation Game* announces what will become an all-too-predictable programme in one long Barker novel after another: the trumping of intelligent plot development by action and special effects, and the flattening of credible characters. Horkheimer and Adorno's strictures on the culture-industrial movie are depressingly applicable to Barker's fantasy programme: 'Often the plot is maliciously deprived of the development demanded by characters and matter according to the old pattern. Instead, the next step is what the script writer takes to be the most striking effect in the particular situation. Banal though elaborate surprise interrupts the story-line.'[24] The frequency with which Barker resurrects dead characters in his stories seems symptomatic of a writer who has become deeply uncomfortable with the tax on invention which narrative finality of any sort imposes.

Barker has never written a fully-fledged realist novel. It is my contention that his refusal to do so has come less out of a positive non-realist vision and more out of profound artistic insecurity. Put crudely, non-realism has allowed him to get away with murder. A work like *Galilee* is hard to read precisely because one senses the masterpiece of historical fiction it could have been had it not been so maddeningly aim-inhibited by its own author. Like *The Damnation Game*, *Galilee* contains a realist-world schema far darker than anything the supernaturalist Barker has to throw at it. Thus, for instance, the portion of

Charles Holt's Civil War diary where he describes the horrors in his house in Charleston:

> My house, my precious house, had been used as a place for the dying and the dead … The surgeons' accomplices had dug holes there [in the middle of the garden], to bury the gangrenous parts hacked from the wounded. They had done their job poorly. Upon their departure dogs had come up and dug this horrid meat, and picked it clean … in places the dirt was freshly turned, and as yet undevoured trophies lay. A leg, its foot still booted. An arm, severed at midbicep.[25]

In Garrison Geary, the man who likes hiring prostitutes to play dead so that he can play 'the horny mortician',[26] we might have had a sociopathic protagonist of Bret Easton Ellis quality. Barker was surely capable of going there. But he was so busy overdeveloping things on the non-realist front that he left such realist possibilities chronically underexploited. *Coldheart Canyon* is another missed opportunity. In the plastic surgery martyrdom of fading Hollywood star Todd Pickett, Barker could have had a triumph of realist satire in the *Sunset Boulevard* mould. In the event, the only thing that keeps the novel from collapse is Barker's decision to limit his characters' exposure to the mini-secondary-world mural (which magically contains the Duke of Goga's hunting forest). This points us to what is something of a law in Barker's novels. Things go better when exposure to magical spaces – Cesaria's skyroom in *Galilee*, Rukenau's castle in *Sacrament*, the mural world in *Coldheart Canyon* – is limited, controlled, localised, *stinted*. Barker's better novels are those in which it is possible to go for long stretches forgetting that one is in fact reading a non-realist work. His very best writing is that which tends towards a gentle magic realism.

The full-blown secondary-world schemas that underwrite *Weaveworld*, *Imajica*, and *Abarat*, by contrast, bring out Barker's worst literary tendencies. For all the appealing elements of each – the amnesiac angel towards the close of *Weaveworld* is especially well done – the overall effect is dispiritingly weak. *Imajica* surely represents the nadir of Barker's career (at least until 2007's egregious *Mister B. Gone* with its endless appeals to the reader to stop reading). We will likely never know what Barker might have achieved had he renounced the juju, even once, and turned his hand to realist fiction. To speculate further would be idle. There are however two actually existing Barker works whose non-realist temper can be said to be fully vindicated on aesthetic grounds.

The first is *Sacrament* (1996), surely Barker's masterpiece. Written in the wake of the death of Barker's cousin Mark, it transmits a resonant sombreness and a supernatural premise that concentrates, rather than dilutes, what Barker's Liverpool lecturer had called 'the human drama'. This is perhaps the one Barker adult novel that does not leave one wondering how much better it might have been as an exercise in realism. The character of Will Rabjohns is brilliantly realised and his story richly embedded in a coherent thematic complex (death,

AIDS, homosexuality, extinction, fertility). The scene where Will takes his final farewell from his ex-lover Patrick, who is committing assisted suicide, is unforgettably moving. This is Barker at his tender, intuitive, large-hearted, imaginative, and spiritual best. It is immeasurably superior to the kind of over-italicised, over-amped magic he hits us with elsewhere in his oeuvre. *Sacrament* also discloses an all-important truth: the truly edgy, outsider, countercultural aspect of Barker was never the horror, the sensationalism, the excess, the shapeshifting fantasy set pieces, but the deeply unfashionable commitment to a neo-Blakean Christianism. *Sacrament* stands magnificently as what theologians used to call a sign of contradiction.

The other Barker work that will, I suspect, endure is the children's novel *The Thief of Always* (1992). An engaging time-slip fantasy in the *Tom's Midnight Garden* tradition, it represents Barker in full control of his material. Because he is writing for the juvenile market here, Barker does not have the option of hiding behind supposedly edgy adult effects (extreme violence, gore, and sexual content). Instead he must rely on the strength of a strong premise (which he has) and its artful development (which he effects). There is more power and pathos in the treatment of time in *The Thief of Always* than in all the hours of the Abarat put together. The masterly evocation of schoolboy tedium which opens the book – 'The great grey beast February had eaten Harvey Swick alive. Here he was, buried in the belly of that smothering month, wondering if he would ever find his way out through the cold coils that lay between here and Easter'[27] – recalls the control and wit that Barker had showcased, but been unable to sustain with any degree of consistency, in *Books of Blood* (one thinks, for example, of the superb opening sentence of 'The Forbidden').

The Thief of Always is perhaps most significant for the way it seems to code a certain awareness on Barker's part of the wrong turn he himself has taken as a writer. Young Harvey Swick's need to break out of the House of Illusions, with its cyclical tedium of tricks, ideas, and effects, and to find his way back to the real world, gives us a rather pointed allegory for his author's own entrapment himself in the horror-fantasy machine: 'If he'd remained in the House of Illusions, distracted by its petty pleasures, a whole lifetime would have gone by here in the real world, and his soul would have become Hood's property. He would have joined the fish circling in the lake; and circling; and circling. He shuddered at the thought.'[28]

Unlike Harvey, Barker never seems to have pondered the possibility that freedom may sometimes be a matter not of escaping *from* the real world but of escaping back *to* it. When at the top of his game as a writer, he has achieved uncannily powerful results from the dauntless colliding of genres and the generation of productive tension between realism and non-realism. More often than not however – and this the thesis of this essay in a nutshell – the signature over-dominance of the non-realist mode has served to limit rather than potentiate his art.

Notes

1 Clive Barker, *Subtle Bodies*. In *Forms of Heaven: Three Plays* (London: HarperCollins, 1996), pp. 229–378, here p. 245.
2 Clive Barker, 'The Madonna,' *Books of Blood*, Volumes 4–6 (London: Warner, 1988), p. 73.
3 Cf. Clive Barker, *Imajica* (London: HarperCollins, 1991), p. 628.
4 Quoted in Douglas E. Winter, *Clive Barker: The Dark Fantastic* (London: HarperCollins, 2001), p. 305.
5 *Ibid*. Italics in original.
6 *Ibid*. p. 171. Italics in original.
7 *Ibid*.
8 Clive Barker, 'The Midnight Meat Train,' *Books of Blood*, Volumes 1–3 (London: Warner, 1988), p. 13.
9 Clive Barker, *The Hellbound Heart* (London: Fontana, 1991), pp. 69–70.
10 Barker, *Imajica*, p. 666.
11 Chris Ryall and Gabriel Rodriguez, *Complete Clive Barker's Great and Secret Show* (San Diego: Idea & Design Works, 2007).
12 Clive Barker, *Everville* (London: HarperCollins, 1994), p. 94. Italics in original.
13 Barker, *Books of Blood*, Volumes 1–3, p. 54.
14 Barker, *Books of Blood*, Volumes 4–6, p. 65.
15 Barker, *Books of Blood*, Volumes 1–3, p. 90.
16 *Ibid*.
17 Barker, 'Introduction,' *Books of Blood*, Volumes 1–3, p. xii.
18 Quoted in Winter, *Clive Barker: The Dark Fantastic*, p. 315.
19 Barker, *Imajica*, p. 398.
20 Clive Barker, *The Damnation Game* (London: Sphere, 1986), p. 4.
21 *Ibid*. pp. 73–4.
22 *Ibid*. p. 105.
23 *Ibid*. p. 285.
24 Max Horkheimer and Theodor W. Adorno, *Dialectic of Enlightenment: Philosophical Fragments*, ed Gunzelin Schmid Noerr, trans. Edmund Jephcott (Stanford, CA: Stanford University Press, 2002), p. 109.
25 Clive Barker, *Galilee* (London: HarperCollins, 1998), pp. 366–7.
26 *Ibid*. p. 411.
27 Clive Barker, *The Thief of Always* (London: HarperCollins, 1992), p. 4.
28 *Ibid*. p. 122.

11

Clive Barker's late (anti-)horror fiction: *Tortured Souls* and *Mister B. Gone*'s new myths of the flesh

Xavier Aldana Reyes

Clive Barker once explained that, for him, 'Horror is over and again about the body.'[1] It should be obvious, even to the casual reader, that his back catalogue as a writer, director, and illustrator more than corroborates this statement. From the extreme landscapes of his directorial debut *Hellraiser* (1987), where corporeal pleasure mingles dangerously with pain and mutilation, to the horrors of the elective rejuvenating surgery gone wrong in the novel *Coldheart Canyon* (2001), his oeuvre reflects a long-standing preoccupation with anxieties surrounding the nature of embodiment. In a sense, if Barker has been reluctant to continue to associate himself with horror, preferring to be known as a dark fantasist, his fascination with the body is something that still pervades his work and which he has never repudiated.[2] In the later fiction, particularly the novella *Tortured Souls: The Legend of Primordium*, which accompanied a series of six action figures distributed by McFarlane in 2001, and in his widely publicised return to horror with *Mister B. Gone* (2007), this has become a major motif deserving of critical attention. As I will argue, corporality in Barker serves to articulate a characteristic type of fleshy horror – what I have elsewhere called 'body gothic' – that became the writer's trademark after the huge success of the *Books of Blood* (1984–85).[3] However, this proposition needs further qualification. Unlike other writers who became popular during the splatterpunk years in the mid-to-late 1980s, Barker's treatment of the body is not purely exploitative. His corporeal experiments, often destructive and bloody, tend to lead to a species of transcendence from a bounded conception of reality. Horror allows Barker to explore the limits of the body, and hence, of the human. This is not the case because he sees corporeality as a bad thing – quite the contrary.

In a piece written for an exhibition named *One Flesh* (1997), Barker went some way towards explaining why the body, in its most materialist guise, is so meaningful to him. Even though Christianity has been a huge influence in his imagery and thematic concerns, corporeality, for Barker, offers a sense of ontological belonging that is truly universal, a commonality premised on our very existence as sentient beings who live and interact with each other through our respective bodies. In his words:

> Flesh is our indisputable communality. Whatever our race, our religion, our politics, we are faced every morning with the fact of our bodies. Their frailties, their demands, their desires. And yet the erotic appetites that spring from – and are expressed through – those bodies are so often a source of bitter dissension and division. Acts that offer a glimpse of transcendence to one group are condemned by another. We are pressured from every side – by peers, by church, by state – to accept the consensual definition of taboo; though so often what excites our imaginations most is the violation of taboo.[4]

To say that Barker's artistic vision centres on the body is, however, not sufficient. It is true that desire and lust, for example, orchestrate a lot of the actions and results in his stories, and that his monstrous bodies often deconstruct the assumed 'normality' of their human counterparts. But Barker is also preoccupied with excess and taboo, especially as it is connected to a liberation from normativity and ideology. In other words, his flights of fancy are attempts to explore the intricacies of the human beyond the possibilities offered by the here and now. The physical limitations structuring our lives are often subverted through imaginative and original bodily assemblages, such as that of one of his most recent characters, *Abarat's* (2002) Christopher Carrion, whose nightmares crawl out of his brain to gain a semi-corporeal presence. Barker's outlandish, often grotesque, bodies may also accompany larger feats of the imagination involving the creation of new worlds, most notably the mystical dream sea of Quiddity in *The Great and Secret Show* (1990) and *Everville* (1994). In this chapter, I want to turn to his later fiction, partly because it has received less critical attention than his earlier stories and novels, but also because *Tortured Souls* and *Mister B. Gone* show a sustained engagement with the body which continues to escape the boundaries of classic horror to form its own elaborate mythologies.[5] As such, both novels are perfect examples of the type of fiction that made Barker famous during the first part of his career, namely, what biographer and writer Douglas E. Winter has called 'anti-horror'.

Winter, who proposed the term after the publication of the *Books of Blood*, sought with its application to Barker's work to differentiate it from that of other horror writers who were, to his mind, more interested in the exploitative aspects of the genre. Since Barker was, at one time, connected to the splatterpunk movement, this was a matter of some urgency, especially as splatterpunk designated horror at its most extreme.[6] According to Winter, the horror genre has traditionally relied on the premise that the universe is 'ordered' and that 'goodness is found in sanity, conformity and the ordinary'.[7] As a result, chaos, difference, and ambivalence are associated with evil and they must be destroyed or exorcised if the status quo (order) is to be restored and happiness attained. Anti-horror, then, is 'a knowing deconstruction' of these principles:

a conscious subversion of formula that rejects the Manichean simplicity of God and Devil, good and evil, pushing the reader into a realm of ambiguity, forcing us to confront the real world, outside and within – a place of possibilities, some dark and dangerous, others bright and beautiful, and all of them liberating. The intent of this fiction is not to horrify (although the effect is occasionally inevitable) but to force the reader to imagine.[8]

What is important to note here is not the potential dismissal of anti-horror's capacity to generate fear, shock, or disgust; this is an art Barker has been duly praised for and which should not, in any case, be condemned as a low-brow or less ambitious endeavour. Winter's reading of the *Books of Blood*, particularly the last three volumes, puts forward the interesting idea that, although initially presented as horror, Barker's stories actually undermine the genre's conservative foundations. Even more important is the suggestion that anti-horror might be seeking to have an emancipatory power and to become a paragon of anti-hegemonic and postmodern discourses of diversity. Contrary to older theorisations of horror, which tended to pit it against terror, and focus on its claustrophobic and annihilating qualities, the genre is presented as an eye-opening and rebellious exercise in the negotiation and questioning of boundaries.[9] These are, as I am arguing, primarily corporeal and do not shy away from gore. In fact, as Linda Badley has noted, splatter plays a crucial role in the construction of 'an iconography of confrontation and paradox' that can open up discussions about taboo subjects such as gender politics, sexuality, violence, or censorship.[10]

Although not all of Barker's work may be best understood under the anti-horror rubric, my contention is that it has gained relevance in the late fiction specifically promoted as horror. Moreover, it is perhaps the case that, precisely because the liberating aspect of anti-horror has become central, the lukewarm critical reaction to a playful work like *Mister B. Gone* may be a result of fears that Barker could have lost his extreme transgressive edge. I begin with *Tortured Souls* because, although a peripheral work, having been conceived alongside a toy line, it constituted a return to familiar territory and packed more obvious visceral punches than *Mister B. Gone*.

Torturing and tortured souls

The Cenobites, characters who straddle the line between the torturer and the tortured, are possibly Barker's most famous creation; their stories have developed over ten films and an equally impressive number of comics.[11] The various flayed and grotesque bodies of the characters that populate *Tortured Souls* (also known as *Animae Damnatae*) owe a great deal to the lead villains in *The Hellbound Heart* (1986) and their cinematic interpretation in *Hellraiser*. In fact, they could be seen, at least iconographically, as their second permutation, the former being the enemies in the video game *Clive Barker's Jericho* (2007), for which Barker produced the basic plotline.[12] In *The Hellbound Heart*, the Cenobites, also described as 'theologians of the Order of the Gash', are extradimensional creatures who may be summoned through a little puzzle box called the 'Lemarchand Configuration'.[13] Attractive to humans who want to push the limits of human experience, the Cenobites experiment with flesh and nerve-endings and promise an experience of pleasure unlike any that may be experienced on Earth. Their appearance betrays their profession: 'scars … cover … every inch of their bodies; the flesh cosmetically punctured and sliced and infibulated, then dusted down with ash'.[14] Seeing them has a series of mixed effects on Frank, who confesses that he feels nauseated by their 'decrepit' look, 'deformity' and 'self-evident frailty'.[15] In *Hellraiser*, the visceral quality of these descriptions is intensified and filtered through sadomasochistic imagery.[16] The Cenobites appear in black leather clothing, garments which are torn in places and display open wounds. The skin is lifted so that the underlying muscle tissue and cartilage is revealed, and held in place by hooks and other metallic implements. The result is a highly elaborate and aesthetic monster that breaks down all boundaries between inner and outer body, and opens up corporeality for voyeuristic inspection.

The design for the characters in *Tortured Souls* followed the same principle: human flesh is manipulated, turned into a canvas or mosaic in which the inner and outer bodies mix, often incongruously.[17] The final painted figure for Agonistes, the ancient entity that can reshape the bodies of others and which was possibly created by God, recalls Chatterer and his grotesque lipless grin. His facial skin has been extracted completely ('scalped') and is held by metallic rods above his head. His eyes are blinded by hooks that push deep into his eye sockets and a dark leather contraption clamps the flesh away from the periphery of his mouth. The result is a creature both monstrous and human – the monstrosity is created by pushing the flesh, in what appears to be an otherwise human body, to disfiguring extremes. Agonistes' face, like his right arm, is made entirely of muscle tissue, the skin flayed and discarded, and is itself pulled in artificial and contrived ways. Like a martyr and, most importantly, like the Cenobites, his body is condemned to eternal suffering, as the flesh is precluded from healing and from returning to its natural state by hooks and cylinders. The rest of the characters, from the Scythe-Meister to Venal Anatomica, display similar transfigurations; they are nightmares of flesh, blood, metal, and leather with a single intention: to 'become a benchmark in horror toys', to be the scariest and most extreme ever made.[18] Their innovative collection of wounds constitutes a mythological extension of the corporeal nightmares in *Hellraiser*, the main difference being that the characters in *Tortured Souls* rely more heavily on a faux-futuristic aesthetic that also draws on mad science horror. However, the similarities are such that one could be forgiven for mistaking Agonistes for simply another, more evolved, Cenobite.

The novella that accompanied the articulated figures, published in six chapters and broadly related to each of them, is a fable thematically concerned with the recreation of the body under new plastic conditions. Like *Hellraiser*, *Tortured Souls* proposes a new carnal mythology introducing a pantheon of transmogrified superhumans. The action takes place in Primordium, the first city ever built and run by a dynasty of cruel and corrupted Emperors, the Perfettos. In this city, the aforementioned Agonistes, a two-and-a-half-thousand-year-old 'transformer of human flesh, a creator of monsters' who could be one of God's unwholesome experiments, operates freely.[19] His hands are capable of turning supplicants, who come to him of their own free will, into 'objects of perverse beauty', 'their bodies remade in fashions that they have no power to dictate'.[20] As in *The Hellbound Heart* and *Hellraiser*, individuals need to find him and consciously sign over their flesh so it may be 'rem[ade] in the image of their terror' and that of their enemies.[21] Supplicants, who include historical and religious figures such as Judas Iscariot and Pontius Pilate, resort to Agonistes' services due to insecurity and in the hope that they might be able to thus take revenge on those who have mistreated them. They also sometimes regret the decision to be 'empowered' by Agonistes' 'scalpels' and 'torches' and beg to be killed; the process, which includes 'cutting, infibulating, searing, cauterizing, stretching, twisting [and] reconfiguring', is particularly painful.[22] The surgery is described as an 'art', that of the creation of 'new flesh', and imitates the work of God himself.[23]

One of Agonistes' creations is the Scythe-Meister, the reconfigured version of Zarles Kreiger, a low-life criminal and killer of political figures who changes his ways after he strikes up a relationship with Lucidique, the daughter of a Senator he assassinates. After making Zarles conscious of the unfairness of a decadent government which exploits the lowest strata of the city, Lucidique convinces him to try to turn Primordium into a Republic by means of violence. After Agonistes' treatment, he is no longer capable of rejoining the human race: bodies that have been transformed by the divine scalpel inevitably terrify others, so that walking around Primordium has to be done in the dark, if one is to go unnoticed. Apart from a 'bacterial brightness' that coats his skin with a 'sickly luminescence', the Scythe-Meister sports raw wounds 'designed never to heal'.[24] Although the changes he has undergone are not made explicit in the novella beyond the fact that, in him, '[s]ilver bond[s] with bone and nerve; gold and bronze the same', the final figure cast for the toy line can give an indication of what these involve.[25] Like Agonistes, his skin is pulled away from the face, and the eyes have been blinded; the mouth is exposed, as a metallic strap connecting it with his forehead pulls from below and freezes it forever in a rictus of pain. As with Lucidique, also eventually transformed beyond recognition, his new appearance is so monstrous that it ultimately ostracises Zarles from the society of those who have not been surgically altered.

The other notorious grotesqueries in the novella are Doctor Talisac and his offspring, hidden away from the world in the Hospice of the Sacred Heart, a gothic underground laboratory. Like Victor Frankenstein, Talisac's raw materials are corpses, found in various states of amputation. A monster-maker, Talisac has managed to fashion himself an external, semi-translucent womb, out of which grows the Mongroid. The latter is an aberration of creation resembling a gigantic mouth, a crab homunculus made of his DNA, and who is referred to as the 'infant of the Second Coming'.[26] But if these designs do not sound dark enough, Talisac himself incarnates the corporeally macabre: he hangs by his mouth from a device whose purpose is unclear and, as I have mentioned, boasts an external reproductive system that makes him a true creator. The three generals who compose the military junta which controls Primordium after the Great Insurrection approach him precisely because he is the only creature capable of giving life to 'a fiend to put fear into the heart of the Devil himself', '[s]omething to scour the city of its monsters by being still more monstrous'.[27] The result is Venal Anatomica, who has 'death's face', wounds that bleed constantly where 'nails [have been] crudely hammered', and who smells of 'disease, of corruption, of death'.[28]

Interestingly, the novella makes a distinction between Venal Anatomica and the Mongroid, and Lucidique and the Scythe-Meister. Whilst the latter are presented as scary and cruel monsters, they are wholesome by comparison. They have been reconfigured out of their own flesh and thus are evolved versions of themselves. Venal Anatomica, on the other hand, is 'a charnel-house child', 'made of parcels of rotten flesh and nerve and bone, all nailed together and given a foetid breath'.[29] The Mongroid is no better than a failed experiment, not quite what Talisac had in mind when he set out to create a feral child, and ends up cruelly eating his creator in *Tortured Soul*'s most gruesome scene. On the one hand, monsters are manipulated to exploit gore and horror through the impossible and brutal mutilations their bodies undergo, which include, in the case of the Mongroid, a belly that can spring open to reveal a collection of sharp teeth. On the other, monsters can have a good heart, are capable of loving each other and, in the case of Lucidique, even of mourning and of avenging their kind. In a sense, as the action in *Tortured Souls* encompasses, almost exclusively, the life of monsters, their otherness becomes less important as the story moves forward. Whilst Barker employs traditional horror techniques and imagery, he also subverts them by presenting sympathetic hybrids with complex psychologies who resist being reduced to a walking nightmare. Even Venal Anatomica, introduced as the ultimate villain, ends his days blinded and crying tears through slit eyes.

Tortured Souls is thus a perfect example of anti-horror. Although it is not short of gruesome descriptions – Mongroid's cannibalistic episode ends with Talisac's innards falling off his body one by one – the novella uses monstrosity in multiple ways and problematises the presentation of nightmarish bodies.

Agonistes' visceral reconfigurations are, after all, introduced as nothing but attempts to 'change [the] world'.[30] Not only are his methods empowering, they are also potentially connected with progress and the desire to put an end to shameless profiteering by the ruling elite. The Scythe-Meister's killing spree ultimately brings down the corrupt dynasty of the Perfettos, starting the Great Insurrection, during which the members of the clergy and other corrupt institutions are hunted down by the populace. Similarly, Lucidique is saved from certain death by Agonistes' intervention and turned into a 'strong, supple and powerful' 'living weapon' that wreaks revenge on the gangster Cascarellian.[31] The flesh nightmares explored in *Tortured Souls* appear as liberations from a reality that proves too obstructive for their main characters, a species of mortal coil. Its shedding, via re-articulations connected to the person's history and traits, seems to equate to a form of divinity or, at the very least, immortality, as the narrative spells out at the very end.[32] *Tortured Souls* also plays with religious scripture in a perverse way, referring to the second coming and to Lazarus' resurrection in two different instances. It is possible, therefore, to understand Barker's characters as an attempt to imagine a new mythology of monstrous deities that relies on the body as both the clay on which to mould great horrors and the final door to transcendence.

The novella revisits the territory already explored in *The Hellbound Heart* by providing an alternative profane mythology concerned with the creation of new societies and the destruction of older ones. This leads to a form of horror that is not annihilating or pessimistic, but which, instead, provides new ways to rethink the body beyond its 'normative' status. Barker's interest in destroying the body is countered by a marked preoccupation with reconfiguring it in liberating ways, often involving the grafting or coming together of unusual assemblages – in this case, metal/human, but also animal/human in *Coldheart Canyon*. Such a preoccupation stems from a need to revitalise old myths, often from Biblical or otherwise religious extraction, through a corporeal lens that is original in its rethinking of the possibilities and limitations of the human body. This is a constant in his work. It merely becomes obvious in his horror fiction because it tends to deal with monstrosity, otherness, and the fear generated by difference much more explicitly.

Mister B. Gone

Mister B. Gone was, until the publication of *The Scarlet Gospels* (2015), the last novel of Barker's to be marketed as horror, so it is susceptible of the type of corporeal reading that I have outlined above.[33] However, as the writer himself has noted, the text is, in large part, a comedy and purposely defies clear-cut genre boundaries.[34] I consider it in this chapter because, apart from being an exponent of his late horror fiction, Barker's bodily preoccupations take a marked metaphysical bent in it. The trapping of a demon in the body of the book itself (the one that potential readers have in their hands), is used as an excuse to explore the legacy of human consciousness beyond carnal existence. Whilst the novel is still interested in the grotesque body of its demon protagonist, Barker once again goes beyond the mere surface exploration of monstrous embodiment to focus on the role of imagination in the creation of our bodies and our own understanding of ourselves. The horror genre, indebted as it is to gothic monsters, fantasy, and the uncanny, allows him to imagine corporeality outside its current boundaries. The fact that horror is a genre that can push the envelope and does not need to worry about its effects on the reader means that Barker can investigate the more visceral and grisly implications of his fleshly vision. *Mister B. Gone* offers an interesting counter-narrative that manages to put forward an original concept – a 'brutal' and 'intimate' kind of scare – whilst continuing to build on the author's characteristic mythology.[35]

Mister B. Gone opens with a three-word exhortation: 'Burn this book.'[36] The demand – which initially takes the shape of seductive persuasion but later becomes a 'real' threat – punctuates a novel which has no chapter breaks. The narrator is one minor medieval devil, Jakabok Botch, or Mister B., as he later comes to be named, who speaks directly to the person reading his lines. Allegedly penned in 1438 and the first book to be produced by Gutenberg's press, *Mister B. Gone* presents itself as a forbidden found manuscript and confessional similar to the ones found in canonical gothic novels like Ann Radcliffe's *Romance of the Forest* (1791). It tells the morbid tale of one evil spirit, who dwells near the Ninth Circle of Hell, and his unlucky exploits in the fourteenth century once he is 'fished out' by a corrupt priest. Once freed, Jakabok meets another evil spirit, Quitoon, with whom he wreaks havoc in the land. After a disagreement, both demons meet in Mainz, Germany, where they are witness to the war waged between Heaven and Hell over Gutenberg's press. In the aftermath, Jakabok is captured and turned into words: his essence is then magically contained in the book itself, which goes on to address curious onlookers.

This breaking of the fourth narrative wall – 'I'm staring out of the words right now, moving along behind the lines as your eyes follow them' – aims to involve the reader viscerally by turning reading into a dangerous experience, hindered at every step by more warnings and imprecations.[37] In the Lovecraftian tradition, Mister B. also explains that the book contains passages so 'terrifying that your sanity won't hold once you see them.'[38] This continued interpellation has a double effect. On the one hand, like much horror, it creates the impression that the reader is being dared to read the contents because of their graphic, titillating, and forbidding nature. This is the equivalent of the 'extreme editions' of films, which purport to offer even bloodier versions of already violent narratives. On the other hand, to persevere in the book's reading also entails accepting, even if purely fictitiously, a form of curse, for Mister B.'s words are intimidating and suggest that negative consequences are inescapable. Of course, as we find out, Mister B. is actually enticing the reader, as only by sharing his life and deeds can he be remembered. In a sense, then, we must differentiate between the intradiegetic and extradiegetic readers here. The novel seems to imply a reader who persists in the knowledge that they will come to harm, whilst the actual reader knows fully well that this is a novel written by Clive Barker and which can have no real effect on their lives. The reading impetus is very different in the case of the extradiegetic reader: to continue to engage with the narrative is a decision partly influenced by the desire to know what happens to the interpellated subject. This does not mean that Mister B.'s story is not interesting in itself, but rather that his admonishments set up a series of expectations regarding the gradual damning of the reader. Proceeding with the book, hence, feels twice as illicit, because the contents are advertised as horrific, but also because a direct sense of peril is foregrounded. The experience of reading *Mister B. Gone* is framed around finding out more about terrific deeds and losing one's mind in the process.

The book is peppered with violent exploits appropriate to the subject matter. When free to roam the Earth, Jakabok does much mischief to the humans he encounters, and some of his tricks are particularly nasty. There is, for example, an episode where he and Quitoon bathe in the blood of infants, another where Jakabok boils a woman alive, and yet another where Quitoon cuts someone in half with a sword. These occurrences, despite being advertised as 'not for the squeamish', are rare and not always described explicitly.[39] The 'grisly details' that are meant to make the reader 'a little sick to [the] stomach' are not fore-grounded in the same way that they were in, for example, the *Books of Blood*, although they still colour the narrative.[40] In keeping with dark fantasy and horror, Mister B. is a demon, albeit a minor one, and thus his body is also paraded for its grotesque value. A 'creature of marvelous [sic] ugliness', he is the owner of a double tail, is covered in reptilian yellow and vermillion scales, and has tiny black spines running up his back.[41] After an unfortunate accident, he also sports a face he describes as a 'mass of keloid tissue' and 'a chaos of bubbles', a mouth whose lips have been scarred, a nose that is mostly nostrils, and eyes that are 'holes, without lashes or brows'.[42] The latter 'constantly run with grey-green mucus so that there isn't a moment … when [he] do[es]n't have rivulets of foul fluids running down [his] cheeks'.[43] All of these physical traits do not go unnoticed, especially on Earth, where he can easily slide into the role of terrorising creature.

But, for all its stock grotesquerie, the monstrous body in *Mister B. Gone* is not purely a vehicle for horror. As his earliest memories show, Mister B. was a very unhappy, friendless demon child disfigured after he fell, face forward, on a pile of his own burning writings. The fact that this fire was started because his stories – unpleasant tales of patricide and torture which helped him sublimate his hatred for his father – were found to be more than objectionable by his mother, adds a touch of pathos to the story. Additionally, Mister B. and Quitoon's bodies are the victims of numerous acts of violence perpetrated by humans. Although they can 'survive extremely vicious maimings and mutilations', their demonic bodies still bleed and suffer pain, which often comes from human cruelty and ignorance (brought on by superstition).[44] The many 'blows, cuts, kicks, curses, and wads of phlegm' Mister B. is subjected to can therefore generate sympathy – as when bits of him are cut off and kept as trophies – and be perceived differently from similar attacks on the human body. Since Mister B.'s body is supernatural, the reader is more likely to feel curiosity towards the effects that violence will have upon it than to partake vicariously of the corporeal attacks. For example, when he speaks of his 'organs of regeneration', the reader may be more interested in the fantastic possibilities of a self-healing body than in gore.[45]

Mister B. is not a totally redeemable character, however, since he does commit crimes, brings death to various people and is, after all, a demonic figure. He is presented as a contradictory and conflicted individual, and this is, in itself, noteworthy. His complex characterisation, with plenty of recognisable human traits, means that it is difficult to accept him as merely a demonic figure to be feared. Moreover, in the conclusion to the novel, it is revealed that Mister B.'s pleas for the burning of this particular book have not been a scare-mongering stunt but the demon's way of seeking his own liberating exorcism.[46] His essence has been trapped in the pages of the book, turning it into a 'prison of pages' from which he cannot be released by means other than fire.[47] This is not coincidental. The action macabrely echoes the earlier burning of his own tales and thus figures as another desperate cry for attention and help. As Mister B. confesses towards the end of the narrative, his weakness is that centuries of loneliness have made him crave company, and the telling of his life has, in itself, become contagious: 'the more I told, the more I wanted to go on telling and the more I wanted to go on telling, the more I wanted to tell'.[48]

Mister B. Gone is, therefore, more than a straightforward horror novel chronicling the life of a fictional demonic memory. Its 'burn this book' premise also stretches beyond a simple stylistic gimmick to make a bold point about the nature of reading and the type of immortality sought in committing thoughts to paper. On the one hand, *Mister B. Gone* is introduced as a unique text, whose pages and ink are imbued with the essence of a demon; its narrator is allegedly able to 'rearrange the words on the pages you ha[ve] yet to read'.[49] On the other hand, Mister B.'s tale is obviously a more universal exploration of the role of reading and writing, not least because Barker takes the trouble of locating the story at the inception of the first mass printing press.[50] As Mister B. puts it towards the ending, the reader should not 'abandon me on a shelf somewhere, gathering dust, knowing I'm still inside, locked away in the darkness'.[51] The only way to liberate Mister B., of course, is to burn him. But on a less literal level, it is to remember him. His memories, his adventures and misadventures, his right and wrong choices, can, like all writing, be kept in the collective memory and thus potentially help them survive through the centuries. Although Mister B.'s main goal is to disappear, to escape a prison of paper, his desires and flaws make a larger point about the transient nature of existence and the human struggle to remain through our writing. As the narrator puts it, 'words [are] a part of [us], part of [our] mind and memory'; 'Only when the last syllable has been spoken, … we can reasonably assume the world will have ended. Created with a word, and … maybe destroyed by one'.[52]

Clive Barker's anti-horror is preoccupied with the creation of important mythologies that replace the ephemerality of the flesh, which, as he has thoroughly recorded in many of his books, is very physiological. However, precisely because he is not scared of the material nature of the body, his gods and demons have sported a very original and idiosyncratic look that transcends the horrific. As with *Cabal* (1988) and his *Books of Blood* ('The Madonna', 'The Skins of the Fathers'), and even later with his *Abarat* series, there is pity to be had for the monster, because s/he is intrinsically related to the human. Monsters in Barker can, occasionally, take on the role of 'other/ed' and 'abject/ed' attackers, but, most of the time, they are eminently embraced for their ability to negotiate universal anxieties connected to the passing of time, death, the embodied nature of life and to complicate normativity.[53] Barker's stories, then, are closer to the parable than to traditional horror, and transcend Manichean accounts of Good and Evil. Although I would be reluctant to suggest that Barker's anti-horror is in direct opposition to popular horror, as that would perpetuate the misguided notion that the latter is necessarily conservative and reactionary, his work is rich and shows a considerable breadth of imagination that has won him the appellative 'visionary'.[54]

Barker has built his own pantheons of mythic monsters that explore the limits and limitations of what it means to be human. In fact, one of the conclusions that may be derived from *Mister B. Gone* is that the acts of the humans and demons in the novel are not so easily differentiated. Both this book and *Tortured Souls* demonstrate that Barker's late 'official' returns to the genre are still imbued with his obsession with the flesh and its ability to speak about the human condition in Biblical grandeur.

Notes

1 Clive Barker, interviewed in Richard Lupoff, Richard Wolinsky, and Lawrence Davidson, 'A Talk with the King', in James Van Hise (ed.), *Stephen King and Clive Barker: The Illustrated Guide to the Masters of the Macabre II* (Las Vegas, NV: Pioneer Books, 1992), pp. 79–95 (p. 84).
2 My point here is that, while Barker was initially marketed as a horror writer throughout the publication of the first three volumes of the *Books of Blood* (London: Sphere, 1984), he has, later on in his career, challenged this label. I am not suggesting

that Barker has repudiated horror, as he readily concedes that there are horror elements in his novels. He even produced a very thorough guide to the genre, *Clive Barker's A-Z of Horror* (London: BBC Books), as late as 1997.

3 See Xavier Aldana Reyes, *Body Gothic: Corporeal Transgression in Contemporary Literature and Horror Film* (Cardiff: University of Wales Press, 2014).

4 Clive Barker, 'One Flesh Exhibition', in Phil and Sarah Stokes (eds), *Clive Barker: The Painter, the Creature, and the Father of Lies* (Northborough, MA: Earthling Publications, 2011), p. 219.

5 Barker has often been referred to as a 'mythmaker'. See, among others, Suzanne J. Barbieri, *Clive Barker: Mythmaker for the Millennium* (Stockport: British Fantasy Society, 1994).

6 The cover for Joe R. Lansdale's *The Nightrunners* (Arlington Hts., IL: Dark Harvest, 1987) reproduces a quote from *Fangoria* magazine, which reads 'You have to turn to someone like Clive Barker to equal the repulsive and vivid imagination Lansdale has at his command'. For more on the splatterpunk movement, see *Body Gothic*, pp. 28–51, where I also discuss Barker's relation to the splatterpunk movement.

7 Douglas E. Winter, *Clive Barker: The Dark Fantastic* (London: HarperCollins, 2001), p. 190.

8 *Ibid*. p. 191.

9 In this respect, Ann Radcliffe's dyadic model in her influential 'The Supernatural in Poetry' is perhaps the most important early distinction between the two terms. According to her, 'Terror and Horror are so far opposite that the first expands the soul, and awakens the faculties to a high degree of life; the other contracts, freezes and nearly annihilates them'. See Ann Radcliffe, 'The Supernatural in Poetry', in E. J. Clery and Robert Miles (eds), *Gothic Documents: A Sourcebook 1700–1820* (Manchester: Manchester University Press, 2000), pp. 163–72 (p. 168). This idea was later used to differentiate between her own work (often referred to as the 'supernatural explained', and thus, connected to terror) and that of Matthew Lewis, whose *The Monk* (1796) has become the foremost exponent of horror. For more on this distinction, see Xavier Aldana Reyes, 'Fear, Divided: Terror and Horror – The Two Sides of the Gothic Coin', *Emagazine*, 68 (2015), pp. 49–52.

10 Linda Badley, *Writing Horror and the Body: The Fiction of Stephen King, Clive Barker, and Anne Rice* (Westport, CT: Greenwood Press, 1996), p. 74.

11 The last instalment in the film franchise is *Hellraiser: Revelations* (Víctor García, 2011), but *Hellraiser: Judgment* is set for 2017 release. Epic Comics published twenty issues from 1989 to 1992, plus a number of special issues and adaptations. Another comic series, this time published by Boom! Studios, was launched in 2010 and is on-going at the time of writing. It is important to note that the degree of Baker's involvement in these different works varies greatly.

12 Although *Jericho* is not specifically related to *The Hellbound Heart* cosmogony, the look of some of the characters is derived directly from that of the Cenobites. For example, Arnold Leach, a former scholar of arcane books turned flying demon, has wings that have been fashioned from the skin on his back, and his eyes and mouth are pulled by metal hooks that borrow directly from *Hellraiser*.

13 Clive Barker, *The Hellbound Heart* (London: HarperCollins, 2008), p. 5.

14 Barker, *The Hellbound Heart*, p. 7.

15 *Ibid.* p. 9.

16 As is well known, Barker famously took inspiration from the S&M community. This is evident in his sketches for the lead Cenobite who would eventually become Pinhead (Doug Bradley) in the film franchise.

17 Unsurprisingly, the tagline for the second line of *Tortured Souls* toys promised 'a further redefinition of human flesh as canvas'. See the official McFarlane toys page for the series, *Spawn.Com: The Home of McFarlane Toys*, www.spawn.com/toys/series.aspx?series=179. Date accessed: 7 July 2014.

18 Clive Barker, interviewed in 'Clive from New York,' *Spawn.Com*, 13 February 2001, www.spawn.com/news/news.aspx?id=5174. Date accessed: 7 June 2014.

19 Clive Barker, 'Book One: The Secret Face of Genesis,' part I, in Clive Barker, *Tortured Souls: Six Destinies* (Tempe, AZ: Todd McFarlane, 2001), n.p. The novella was also published in one volume by Subterranean Press in 2015.

20 *Ibid.*

21 *Ibid.*

22 *Ibid.*

23 Barker, 'Secret Face of Genesis,' part II.

24 Barker, 'Book Four: The Surgeon of the Sacred Heart,' part II.

25 'Surgeon of the Sacred Heart,' part IV. His and Lucidique's bodies are also later described by passers-by who spy on their love-making in part II of 'Book Five: The Haunter of Primordium' as 'one third human, one third metallic, one third the no man's land between flesh and devices made to strip it and slash it and scour it'.

26 Barker, 'Book Six: The Second Coming,' part I.

27 Barker, 'Surgeon of the Sacred Heart,' part V.

28 Barker, 'Haunter of Primordium,' part II, and 'The Second Coming,' part II.

29 Barker, 'The Second Coming,' part II.

30 Barker, 'Book Two: The Assassin Transformed,' part VI.

31 'Surgeon of the Sacred Heart,' part II; and 'Book Three: The Avenger,' part IV, respectively.

32 The last line is 'It was a land of immortality.' See 'Second Coming,' part VI.

33 *The Scarlet Gospels* is Barker's last horror novel but it came out too late in the writing of this chapter for it to be included in any significant way. My reading of his late (anti-)horror fiction still stands, however, especially because *Gospels* continues the mythology developed in *The Hellbound Heart* and situates part of its action in a hell reminiscent of the one in *Mister B. Gone*.

34 Barker has, in retrospect, proposed that it might have been a mistake to market the novel as horror, as this created certain expectations from a reading public who wanted a new *Books of Blood*. Clive Barker, interviewed by Lucy A. Sneider, 'It's All Part of the Fun,' in *Clive Barker: Revelations*, 2009, www.clivebarker.info/mbgbarker.html. Date accessed: 7 June 2014.

35 Clive Barker, interviewed by Madeline Puckett at *Fangoria* Weekend of Horrors, 20 May 2007, rpt. in *Clive Barker: Revelations*, www.clivebarker.info/mbgbarker.html. Date accessed: 7 June 2014.

36 Clive Barker, *Mister B. Gone* (London: HarperCollins, 2007), p. 1.
37 *Ibid*. p. 43.
38 *Ibid*.
39 *Ibid*. p. 45.
40 *Ibid*.
41 *Ibid*. p. 16.
42 *Ibid*.
43 *Ibid*.
44 *Ibid*. p. 97. Significantly, Mister B. makes a point of emphasising that human genius is often found in war machines and torture instruments, p. 109.
45 *Ibid*. p. 98.
46 This exorcism is also metaphorical and related to guilt: Mister B. sees writing things, 'setting [them] down in pages', as a way of 'purging all that you witness', p. 45. Hence, the story is not purely a biography, but a confession seeking some form of redemption.
47 Barker, *Mister B. Gone*, p. 247.
48 *Ibid*. p. 246.
49 *Ibid*.
50 I have no space here to develop the implications of the figure of the self-effacing writer. The novel is written by Clive Barker and bears his name, and yet, to all accounts, the writer and narrator is Mister B. The role and responsibility of authorship seems to be a topic that permeates some of Barker's writings, too. See Katarzyna Ancuta, 'Pain into Pleasure or the Horror of Creation: Notes on Reading Clive Barker's *The Great and Secret Show*,' in Wojcicch Kalaga and Tadeusz Rachwał (eds), *(Aesth)etics of Interpretation: Essays in Cultural Practice* (Katowice, Poland: Wydawnictwo Uniwersytetu Śląskiego, 2000), pp. 159–70.
51 Barker, *Mister B. Gone*, p. 247.
52 *Ibid*. p. 10.
53 This embrace of the monster, as opposed to its downright dismissal, has, as K.A. Laity notes, allowed for wider explorations of, for example, sexual difference and queer identity. See K.A. Laity, 'Imagineer: Clive Barker's Queering of the Conservative Bent of Horror Literature,' in Ruth Bienstock Anolik (ed.), *Horrifying Sex: Essays on Sexual Difference in Gothic Literature* (Jefferson, NC: McFarland, 2007), pp. 248–58. See also Christian Daumann, *Wonderlands in Flesh and Blood: Gender, the Body, Its Boundaries and Their Transgression in Clive Barker's* Imajica (München, Germany: AVM, 2009).
54 See Michael Beeler, 'Clive Barker: Horror Visionary,' *Cinefantastique*, Vol. 26:3 (1995), pp. 16–22.

12

The Devil and Clive Barker: Faustian bargains and gothic filigree

Sorcha Ní Fhlainn

Nothing ever begins. There is no first moment; no single word or place from which this or any other story springs. The threads can always be traced back to some earlier tale, and to the tales that precede that; though as the narrator's voice recedes the connections will seem to grow more tenuous, for each age will want the tale told as if it were of its own making. (Clive Barker)[1]

Faustus is gone: regard his hellish fall,
Whose fiendful fortune may exhort the wise
Only to wonder at unlawful things
Whose deepness doth entice such forward wits
To practise more than heavenly power permits. (Christopher Marlowe)[2]

When you attempted to live beyond death, you entered my domain. You should be very careful what you wish for … it just might come true! (*Hellraiser: Deader*)[3]

Clive Barker's works frequently invoke fundamental elements in the gothic tradition. As both an author and artist, Barker enjoys crossing generic boundaries and expectations, borrowing, blending, and manipulating motifs of the gothic, the *fantastique*, the fairytale, and the quest narrative in order to achieve his vivid and very particular vision. These gothic excesses are core to realising his vision on the page, enabling him to tailor his stories to readers of all ages. The gothic and its grotesquery combine elements frequently shared with mainstream horror fiction, and bring with it attributes and embellishments which reveal the dark textures of Barker's polymathic creations. Read through a gothic framework, Barker's stories are indebted to gothic spaces or figures; we frequently expect to encounter lost worlds, magical doorways, rictus-grinned strangers, frightening demons, and magical beasts, to name but a few, all made familiar by the excesses of the gothic literary tradition. One of the most frequent Barkerian examples of this is found in an expression of desire and bodily transcendence, an appetite to transcend the banal in pursuit of the extraordinary. The pursuit of this transcendental experience operates as a gateway into the gothic, through which a profound sense of unease, disorientation, and encroaching darkness is expressed. Barker oscillates between genres (horror and fantasy) and modes (the gothic), between narrative expectations, gleeful perversities, exploiting realist and anti-realist tensions, and self-categorises his own material as betwixt and between styles, where the gothic and the fantastic meet – a self-imposed descriptor of *dark fantastique*. The *fantastique* as a genre defines itself as the encroachment of the supernatural upon the banalities of the everyday world, and this is without question a frequent signature in Barker's fiction. However, these intrusions upon the everyday are heavily laced with gothic aesthetics and reveal a strong connection to its literary heritage, be it with the return of demonic forces, or the waging of one's soul for a forbidden experience, or the desire to achieve dark power or immortality. To reveal Barker's invocation of fundamentally gothic conventions, this chapter uncovers the gothic excesses in his early and seminal novel(la)s – *The Damnation Game* (1985), *The Hellbound Heart* (1986), *The Thief of Always* (1992), and more recent novels *Coldheart Canyon* (2001) and *The Scarlet Gospels* (2015) – each of which are indebted to the Faustian pact. Barker's gothic imagination manifests in the repeated use of the Faustian bargain archetype which, according to Eric Hadley Denton, 'is at the enstaked heart of the gothic plot'.[4] His invocation of this gothic device is both frequent and irrefutable across his polymathic career, requiring close inspection.

A gothic arrangement

The Faustian pact is a key strategy for Barker to explore the corrupting nature of desire and the twisted path towards the sublime; Barker may be a postmodern writer whose *bricolage* of genres combines borrowed traits from fantasy and horror, yet his journeys are not about reinstating the patriarchal order but rather transcending it. For Barker, the seduction of discovery – knowing the self, experiencing the power of the imagination, or embracing the other – and experiencing the flesh we inhabit stand in for our shared mortal condition. The flesh is textual for Barker – for him it encompasses pain and suffering, difference, erotic sensuality, race, metamorphosis, violence, irony, and monstrosity – and the soul, housed within this expressive flesh, is prized above all else (despite Barker's renunciation of any theological influence). Fundamentally, Barker is repeatedly drawn to the infernal in his works – demons from another world penetrate our own in *Hellraiser* and are keen to demonstrate their pleasures on those willing to submit to their transformative and physically destructive limit experiences. These moments of horror and sexual ecstasy are repeated throughout much of his later fiction too; Barker is truly wedded to the pursuit of forbidden knowledge and experiences – the tell-tale mark of trading with infernal forces. If, as Heidi Stregnell notes, 'the essence of the gothic mode is

... the fall from innocence or the bargain with the devil, that is, the Faustian pact,[5] then it is clear to contend that this gothic trait is entrenched in Barker's fiction and films, and remains as a staple feature from *Books of Blood* ('Down, Satan!' and 'Hell's Event') to *The Scarlet Gospels*.[6] Rather than clarify or delimit Barker's unique brand of fiction, for some readers, the term 'gothic' complicates their relationship with his fiction. Many critics and fans wish to align his works within the more patriarchal domains of fantasy and horror fiction, while the gothic, as a site of resistance for generic rigidity, opens Barker's fiction up to more complex, feminine, and queer readings.

Barker himself recognises these infernal traits and thirst for experience in his own writing too, remarking on Marlowe's play *The Tragical History of Doctor Faustus*: 'It is not that the old stories are the *best* stories; rather that the old stories are the *only* stories. There are no new tales, only new ways to tell.'[7] Barker's postmodern reimagining of the old tale retold delights in confounding and resisting firm categorisation, combining motifs of meta-fantasy and exploring dark gothic fissures, frequently prompting a sickening sense of foreboding, and triggering feelings of disgust and corporeal unease. Barker's visions of other worlds are frequently sources of wonder, but to glimpse these places always comes at a price. The temptation to wander into his other worlds is often too strong to resist, and the sights they offer are too wondrous to ignore. His monsters are so closely aligned with our everyday emotional experiences – they are frequently marginalised, isolated, wronged or abandoned, unloved, dejected, which on occasion spills over into vengeance for power to compensate for their abjection. Barker's characters are all about feeling, of attaining emotional understanding – the creatures may often be fantastical, but they are not beyond emotional recognition; they often elicit our empathy despite their monstrous acts or 'othered' state. Barker is, then, a true postmodernist in his deployment of the gothic in new subjective ways – we understand and often empathise with Barker's monsters because they are us; they are all too human and we readily recognise their appetites and desires for new knowledge and experiences. Gary Hoppenstand recognises these traits in Barker also, locating his particular storytelling as 'tales of death and life ... connected to our most distant memories, our darkest fears and our brightest hopes. For Barker ... what is new is actually quite ancient.'[8]

This fusion of the ancient with the modern recalls the very essence of the gothic mode – the resurrection and recycling of styles and aesthetics – 'the ability to blend or fuse the old with the new' – all of which 'discloses the tremendous might behind [Barker's] artistic punch, the efficacy that supports the telling of tales we already know, but haven't heard before.'[9] Jerrold E. Hogle's understanding of the Gothic provides a means through which we can further affirm Barker's own fiction within the mode, despite the critical reluctance with its (perceived) trappings. Many of Barker's stories, films, and novels – *Coldheart Canyon*, *The Hellbound Heart*, and *Lord of Illusions*, among others

– contain these familiar patterns which Hogle defines as an overarching element of the Gothic:

> These hauntings can take many forms, but they frequently assume the features of ghosts, specters [sic], or monsters (mixing features from different realms of being, often life and death) that rise from within the antiquated space, or sometimes invade it from alien realms, to manifest unresolved crimes or conflicts that can no longer be successfully buried from view. It is at this level that Gothic fictions generally play with and oscillate between the earthly laws of conventional reality and the possibilities of the supernatural … often siding with one of these over the other in the end, but usually raising the possibility that the boundaries between these may have been crossed, at least psychologically but also physically or both.[10]

Many of Barker's works situate their frisson between horror and wonder – his gory spectacles may indeed be the product of a decade that experimented with extreme representations of body horror, but his special worlds and monstrous creations clearly originate from the gothic sublime. Together, these combined elements separate Barker's work from his contemporaries and distinguish his own unique literary brand and style. Barker states: 'Horror Fiction tends to be reactionary. It's usually about a return to the status quo – the monster is the outsider who must be banished from the sanctum. But over and over again, I've created monsters who come from the outside and who call out to somebody to join *them* in the sanctum.'[11] As Hogle suggests, the Gothic is frequently about opening forbidden doors to other realms of the imagination – monsters that invade or corrupt the safe spaces of the family, the home, and the rational mind. Barker adopts this approach to encourage the reader to see the extraordinary in the everyday and to empathise with the monsters that lurk within our own skins. True to the gothic form, he often hides the keys, doors, or portals to other worlds in plain sight, but these wonders frequently blur spaces best kept apart, with access to such miracles kept in the hands of a few, usually the everyday misfit or gifted seer whose adventures lead them towards an apocalyptic battle of the soul. Barker's embrace of the monster and the outcast, refuting the reinstatement of normality in favour of wonder, firmly situates his fiction within the folds of the postmodern Gothic. As Judith Halberstam affirms:

> The postmodern monster is no longer the hideous other storming the gates of the human citadel, he has already disrupted the careful geography of the human self and demon other and he makes the peripheral and the marginal part of the center. Monsters within postmodernism are already inside – the house, the body, the head, the skin, the nation – and they work their way out. Accordingly, it is the human, the facade of the normal, that tends to become the place of terror within the postmodern Gothic.[12]

This empathy with the 'other' and the unmasking of the tyranny of the 'normal' is an expected subversion with the postmodern Gothic, with *Cabal* (1988) and

Nightbreed (1990) serving as prime examples in Barker's early work. The diversity of the Nightbreed and their acceptance of Boone (Craig Sheffer) stand in stark contrast to the banal forces of law, order, and unquestioned authority that seek to eradicate any marker of difference. Moreover, his works repeatedly return to fundamental sites of gothic disruption, piercing through the veil of everyday norms (the home, familial bonds, romantic relationships, boredom with bodily and/or sexual experiences, or feelings of meaninglessness), and using expected gothic signifiers to peer beneath the banal veneer of normalcy. For all of its gory excesses, *The Hellbound Heart* (and its film adaptation *Hellraiser* (1987), directed by Barker) is rooted in a forbidden sexual relationship, murder, a home and a marriage transformed by a visceral resurrection in the attic, complete with an encounter with Mephistophelian demons who return to claim their prize. In conjunction with his emphasis on physical horror and pain in many of his most celebrated works wherein he excitedly pores over a fleshy canvas ripe for rearrangement, metamorphosis, or destruction, Barker's stylistics cite core gothic tropes to articulate repeated concerns with sex, corruption, violence, and power. These transformations can be troubling but also visually exquisite and profoundly erotic.[13] In the framing narrative for *Books of Blood*, Barker explicitly uses the canvas of the human body to inscribe the stories of the dead onto living flesh, the eruption of supressed and misrepresented dead voices carving their own tales onto Simon McNeal's living flesh book. The forbidden gothic book is updated and transformed here into a visible text (a provocative invitation for the reader), cut into living human flesh with the words formed by McNeal's congealing blood. This invitation to read these gothic body tales is stark from the outset, gleefully punned in Barker's epigraph: 'Everybody is a book of blood – wherever we're opened, we're red.' We're all ripe for potential transformation. As Gary Hoppenstand notes on this framing story:

> Horror is a mode of communication, a method of symbolically expressing a number of elements associated with mortality. […] Simon McNeal is transformed by the dead into a living textbook of horror stories. McNeal's very body serves as Barker's philosophical touchstone for all of his short fiction (and even his novels); McNeal is a fictive character who literally embodies dark fiction. His tragedy is that he forfeits his identity, mean and self-centred though it may be, for the sake of miracle.[14]

Barker acknowledges and pastiches Ray Bradbury's short story collection *The Illustrated Man* (1951) here by using the opening story as a device through which the remainder of the text is read, deciphered, and framed. 'The Book of Blood' alludes not only to past masters such as Bradbury, but frames the collection of short stories around 1980s contemporary anxieties and concerns by actively inscribing the hidden stories of the dead onto living flesh to express the decade's concerns about hedonism, social disenfranchisement, and political anger. The carved body marked by suppressed voices stands in not only for the ostracised queer body in 1980s Britain made viscerally visible in the body politic, but also reads as a revolutionary statement concerning contested subjectivities, obscene stories, and sexual narratives that refuse to remain hidden. The horror in mocking these suppressed dead voices in the framing narrative is unleashed when McNeal lies about his abilities as a psychic medium and the dead take revenge on his body for such misrepresentation. For Barker, the ignored and the repressed always find a way to seep through the cracks between our world and another that lies just beyond.

Immortality and the infernal

In his 1997–98 six-part television series *Clive Barker's A-Z of Horror*, Barker concluded the final episode with a teasing thought: 'All of us yearn for immortality, for ourselves or a loved one. But, as the sages say, be careful what you wish for – it might come true.'[15] Barker frequently entwines the invocation of the infernal with the desire for immortality, a pact with the damned that confers humanity's deepest wishes, all the while revelling in its nightmarish and often visceral consequences. On occasion, the infernal Faustian pact is not made to experience immortality, but rather to engage in a limit experience beyond human attainment or understanding. In Barker's most celebrated film, *Hellraiser*, adapted to the screen directly from his novella *The Hellbound Heart*, he underscores his fascination with Faust and infernal bargains when the Cenobites return to claim Frank Cotton, who escaped their clutches in Hell. Frank is a jaded sexual hedonist, disappointed by all the fleshy pleasures he has experienced in this world. He calls upon the Cenobites, purveyors of Faustian desired delights summoned by a mysterious Pandora's box, only to be torn apart by hooks and chains in his brutal encounter with the hierophants of Hell. Soon after, Frank, resurrected by droplets of spilled blood (and semen, in the novella), and nurtured by his former mistress Julia, begins to reform his fleshy body through consuming the flesh and blood of innocent victims she ensnares for him. Kirsty – Rory's friend in the novella, and subsequently recast as Larry's daughter and Frank's niece in the film adaptation, to underscore the incestuous nature of Frank's gothic sexual excesses – discovers the visceral horrors in the attic of the house and strikes a deal with the returning Cenobites: she will coerce Frank to reveal himself and the Cenobites will be certain they have reclaimed their escaped prize. It is a common convention for those who enter into Faustian bargains to try to find a way to break the bargain once the infernal magic has worn thin or the coveted prize is revealed as a hollow or duplicitous endeavour. Trickery and deceit are always to be expected in Faustian agreements, and Barker's demons are fully aware of the slippery nature of human desire to escape the promised surrender to the infernal. Near the conclusion of the novella *The Hellbound Heart*, Kirsty, driven by boredom, accidentally unlocks the 'Lemarchand Configuration'.[16] The Cenobites appear to her, explaining that 'The box is a means to break the surface of the real … you did it in ignorance … but there's no help for it … no way to seal the Schism until we take what's ours.'[17] Kirsty protests that they have made a mistake and offers Frank, who had previously escaped their clutches, in her stead. Aware of the duplicitous nature of bargains, the Cenobite reluctantly agrees to her proposition and cautions her they *may* return: 'No tears, please. It's a waste of good suffering … Deliver him alive to us then … and make him confess himself. And maybe we won't tear your soul apart.'[18] Kirsty is (temporarily) exempted from the trappings of this Faustian pact because she does not harbour the dark desires that the Cenobites offer. Cleverly ensuring her own survival, she is able to sidestep entering into a Faustian pact of her own by ensuring the original arrangement with Frank is duly honoured, in order to protect herself from both the Cenobites' sadism and Frank's increasing sexual depravity. She is spared from witnessing Frank's final and brutal annihilation but is made the reluctant keeper of the Lament Configuration as a cautionary reminder of the ordeal.

Due to the success of the film adaptation *Hellraiser* (and the early *Hellraiser* sequels), this is the most known example of Barker's references to the Faustian pact in popular culture. His return to this 'old story' of Marlowe's *Doctor Faustus* is a consistent and rich theme, an enduring human impetus to desire and to experience something beyond our grasp, offering the soul in return for such empty promises and illusions. Unbridled capitalism and commodification are at the root of many of Barker's Faustian works, and are explicitly evident in *Hellraiser*. As Patricia Allmer notes: 'Like the symbolic exchange which inaugurates the narrative, relationships between the characters, in both the novella and film, are also built on the principles of demand and supply. Frank's love affair with his sister-in-law, Julia, whose help he needs to be rescued from the Cenobites, is built on bargaining and possession.'[19] As Allmer highlights, the transactional nature of both the 'Lemarchand Configuration' and the incestuous exchange of women as sexual commodities confirms that these horrors are rooted in concepts of 'rightful' ownership and sexual access to women in a domestic extension of the free market. This is particularly evident in Frank (Sean Chapman) and Larry's (Andrew Robinson) separate sexual claims on Julia (Claire Higgins) as an owned or stolen sexual conquest. Furthermore, Julia's own method to ensnare victims for Frank subtly suggests she is perceived by her chosen male victims as a prostitute – to be bought and sold for temporary pleasures. Larry's sexual claim is legitimised through his marriage to Julia, whereas Frank's sexual proclivities rest upon forbidden eroticism, pain, and pseudo-incestuous lust through his familial bond as Julia's brother-in-law and Larry's sibling – Frank literally defiles Julia as a means to destroy Larry's claim on her; Julia's own sexual awakening with Frank becomes an addiction she actively feeds. At the climax of the film, Frank (wearing Larry's stolen skin) violently discards Julia, only to extend his lewdly incestuous capitalistic gaze further by threatening to sexually consume his own niece, Kirsty. This moment is explicitly made horrific in Frank's signature taunt made perilously real in his horrific drawl, 'Come to Daddy!' Frank's sexual exchanges and appetites hinge upon entrapments and ownership of another's body as commodity within a violated gothic domestic sphere, which Allmer convincingly reads as an extension of gothic enslavement to capitalistic appetites, property inheritance, and broken 'promises and contracts'.[20] Read this way, *Hellraiser* is bound up in hyper-consumerist expression of the Faustian pact in which fetish reduces bodies to that of exchanged goods – a process which continues unabated with the sale of the Lament Configuration again at its conclusion.

Barker's later novels shift their locations to tailor them to specific re-imaginings of Hell. These relocations, from allegory and satire to a literal wasting landscape, include the wonder-house in *The Thief of Always*, the horrors of Hollywood (arguably Hell on Earth) in *Coldheart Canyon*, and Barker's own version of a Judeo-Christian underworld city in *The Scarlet Gospels*. It is interesting to note the varied but consistent theme of the infernal pact within each tale, all ripe with tell-tale gothic signifiers. In *Weaveworld* (1987), for example, its most cruel Faustian bargain hinges upon raw emotional manipulation, traced through grief and isolation. Shadwell, the infernal Mephistophelian salesman, bears a coat which contains a magical, scintillating lining capable of conjuring treasured items from thin air (in the memorable case of Cal's bereaved father, Brendan, Shadwell offers him love-letters from his departed wife); his sales-pitch entrances his victims with these coveted, and often irretrievably lost, items. In *Weaveworld*, the emotional punch of Barker's short invocation of the Faustian bargain is memorable because it hinges upon a universal emotion – the desire to recapture love that has been lost to death.

In 1985, during an interview with Kim Newman on his first novel *The Damnation Game* (1985), Barker famously stated that it is a retelling of *Faust* without Mephistopheles. Barker states, 'Everybody is morally tainted. I wanted to do a covenant with the devil story without a devil.'[21] In the novel, each character grapples with their own form of addiction and moral slippage: Marty Strauss is a thief whose addiction to gambling led to his incarceration for theft; Joseph Whitehead sold his soul for influence and avarice; Carys Whitehead, his daughter, is a seer and heroin addict; Mamoulian, the infernally inflected European stranger who wields the power of immortality, has committed murder to acquire his forbidden knowledge; and Breer, Mamoulian's acolyte, is rendered gothically abject as a cannibalistic, murderous paedophile. Updating the Faustian tryst for the 1980s, Barker presents humanity as enslaved to various insatiable appetites and dark temptations, subjectively appropriated and expressed through the novel's contemporary anxieties about the growing threats of neo-liberalism, drug addiction, and social isolation. Nearing the climax of the novel, Barker declares what we have suspected all along: Hell will be of our own making, and it will be a familiar yet uncanny place:

Hell is reimagined by each generation. Its terrain is surveyed for absurdities and remade in a fresher mould; its terrors are scrutinized and, if necessary, reinvented to suit the current climate of atrocity; its architecture is redesigned to appal the eye of the modern damned. In an earlier age, Pandemonium – the first city of Hell – stood on a larval mountain while lightning tore the clouds above it and beacons burned on its walls to summon the fallen angels. Now, such spectacle belongs to Hollywood. Hell stands transposed. No lightning, no pits of fire.[22]

Marty Strauss is a thief paroled from prison and tasked with protecting his wealthy and reclusive employer Joseph Whitehead from a malevolent threat. This threat is embodied by an infernal conjuror, Mamoulian, whose former alliance with Whitehead has soured, and who now seeks payment on a historical arrangement that has come due. As expected with Faustian bargains, Whitehead seeks to defer their special arrangement indefinitely. To aid Mamoulian on his quest to fulfil the bargain with Whitehead, he enlists the help of Anthony Breer, a librarian who, unbeknownst to himself, has been resurrected by Mamoulian after his suicide. Mamoulian possesses the ability to take or confer life at will. Breer becomes a brawny lackey to inflict pain and horrific destruction at the conjuror's request. Mamoulian's own distaste for the human body and its fleshy appetites is acutely expressed by Barker through Breer's ever-rotting animated corpse. While Mamoulian is too ethereal for the human world, Breer's own body is too fleshy, abjectly expressed by its increasing putridity – his brawn, his abject violence towards humans and animals, and his sexual deviance, all stain his flesh as an accumulation of too much sin. Unaware that he is a walking corpse – Barker refrains from using the word zombie here, but it is an accurate gothic appropriation – Breer, in tragicomedy moments, uses aftershave to mask his pungent decay. Throughout the novel, sickening horrors of the flesh are acutely emphasised, yet Barker's true source of horror in *The Damnation Game* lies in the price of immortality – it is laced with the cruelty of other people, frequent betrayals, and palpable loneliness, which Mamoulian describes: 'Don't you see how terrible it is to live when everything around you perishes?'[23] Inverting expectations further, Mamoulian, rather than inflict death or claim Whitehead's soul, wishes to reclaim Whitehead as an immortal companion, to ease the burden and isolation of their unnatural and prolonged existence as they near the end of their exhausting deferral of death. He continues, 'you start to long … for someone to take pity on you, someone to embrace you and share your terrors. And, at the end, someone to go into the dark with you.'[24] For Mamoulian, immortality has become an overbearing endurance of betrayal as each of his gifted charges have abandoned him, and he can no longer bear the torment of perpetual loneliness. Whitehead and Mamoulian are bound together, by immortality and by their shared history, becoming an explicit Barkerian theme which is later echoed in Barker's film *Lord of Illusions* (1995) between cult-leader Nix (Daniel von Bargen) and the magician Swann (Kevin J. O'Connor). Despite the reuse of this theme of immortality and abandonment elsewhere in Barker's fiction and films, Mamoulian remains Barker's most sympathetic immortal; he fears his own abandonment and the emptiness of dying alone in a poignant manner that is, at times, unbearably human.

Much to Mamoulian's rage, Whitehead used Mamoulian's sacred teachings to attain immortality to feed his own acquisitive appetites and to extend his influence and power rather than reach for loftier or purer goals: 'He cheated me! He squandered all my teachings, all my knowledge, threw it away for greed's sake, for power's sake, for the life of the body. *Appetite*! All gone for appetite. All my precious love wasted.'[25] This waste of adoration on Whitehead exemplifies the corruptive power of Mamoulian's Faustian gift once it is bestowed onto a greedy and ambitious businessman like Whitehead. Whitehead's appetite to succeed at any cost is demonstrative of the growing neo-liberal hold evident in the 1980s through both Margaret Thatcher's profit-driven policies of deregulation and the rise of privatised corporate empires. Figures such as Joseph Whitehead are prone to such temptations due to their unbridled desire to succeed at any cost – it is a trait that Mamoulian recognises in his most gifted opponent during their first and only game of cards: 'Every man is his own Mephistopheles, don't you think?' Mamoulian tells Whitehead. 'If I hadn't come along you'd have made a bargain with some other power.'[26] While the novel does not contain a literal Mephistopheles, there is enough gothic suggestion surrounding Mamoulian's magical capabilities to adapt this Faustian structure into a modern setting without the need to explicitly address the existence of God or the Devil. The underlying truth in Barker's fiction is that we are all open to the seductive charms of power and immortality – we can all act as authors of our own particular damnation. The addictions that fuel *The Damnation Game* – gambling and the seduction of chance, substance abuse, predatory urges, and the desire to know what lies beyond the veil of existence – are explored as an escape from the crushing mundane reality of everyday misery, only to be turned into a veritable prison of their own making (this is quite literally the case for Marty at the outset of the tale). Each character is, in turn, betrayed by their appetite. For Barker, as Hoppenstand notes, 'The path to miracles … is not without its price.'[27] Barker revisits this explicit gothic motif again, for a new, younger audience, in his first children's fable, *The Thief of Always* (1992).

In the 1990s, it was an extremely unusual move for an established author of gothic horror novels to publish any material for a younger audience. This remarkable shift is testament to Barker's ability to predict trends and to effortlessly shift within the publishing world (and its strictly demarcated audiences), while maintaining his own authorial vision. *The Thief of Always* hinges upon his now established thematic style of insatiable appetites, stolen time, and immortality. Young Harvey Swick is whisked away by the smiling tempter Rictus to Mr Hood's Holiday House, a hidden house of endless delights. To tempt Harvey to visit the house, Rictus describes it as a place of wonders, a space only bound by a child's imagination and desire. Foreshadowing the true nature of the house and its malevolent magic,[28] Rictus is shrouded in gothic suggestion with traces of a grooming child predator:

> 'I know a place where the days are always sunny,' [Rictus] said, 'and the nights are full of wonders.' 'Could you take me there?' … Harvey started to ask him if he'd be coming back soon, but stopped himself in the nick of time. '*No questions, boy!*' Rictus said, and as he spoke the wind seemed to fill up his coat. It rose around him like a black balloon, and he was suddenly swept out over the windowsill. '*Questions rot the mind!*' he called back as he went. '*Keep your mouth shut and we'll see what comes your way!*'[29]

Rictus' black ballooning coat and effortless flight immediately recall the familiar image of the vampire – a gluttonous metaphor which aptly defines Harvey's experience of Mr Hood's magic and malevolence. At Mr Hood's House, Harvey enjoys days of abundance and childhood indulgence, complete with an excessive assortment of comfort foods and endless gifts and toys. The house seems alive to Harvey, and initially it accommodates his every wish. Each day in the house, described by his fellow housemate Wendell as 'the House of Always',[30] is an experience of gothic time, seen through sped up and changing seasonal weather – crisp spring mornings, hot summer afternoons, autumnal Halloween evenings (with bonfires), and snowy Christmas nights. Barker frequently likes to play with gothic time in his other novels too: in the *Abarat* series, each of twenty-five archipelago islands in this world represent each hour of the day, with the mysterious 25th island of Odum's Spire at its centre. Time is magically fractured across the whole world of the Abarat islands, and can be navigated freely, enabling a geographical mapping of time travel. Conversely, gothic time is contracted and distilled in the Hood House where a year passes by in a single day, and the true horror of this time lapse goes largely unquestioned by the resident children. Again, emphasising the Faustian theme, Mrs Griffin, Hood's kindly housekeeper, reminds Harvey of the supernatural ability Mr Hood has in meeting his every whim and desire: 'Mr. Hood knows every dream in your head.'[31] Soon after his arrival at the house, Harvey questions the rules that govern the house's magical wonders and the true nature of the elusive Mr Hood. He realises that the house seems wholly uncanny and alive, that it is a 'haunted place… [and] [w]hoever, or whatever, the haunter was, Harvey could not be content now until he'd seen its face and knew its nature.'[32] It soon becomes apparent to Harvey, Wendell, and Lulu that the house uses tricks to deceive them, holding them hostage and feeding on their youthful souls to fuel its deceptive magic while nourishing its elusive, immortal owner.

The novella repeatedly uses the motif of nourishment and hunger to explore the children's associations with home and warmth and, in sharp contrast, the dangers of excessive consumption when Mr Hood's home imprisons them with the illusion of inconsequential abundance. Questions are hushed up with extra slices of desserts and pies, and cherished presents lost long ago are conjured up to distract Harvey from his increasing desire to return home. It is only when Harvey and Wendell eventually escape the house that the true cost of such gothic excesses and wonders are fully realised. Wendell reveals his horror to Harvey after he returns home to find that his mother is now divorced, 'so old … and fat as a house'.[33] Wendell's mother has evidently overeaten in an attempt to soothe her grief after losing her missing son. Both Wendell and Harvey agree that Mr Hood has a particular taste for children's souls, and deduce that, had they not escaped into the real world to see how time had been stolen from them, Mr Hood would have devoured them whole: 'it almost had us. It almost ate us alive … it's got a taste for us.'[34] The gothic monster that Harvey repeatedly associates Mr Hood with is a vampire – a creature that drains others for its own survival and immortality, and whose appetite is unquenchable. For Harvey, the illusion of false nourishment is laid bare when he confronts Jive, one of the cruel and watchful creatures in the house, who offers Harvey a slice of golden apple pie and ice cream to suppress his anger at Mr Hood upon his return to the Holiday House. Harvey's rejection of this bribe emphasises his maturation and his ability to expose the greedy illusions for what they truly are: 'it's all dust. … Dirt, dust and ashes! All the food. All the presents. Everything!'[35] In typical Barkerian fashion, once the truth about the house's illusions has been revealed to Jive, reminding him what he too is made of, he begins to disintegrate, choking and spewing 'dry streams of dust that ran from his gullet and poured over his fingers. It was like a fatal message, being passed from part of his body to another.'[36] The revelation that the dream house is made from nothing more than dirt and ash, the illusion of solidity and assurance which now melts into air, clearly signals the cycle of maturation towards adulthood for Harvey; he begins to understand the true peril of appetite without thought or consequence (the emptiness of Faustian acquisitiveness), which has led him into the clutches of the monster, Mr Hood.

In his final showdown with Mr Hood, Harvey confronts the monster who exists in the very structure of the Holiday House, and demands that the 'King Vampire' returns the lost time he stole from the children. Mr Hood regards Harvey as his most prized acquisition in the house and refuses to relinquish the stolen years from the children: 'You burn bright, Harvey Swick … I've never known a soul that burned as bright as yours.'[37] Harvey is repeatedly promised that he will achieve immortality if he remains in the house forever as Mr Hood's apprentice – he will, like Mr Hood, become a vampire of sorts, fixed in this permanent gothic time, and made to feed off the souls of new children tempted into the house, repeating this cycle of consumption to maintain immortality. In his desperate final attempt to save his friends, to regain his stolen time from the thief, and to save his own soul, Harvey tricks Mr Hood by having him exert his magic by demanding increasingly impossible wonders;

he demands more food, elaborate toys, and zoo animals, and the four seasons raging all at once, playing upon Mr Hood's magical hubris. The house eventually collapses under the toll of Harvey's demands for these increasingly taxing magical illusions, and the souls of previously captive children are set free once Mr Hood is vanquished. The emptiness of appetite – of childish illusions, endless desires, and want for material possessions at the expense of the priceless love and precious and fleeting time spent with family – is repeatedly emphasised by Barker to underscore the horrors of the Faustian pact for a new audience of younger readers.

Barker returns to this theme again for his adult readers by situating his Hollywood Faustian tale in another magical house in an echo of his children's fable. Moreover, this magical house is filled not just with wonders and illusions, peering beneath the vulgar veneer of Hollywood glamour by exposing its visceral nightmares, but is set in a literary reimagining of Barker's own home. *Coldheart Canyon*, Barker's *roman-à-clef* and self-proclaimed 'Hollywood gothic novel',[38] examines the emptiness and gothic heritage of the glamour of Hollywood, and the horrific lengths people endure to experience fame, all of which stands in for the novel's overarching Faustian temptation and infernal practices. For Barker, Hollywood history is a ripe source for perversity, insecurity, and the desire for immortality, filtered through the power of scopophilia and lurid sexuality. This is Barker's most realistic and recognisable depiction of Hell on Earth, a space rife with greed and corruption, tinged here with elements of magical realism. The Hollywood cast is driven by fear and the allure of immortality – 'Fear of living, fear of dying. Fear of staying, fear of going, Fear of remembering, and yes, fear of forgetting',[39] with the source of power and celebrity filtered through the desire to look, and to be looked at. The tale begins with an enchanted room in Romania, where a hunt scene is captured on an enormous mosaic that seemingly ripples and shimmers, as though it is coming to life. Willem Zeffer, assistant to silent-film starlet Katya Lupi, is enchanted with the room and insists on purchasing the mesmerising artwork, relocating it to Hollywood for the starlet's perverse viewing pleasure. The room is not all that it seems: in its detailed tile work, it captures the scene of an everlasting hunt with cursed huntsmen chasing after a goat-child, later revealed to be the favourite son of Lucifer. The tiled world includes a variety of scenes of sexual perversities, including rape, bestiality, and torture, abominations that drive those who gaze upon the excessive spectacle mad with lust and visual addiction. Though it is never fully explained, the tiled room possesses an infernal quality that derives its power from being seen or witnessed. It is also a contradictory gothic space: 'Though we are in the bowels of Hell, we shall have the eyes of Angels'[40] is inscribed upon its threshold, corrupting and deceiving those who gaze upon its ornate tiles as it transforms into another lush and pornographic world. The space magically shifts into a gothic pastoral scene before the eyes of those who witness the mosaic, monikered 'The Devil's Country', as the hunt comes alive and continues unabated, an antinomy suspended in a frozen moment in time. Time is doubly paradoxical in the enchanted room – it is rendered frozen by artistically creating the world on the tiles, yet it moves and scintillates, brought to vivid life once it is experienced by a spectator. Once inside this magical scene, there is yet another visible layer of gothic time within the mosaic itself – time becomes dislocated, warped, and arrested, rendered in an uncanny and inescapable frozen present visually represented by the suspended eclipsed sun in the sky. This fixed celestial event signals that time in the mosaic is an arrested endless loop, magically perpetuated for centuries; it is only when the cursed huntsman Goga catches Qwaftzefoni, the devil's goat child, and returns him to Lilith, the Devil's wife, that the infernal spell in the room will be lifted, and time and the stars can resume their heavenly course.

The narrative core of *Coldheart Canyon* is primarily concerned with modern preoccupations with celebrity culture and Hollywood icons. Aside from Barker's fantastical world housed in the basement of Katya Lupi's Hollywood mansion, the novel explores the familiar conceits and demands of Hollywood culture and its capacity for wretchedness and hubris. Barker reveals an overt disdain for the Hollywood elite, here comprising of caustic agents, vile studio power-players, and self-centred film stars; Hollywood is clearly its own Faustian bargain of false promises and unending deceit, with liars and flatterers at every wretched turn.

Hollywood star Todd Pickett undergoes a botched plastic surgery procedure to erase signs of ageing to continue his successful film career unabated. Rendered temporarily grotesque while healing from the horrific procedure, Todd's self-loathing fuels his desire to be hidden away from the press; he is soon relocated to an unknown Hollywood home off the beaten track – bitterly monikered Coldheart Canyon by its ghostly inhabitants – the former home of Katya Lupi. Encountering the seemingly immortal Katya, and the monstrosities secreted away in the canyon, including the sadistic sexual appetites of dead Hollywood stars – Rudolph Valentino, Jean Harlow, and Victor Mature among them – that now haunt the grounds and breed perverse creatures with its exotic animals, Todd is seduced by the infernal forces that flatter his (regained) beauty and partakes in many of the Canyon's perversities. The creatures showcased are typically abject Barker hybrids for those familiar with some of his erotic art – the most ghastly of which in the Canyon is a peacock with an exaggerated human phallus which delights in raping those who cross its path. Barker's creatures are demonstrative of the sexual depravity of the ghostly stars in the haunted canyon and the sexual perversity to which they stoop – some bred with animals, and produced monstrous offspring. The ghosts all remain enslaved by their devotion to Katya's infernal room and desire its restorative, infernal magic. Throughout the novel, it is increasingly emphasised that Todd's own vanity will cost him his soul, as his encounters with Katya and the infernal hunt erase his facial mutilations and tantalise his increasingly voyeuristic sexual curiosities.

In contrast to the Hollywood ideal of sleek bodies and sexual promiscuity, but also enslaved to the voyeurism which saturates celebrity culture, Barker reverses expectations by filtering much of the tale through the subjectivity of a benign but resourceful fan. Tammy, head of Todd's devoted fan club is heavily contrasted and othered against Hollywood's impossible standards of femininity; Barker introduces his heroine as a homespun, overweight, and intelligent woman, a literal embodiment of real values beyond illusory Hollywood excess. Tammy's ability to know and value life beyond celebrity status enables her to wield the power to break the infernal Faustian spell, to reject the tempting mirage of Hollywood dreams. In one of the more positive representations of fandom in literature, Barker situates Tammy as a sane and familiar counterpoint to Hollywood toxicity which the novel explicitly satirises.

Filtered through fandom and fame, voyeurism and Faustian magic, the mirage of immortality and the power of the gaze dominate every aspect of *Coldheart Canyon*'s narrative. The cost of gaining access to this infernal erotic display is the addiction it springs within the viewer. Desperate to relive and experience the power of the hunt because of the forbidden and erotic displays it yields, and thus triggering a compulsive pornographic desire to explore it again and again – a hunger to keep looking at any cost – the infernal room binds and addicts anyone exposed to its magic. Victims of their own addiction, reduced to despair once the spectacle in the room is undone, the ghosts of the dead emit '[s]laughterhouse shrieks and plague-pit moans, chattering and curses that were more the din out of a padded cell than anything that should have come from an assembly of once-sophisticated souls'.[41] It is the limit experience of perverse immortality that drives Katya (the novel's coded Mephistopheles), the ghostly Hollywood stars, and Todd towards the room's vivid mosaic. In this respect, the novel returns to the dread of ageing as felt by Wendell at his mother's wizened appearance when he escapes from the Holiday House in *The Thief of Always*. For Harvey, the horror lies in the revelation that time is so easily stolen from him through Mr Hood's tricks in the house, whereas in *Coldheart Canyon*, the youth of Katya Lupi is a Faustian suspension of time – 'that room was the reason she stayed young'[42] – and founded entirely on the endurance of illusion and the refusal to bring Goga's hunt to an end in the infernal mosaic. Mr Hood's greed is expressed through the abundance of material possessions and luscious foods in the house to ensnare the children, while *Coldheart Canyon* relies on the adult fear of ageing and Hollywood's rejection of physical imperfection, and the drastic mutilations undertaken to remain eternally young.

Once the magical spell is spent, time must resume its natural course. It is only when Tammy loses her star-struck adoration for Todd, and rejects the hollow culture of Hollywood, that she can both actively resist the trickery that has imprisoned them and bring about the room's destruction by solving the conundrum of the infernal hunt. It is said that no man could end the hunt – '*how*

could any man catch the devil's child?'[43] Yet, as evidenced in Barker's other
gothic fantasies, it is the power attributed to strong women that solves this
core riddle. Barker may well enjoy the erotic and queer exploration of male
fantasy in his novels, but unlike many of his contemporaries, he also frequently
populates his worlds with strong female characters. Tammy's inclusion is
profound, as she represents female desires and class dynamics which are, too
often, easily dismissed. She is besotted with the *image* of Todd Pickett as the
perfect movie star, and erotically motivated by his status and looks, but, over
the course of the Canyon's supernatural and gothic events, the mirage of fandom
and Hollywood as a dream factory is irreparably punctured. It is her ability to
retain a sense of self-worth and assurance in the face of Barker's haunted
Hollywood space that explicitly elevates her above the shallowness of contemporary popular culture. In the infernal room, Tammy, in an overt sexual display,
traps the lusty goat-child Qwaftzefoni by revealing her ample breasts to him
to retain his scopophilic/pornographic stare, enabling Goga and the huntsmen
to complete their infernal charge. The scopophilic drive in all of us (on which
the industry rests) to adore the rich and famous, to desire the forbidden, and
to surrender to lusty spectacles and illusions, is central to understanding Barker's
interpretation of Hollywood's gothic excesses, for it is all a prison made from
our own desires. Beauty, and its scopophilic addiction, demands to be looked
at, to seduce and corrupt the voyeur; it is not only the novel's scintillating core
idea and Faustian trick, but it also provides the key to its (re)solution by
reverting the mesmeric gaze back onto the illusion – enticing the infernal child
to gaze upon the voyeur. Barker understands the imprisoning and perverse
nature of our Faustian enslavement to voyeurism and seductive and illusory
attainment of immortality.

The banality of immortality

The most recent of Barker's novels, *The Scarlet Gospels*, continues in this vein of
voyeurism and witnessing miracles beyond the call of human understanding.
The access to such miracles always incurs a debt, and taints those who achieve
such wonders. By bringing demons and the devil into focus for this much
anticipated novel, Barker's band of misfits and seers grapple with his most
infamous creation, Pinhead. Returning to Pinhead's tale as Barker envisioned, this
novel reclaims the character from his screen afterlife of sequels and diminishing
returns (by other artists), as it moved further and further from Barker's vision
and source novella. In the same vein as *Coldheart Canyon* and *The Thief of
Always*, *The Scarlet Gospels* is laced with profound gothic excess, rendered here
through extreme violence and communing with the dead, and a literal descent
into a Judeo-Christian version of Hell. The novel opens with the Cenobite
Pinhead murdering the most powerful magicians on Earth, in his attempt to

steal and use their dangerous magic to fulfil his quest to reign over Hell. The
novel graphically details the physical destruction of these powerful sorcerers
by Pinhead's rusty chains and newly acquired black magic; seeking out their
amulets, grimoires, and talismans, the sum of their pooled gothic knowledge
secreted away in sacred manuscripts, Pinhead returns to Earth to claim all of
their magical power for himself as he vows to dethrone his infernal majesty.
Harry D'Amour, Barker's neo-noir styled private eye, is drawn into the tale in
true noir fashion when he chances upon one of the Lament Configurations (also
described as Lemarchand's boxes or Configurations in its preceding novella,
The Hellbound Heart), secreted away in a dead client's house, evidencing the
client's familiarity with the Cenobites and their perverse and fleshy pleasures.
D'Amour knows the powers and horrors these boxes wield to glimpse their
wonders: 'To solve the puzzle box was to open a door to Hell, or so the stories
said. The fact that most of the people who solved the puzzles were innocents
who'd chanced upon them was apparently a matter of indifference to Hell
and its infernal agents. A soul, it would seem, was a soul.'[44] Norma, Harry's
friend and blind psychic seer, is kidnapped by Pinhead as he descends into
Hell to claim Lucifer's empty throne for himself, luring Harry into the demon
underworld to rescue her. This is, of course, all part of Pinhead's plan: much
like 'The Devil's Country' mosaic in *Coldheart Canyon*, Pinhead's own ascen-
sion to power must be witnessed. Ordered by Pinhead to write the gospels
of his coming infernal triumph, Harry, refusing this blackmail, is nonetheless
eventually forced to endure the Cenobite's final confrontation with Lucifer.
As the Cenobite explains, 'I have chosen you, Harry D'Amour … [b]ecause
Hell made you its business. Or you have made Hell yours. Perhaps both. …
You won't simply witness what is going to unfold in Hell from this point
onward; you will make a testament of it, wherein my acts and philosophies will
be recounted.'[45]

This tale largely abandons the structure of earlier Faustian pacts, where the
desire to know such forbidden pleasures is crucial. Pinhead's own pretext is odd
as it violates the expected call on the Cenobites via the Lament Configuration
and the subsequent Faustian bargain; horrified at Pinhead's unsummoned arrival
on Earth, Harry confirms the violation: 'Nobody touched your goddamned
box … you shouldn't be here!'[46] Access to this doorway between Hell and
Earth is neither fetishised nor earned in this novel – it simply appears. Shifting
from his more familiar guise in *The Hellbound Heart* and *Hellraiser*, Pinhead
is now unbound by the rules that previously governed the doorways between
this world and Hell itself: 'I no longer have need for the box and its games …
I have begun my sublime labor [sic].'[47] Perhaps this tale is best understood,
then, as one which seeks to cast off the shackles of Pinhead's debt to the
Faustian tale. The novel in many ways undermines its own Faustian narrative
framework by simply blackmailing Harry D'Amour to descend into the demon
world in pursuit of Norma. D'Amour does not harbour the desire to see or

experience Hell; when made to bear witness to the Cenobite's final battle with Lucifer, such refusals to see do not spare him as he is blinded by the ordeal – he survives but has simply witnessed too many horrors for human eyes to bear – a bitter irony that witnessing the impossible robs Harry of his ability to uncover forbidden and secret knowledge again as a private detective. For Barker's protagonists, including D'Amour, bearing witness to (let alone possessing) forbidden magic is a dangerous and often punitive endeavour, as it was for Faust.

The exploration of Hell in the novel is detailed in a quasi-filmic manner, filled with destroyed landscapes and ruined cities (echoing Barker's earlier descriptions of war-torn Warsaw as Hell on Earth which opens *The Damnation Game*); Barker describes a confusing landscape, with geographical and architectural impossibilities and contradictions (architecturally paradoxical cathedrals and Babel-esque towers built in Lucifer's honour) that drive those who witness it close to madness. This was Barker's initial intention when he began crafting his own version of the underworld:

> Before starting *The Scarlet Gospels*, I went and looked at every book about Hell I could find, to see if there was anything that had anything close to what I wanted. The closest that I got was actually pictures of war-torn cities, cities after destruction by gunfire, heavy duty artillery … The stuff in [*The*] *Scarlet Gospels* is neither Miltonic nor Dante-esque, nor is it Hellraiserian. The Hell I'm creating for that book, I just want it to be real. I want it to have no clear sense of dominions and principalities, no clear sense of order … What would you see of treasures, and pain, and glorious things and inglorious things? Shit and Michelangelo.[48]

For all of its landscapes and demons, Hell in this novel is not its most interesting feature; save for Lucifer's magnificent throne of death – a symmetrical display of seventeen blades forming a gruesome halo, all precisely piercing the fallen angel's youthful body and pinning him to the marble throne – Barker's Hell is largely a bland and vast world. The central conceit for Pinhead's desire for power, and Lucifer's own attempted suicide is rooted in the great Barkerian tradition of trying to escape boredom. The banality of immortality, recalling Mamoulian's cursed isolation in *The Damnation Game*, is a shared sentiment with Lucifer's attempt to find solace in death: 'Lucifer's death sentence was life everlasting. He was beyond death. He found a means to trick his way past immortality.'[49] Lucifer's suspended animation is as close to death as his vengeful God would permit, or that the fallen angel could hope to achieve. His suspended state has led to a political stalemate in Hell which Pinhead intends to usurp. This vacuum of power in the pits of Hell piques Pinhead's insatiable overreach, tempting him to assume the powers of darkness for himself. Pinhead resurrects Lucifer by removing the array of swords which impale him to his gruesome throne, to claim its power. This is a truly Barkerian display of beauty and destruction, visually suggesting at least partial pop culture influence from the Iron Throne and the Rider Waite Tarot's ten of swords.[50] Immortality for Lucifer has become a banal and weary state, the antithesis of imagination, a grinding and cursed existence, which neither pact nor temptation can assuage. *The Scarlet Gospels* concludes with Hell being destroyed during the battle for power between Lucifer and the Cenobite, climaxing with the ultimate humiliation when Lucifer plucks out numerous nails from Pinhead's bejewelled and decorated head. This abject humiliation in the battle for Hell proves to be an empty gesture of hubris and, more tellingly, a reassertion of authorial control by Barker. By destroying Pinhead, Barker can enforce his own desired ending to his most infamous and Mephistophelian tormentor. Barker modifies Pinhead's character (the Cenobite sexually violates and murders Norma for spite, which is quite contrary to his more impartial demeanour in *The Hellbound Heart*), reducing the grandeur of the Cenobite to that of simply another nasty demon. However, the novel's gothic coda of releasing Lucifer from the underworld resists narrative closure and hints at an unexpected conclusion; rather than to assume or merely contain the infernal forces of Hell, Pinhead's failed provocation has instilled in Lucifer the temptation to rediscover the world again. This transgression opens up a new gothic prospect by unleashing evil back onto the world, creating a schism that cannot be undone. As ever, Barker is on the side of the most interesting violators of the everyday world.

Barker's greatest fear in his tales, and the drive to meddle with forces beyond our world, is the threat of boredom; as Hoppenstand keenly observes: 'Exiting banality is what Clive Barker is all about.'[51] The overarching nexus between these tales returns us to the fall of Faust, who wished to behold that which lay beyond human grasp or understanding. The thematic dread of ennui continually tempts his characters to pursue or follow the path towards miracles. In *The Hellbound Heart*, Frank discovers and uses the Lament Configuration to heighten his sexual limit experiences, to relieve his boredom with his excesses; so too does Kirsty solve the 'Lemarchand Configuration' to relieve her boredom, accidentally summoning the Cenobites in the process. Harvey Swick is tempted away from home by the charming miscreant Rictus, who tempts him with the promise of sunny days and seemingly inconsequential unending fun, which overpowers Harvey's better judgement during the dark days of a miserable grey February. *Coldheart Canyon*'s Katya Lupi acquires her infernal room 'The Devil's Country' as a means to consume its magic and becomes increasingly addicted to its infernal spectacle, contaminating all that witness its scopophilic erotic horrors. On the side of the devils, ennui is equally threatening: for Pinhead, too many Faustian delights seem to have jaded the Cenobite's appetite – his desire for power relieves the banality of his prolonged existence and, by hubris, ends the reign of the Cenobites. As if by cruel irony, Lucifer's own elaborate attempted suicide, to suspend his immortal life in a death-like slumber, is to escape the tedious punishment of eternal life in the bowels of Hell. Immortality, then, for Barker, is a terrible fate – it generates intolerable suffering, is frequently wished for but nearly always comes at an unbearable price – as those who seek the thrill of the forbidden, fail to value the experiences and gifts they wield, always wanting more.

Barker's texts continuously invoke gothic templates and Faustian exchanges, reliant upon this signature motif which has strangely been overlooked in his fiction beyond *The Hellbound Heart*. From stealing souls, revealing doorways to other worlds, monsters, infernal arrangements with the devil and his acolytes, to the warping of time itself, fundamentally, it is Barker's use of old stories, what he claims are *the best stories*, like Faust, which distinguishes his original, yet familiar tales. These gothic tales retell variations of the Faustian bargain and rely upon familiarity and universal recognition – a loose design beyond Marlowe or Goethe is enough: 'The threads can always be traced back to some earlier tale, and to the tales that precede that [...] for each age will want the tale told as if it were of its own making ... [and] hidden amongst them is a filigree which will with time become a world.'[52] Clive Barker's gothic filigree has always been hidden in plain sight.

Notes

1 Clive Barker, *Weaveworld* (10th Anniversary edition) (London: HarperCollins, 1997), p. 5.

2 Christopher Marlowe, 'Doctor Faustus – A text,' [1592] in David Bevington and Eric Rasmussen (eds), *Doctor Faustus and Other Plays* (Oxford: Oxford University Press, 1995), p. 183.

3 A Barkerian warning issued by Pinhead (Doug Bradley) at the climax of *Hellraiser: Deader*. Dir. Rick Bota, 2005.

4 Eric Hadley Denton, 'Johann Wolfgang von Goethe,' in Marie Mulvery Roberts (ed.), *The Handbook to Gothic Literature* (New York: New York University Press, 1998), p. 70.

5 Heidi Stregnell, *Dissecting Stephen King: From the Gothic to Literary Naturalism* (Madison: University of Wisconsin Press, 2006), p. 9.

6 Earlier works infused with infernal reference include Barker's play *The History of the Devil* (The Dog Company, 1980).

7 Clive Barker, 'Christopher Marlowe's *The Tragical History of Doctor Faustus,*' in Stephen Jones (ed.), *Clive Barker's Shadows in Eden* (Lancaster, PA: Underwood Miller, 1991), p. 111. Italics in original.

8 Gary Hoppenstand, *Clive Barker's Short Stories: Imagination as Metaphor in the* Books of Blood *and Other Works* (Jefferson, NC: McFarland, 1994), p. 16.

9 *Ibid.* p. 16.

10 Jerrold E. Hogle, 'Introduction: The Gothic in Western Culture,' in Jerold E. Hogle (ed.), *The Cambridge Companion to Gothic Fiction* (Cambridge: Cambridge University Press, 2002), pp. 2–3.

11 Barker quoted by Gregg Kilday, 'Out in America: Film: Clive Barker Raises Hell,' *Out* (March 1995) p. 14, in Harry M. Benshoff, *Monsters in the Closet: Homosexuality*

and the Horror Film (Manchester: Manchester University Press, 1997), p. 262. Italics in original.

12 Judith Halberstam, *Skin Shows: Gothic Horror and the Technology of Monsters* (London: Duke University Press, 1995), p. 162.

13 For more on this, see Brigid Cherry's chapter in this book, which analyses fan responses to Barker's monsters and villains.

14 Hoppenstand, *Clive Barker's Short Stories*, p. 17.

15 Clive Barker, 'F for Final Frame', *Clive Barker's A-Z of Horror* – Part 6, BBC Two, Air date: 3 January 1998.

16 In the *Hellraiser* universe, there are several boxes. The maker of singing birds and toys, Philip Lemarchand created several puzzle boxes, the most famous and prominent of which is the Lament Configuration, which summons demons. In the novella, *The Hellbound Heart*, Barker describes it as the Lemarchand Box (p. 4), but with the prominence of the film series and the expansion of its narrative universe, the Lament Configuration is the generally accepted name for the box which opens infernal doorways and summons demons. In the films, the Lament Configuration can change into elaborate shapes and is decorated with brass and intriguing symbols, whereas the box in the novella is a very subtly marked black lacquer box.

17 Clive Barker, *The Hellbound Heart* [1986] (London: Harper Collins, 1991), p. 106. Capitalisation as in original.

18 *Ibid.* pp. 107–8.

19 Patricia Allmer, '"Breaking the Surface of the Real": The Discourses of Commodity Capitalism in Clive Barker's *Hellraiser* Narratives', in Maria Holmgren Troy and Elisabeth Wennö (eds), *Space, Haunting, Discourse* (Newcastle: Cambridge Scholars Publishing, 2008), p. 16.

20 *Ibid.* p. 17.

21 Kim Newman, 'Clive Barker', *Interzone*, No. 14, Winter 1985/86. Online at: www.clivebarker.info/damnatbarker.html. Date accessed: 9 January 2016.

22 Clive Barker, *The Damnation Game* [1985] (London: Warner, 1997), p. 455.

23 *Ibid.* p. 433.

24 *Ibid.*

25 *Ibid.* p. 434. Italic in original.

26 *Ibid.* p. 485.

27 Hoppenstand, *Clive Barker's Short Stories*, p. 8.

28 I read this exchange as an echo of a similar deception to in the 1940 Walt Disney animated film *Pinocchio*, when 'Honest' John leads Pinocchio away to become an actor instead of going to school.

29 Clive Barker, *The Thief of Always* [1992] (London: Harper Collins, 1996), p. 9. Italics in original.

30 *Ibid.* p. 54.

31 *Ibid.* p. 63.

32 *Ibid.* p. 71.

33 *Ibid.* p. 132. Italic in original.

34 *Ibid.*

35 *Ibid.* p. 164.

36 *Ibid.* p. 165.

37 *Ibid.* pp. 174–5.

38 James Bohling, 'Dreaming of a Nightmare,' *Frontiers*, 27 October 2000, *Revelations: The Official Clive Barker Website*. www.clivebarker.info/coldheartbarker.html. Date accessed: 10 January 2016.

39 Clive Barker, *Coldheart Canyon* (London: Harper Collins, 2001), p. 245.

40 *Ibid.* p. 33.

41 *Ibid.* p. 602.

42 *Ibid.* p. 583.

43 *Ibid.* p. 582. Italics in original.

44 Clive Barker, *The Scarlet Gospels* (London: Macmillan, 2015), pp. 62–3.

45 *Ibid.* p. 159.

46 *Ibid.*

47 *Ibid.*

48 Evan J. Peterson, 'The Company of Monsters: An Interview with Clive Barker,' *The Southeast Review*, Volume 26:2, 2008, *Revelations: The Official Clive Barker Website*. www.clivebarker.info/scarletbarker.html. Date accessed: 9 January 2016.

49 Barker, *The Scarlet Gospels*, p. 255.

50 Barker spent many years producing drafts of *The Scarlet Gospels*, so it is difficult to pinpoint precisely when he devised Lucifer's piercing throne. It does feature echoes in popular culture that are worthy of note: The iron throne in the HBO series *Game of Thrones* (2011–) matches elements of Lucifer's piercing throne with its dazzling array of blades; however, the iron throne itself does not pierce the flesh of its occupant (and according to author George R.R Martin, the throne in his novels is much grander than that depicted in the popular television series). The art of the Rider Waite Tarot's ten of swords displays a pierced prone body punctured with ten erect swords, usually signifying absolute defeat in tarot interpretation; another image it recalls is the pierced body of Saint Sebastian. The combination of these influences (intended or not) inform elements of description for Lucifer's majestic throne.

51 Hoppenstand, *Clive Barker's Short Stories*, p. 8.

52 Barker, *Weaveworld*, p. 5.

Bibliography

Aldana Reyes, Xavier. *Body Gothic: Corporeal Transgression in Contemporary Literature and Horror Film*. Cardiff: University of Wales Press, 2014.

Aldana Reyes, Xavier. 'Fear, Divided: Terror and Horror – The Two Sides of the Gothic Coin.' *Emagazine*, 68 (2015), pp. 49–52.

Aldiss, Brian. *Frankenstein Unbound*. Thirsk: House of Stratus, 1975.

Allmer, Patricia. '"Breaking the Surface of the Real": The Discourses of Commodity in Clive Barker's *Hellraiser* Narratives.' *Space, Haunting, Discourse*. Eds. Maria Holmgren Troy and Elisabeth Wennö. Newcastle: Cambridge Scholars Publishing, 2008, pp. 14–24.

Ancuta, Katarzyna. 'Pain into Pleasure or the Horror of Creation: Notes on Reading Clive Barker's *The Great and Secret Show*.' *(Aesth)etics of Interpretation: Essays in Cultural Practice*, Eds. Wojcicch Kalaga and Tadeusz Rachwał. Katowice, Poland: Wydawnictwo Uniwersytetu Śląskiego, 2000, pp. 159–70.

Anderson, Tonya. 'Still Kissing Their Posters Goodnight: Female Fandom and Politics of Popular Music.' *Participations: Journal of Audience and Reception Studies*. Vol. 9:2 (2012), pp. 239–64.

Artaud, Antonin. *The Theatre and its Double*. Trans. Victor Corti, Montreuil, London and New York: Calder, 1993.

Artaud, Antonin. 'No More Masterpieces,' Trans. Victor Corti, Montreuil, London and New York: Calder, 1993, pp. 56–63.

Artaud, Antonin. 'Theatre and the Plague,' *The Theatre and its Double*. Trans. Victor Corti, Montreuil, London and New York: Calder, 1993, pp. 7–22.

Babouris, Bill. 'Addicted to Creativity.' *Samhain*, Issue 70 (November 1998).

Badley, Linda. *Writing Horror and the Body: The Fiction of Stephen King, Clive Barker, and Anne Rice*. Westport, CT: Greenwood Press, 1996.

Baker, Houston A. Jr. *Blues, Ideology, and Afro-American Literature: A Vernacular Theory*. Chicago: University of Chicago Press, 1991.

Baker, Houston A. Jr. *Workings of the Spirit: The Poetics of Afro-American Women's Writing*. Chicago: University of Chicago Press, 1984.

Balides, Constance. 'Jurassic Post-Fordism: Tall Tales of Economics in the Theme Park.' *Screen*. Vol. 41:2 (2000), pp. 139–60.

Bamford, Paul. 'Clive Barker.' *Contemporary North American Film Directors: A Wallflower Critical Guide*. Eds. Yoram Allon, Del Cullen, and Hannah Patterson. London and New York: Wallflower Press, 2002, pp. 37–8.

Barbieri, Suzanne J. *Clive Barker: Mythmaker for the Millennium*. Stockport: British Fantasy Society, 1994.

Barker, Clive. *Abarat*. New York: HarperCollins, 2002.

Barker, Clive. *Abarat: Absolute Midnight*. New York, HarperCollins, 2011.

Barker, Clive. *Abarat: Days of Magic, Nights of War*. New York: HarperCollins, 2004.

Barker, Clive. *Cabal*. London: Fontana, 1988.

Barker, Clive. *Clive Barker's Books of Blood, Omnibus Edition*, Volumes 1–3. London: Sphere, 1988; and London: Warner, 1998.

Barker, Clive. *Clive Barker's Books of Blood, Omnibus Edition*, Volumes 4–6. London: Sphere, 1988; and London: Warner 1998.

Barker, Clive. *Coldheart Canyon*. London: HarperCollins, 2001.

Barker, Clive. 'Christopher Marlowe's *The Tragical History of Doctor Faustus*.' *Clive Barker's Shadows in Eden*. Ed. Stephen Jones. Lancaster, PA: Underwood Miller, 1991, pp. 111–14.

Barker, Clive. *The Damnation Game*. London: Sphere, 1985.

Barker, Clive. *Everville*. London: HarperCollins, 1995.

Barker, Clive. *Galilee*. London: HarperCollins, 1998.

Barker, Clive. *The Great and Secret Show*. London: HarperCollins, 1989.

Barker, Clive. *The Hellbound Heart*. [1986]. London: Dark Harvest. HarperCollins, 1991.

Barker, Clive. *Imajica*. New York: HarperCollins, 1991.

Barker, Clive. *In Conversation* with Sorcha Ní Fhlainn, a special panel presented as part of the *Clive Barker: Dark Imaginer* conference, 14 July, 2011, Trinity College, Dublin.

Barker, Clive. Interview with Nick Hasted, *Creature*, No. 5 (1986).

Barker, Clive. Interview with Richard Lupoff, Richard Wolinsky, and Lawrence Davidson. 'A Talk with the King.' *Stephen King and Clive Barker: The Illustrated Guide to the Masters of the Macabre II*. Ed. James Van Hise. Las Vegas, NV: Pioneer Books, 1992, pp. 79–95.

Barker, Clive. 'An Introduction: Private Legends.' *The Essential Clive Barker*. London: HarperCollins, 1999, pp. 1–27.

Barker, Clive. *Mister B. Gone*. London: HarperVoyager, 2007.

Barker, Clive. 'One Flesh Exhibition', *Clive Barker: The Painter, the Creature, and the Father of Lies*. Eds. Phil and Sarah Stokes. Northborough, MA: Earthling Publications, 2011, p. 219.

Barker, Clive. Public interview and Q&A at the Irish Film Institute. 13 July 2011. *Clive Barker: Dark Imaginer* conference, Trinity College, Dublin. Public Event.

Barker, Clive. 'Ramsay Campbell: An Appreciation.' *1986 World Fantasy Convention Programme*.

Barker, Clive. *Sacrament*. London: HarperCollins, 1996.

Barker, Clive. *The Scarlet Gospels*. London: Macmillan, 2015.

Barker, Clive. *The Thief of Always*. London: HarperCollins, 1992.

Barker, Clive. *Tortured Souls: Six Destinies*, Tempe, AZ: Todd McFarlane, 2001.

Barker, Clive. *Weaveworld*. London: Collins, 1987.

Barker, Clive and Stephen Jones. *Clive Barker's A-Z of Horror*. London: BBC Books, 1997.

Barker, Paul. *The Freedoms of Suburbia*. London: Frances Lincoln, 2009.

Bassett, Jonathan F. 'Death and Magic in Clive Barker's *Lord of Illusions*: A Terror Management Perspective.' *Studies in Popular Culture*. Vol. 32:1, Fall 2009, pp. 67–78.

Beeler, Michael. 'Clive Barker: Horror Visionary.' *Cinefantastique*. Vol. 26:3 (1995), pp. 16–22.

Benshoff, Harry M. *Monsters in the Closet: Homosexuality and the Horror Film*, Manchester and New York: Manchester University Press, 1997.

Benshoff, Harry M. 'The Monster and the Homosexual.' *Horror: The Film Reader*. Ed. Mark Jancovich. London: Routledge, 2002, pp. 91–102.

Benshoff, Harry M. '"Way Too Gay To Be Ignored": The Production and Reception of Queer Horror Cinema in the Twenty-First Century.' *Speaking of Monsters: A Teratological Anthology*. Eds. Caroline Joan S. Picart and John Edgar Browning. Basingstoke: Palgrave Macmillan, 2012, pp. 131–44.

Benshoff, Harry M. and Sean Griffin. *Queer Images: A History of Gay and Lesbian Film in America*. Oxford: Rowman & Littlefield, 2006.

Blake, Linnie. *The Wounds of Nations: Horror Cinema, Historical Trauma and National Identity*. Manchester and New York: Manchester University Press, 2008.

Blake, William. 'London.' *William Blake: The Complete Illuminated Books*. Ed. David Bindman. London: Thames & Hudson, 2001.

Blumenfeld, Warren J. *Homophobia: How We All Pay the Price*. Boston: Beacon Press, 1992.

Bradbury, Dominic. *The Iconic House: Architectural Masterworks since 1900*. London: Thames & Hudson, 2009.

Brook-Rose, Christine. *A Rhetoric of the Unreal: Studies in Narrative and Structure, Especially of the Fantastic*. Cambridge: Cambridge University Press, 1981.

Brosnan, John. 'Terror Tactics.' *Clive Barker's Shadows in Eden*. Ed. Stephen Jones. Lancaster, PA: Underwood-Miller, 1991, p. 89–93.

Brown, Derren. *Tricks of the Mind*. London: Channel Four Books, 2006.

Burke, Edmund. *A Philosophical Enquiry into the Origin of Our Ideas of the Sublime and Beautiful*. Ed. with an Introduction by Adam Phillips. Oxford: Oxford University Press, 1990.

Burns, Craig William. 'It's That Time of the Month: Representations of the Goddess in the Work of Clive Barker.' *Journal of Popular Culture*. Vol. 27:3 (1993). pp. 35–40.

Cardwell, Sarah. 'Adaptation Studies Revisited: Purposes, Perspectives, and Inspiration.' *The Literature/Film Reader: Issues of Adaptations*. Eds. James M. Welsh and Peter Lev. Lanham, MA: The Scarecrow Press, 2007, pp. 51–63.

Carroll, Nöel. *The Philosophy of Horror or Paradoxes of The Heart*. London: Routledge, 1990.

Carter, Angela. *The Sadeian Woman: An Exercise in Cultural History*. London: Virago, 1979.

Cherry, Brigid. 'Beyond "Suspiria": The Place of European Cinema in the Fan Canon.' *European Nightmares: European Horror Cinema Since 1945*. Eds. Patricia Allmer, Emily Brick, and David Huxley. London: Wallflower Press, 2012, pp. 25–34.

Cherry, Brigid. 'Broken Homes, Tortured Flesh: *Hellraiser* and the Feminine Aesthetic of Horror Cinema.' *Film International*. Vol. 3:17 (2005), pp. 10–21.

Cherry, Brigid. 'Imperfect Geometry: Identity and Culture in Clive Barker's "The Forbidden" and Bernard Rose's *Candyman*.' *Monstrous Adaptations: Generic and Thematic Mutations in Horror Film*. Eds. Richard. J. Hand and Jay McRoy. Manchester: Manchester University Press, 2007, pp. 48–63.

Cherry, Brigid. 'Subcultural Tastes, Genre Boundaries and Fan Canons.' *The Shifting Definitions of Genre: Essays on Labelling Films, Television Shows and Media*. Eds. Mark Jancovich and Lincoln Geraghty. Jefferson, NC: McFarland, 2007, pp. 201–15.

Cherry, Brigid. 'Refusing to Refuse to Look: Female Viewers of the Horror Film.' *Identifying Hollywood Audiences*. Eds. Richard Maltby and Mervyn Stokes. London: BFI, 1999, pp. 187–203.

Cherry, Brigid and Brian Robb. 'Birth of the Nightbreed.' *Starburst*. Vol. 11:11 (1989).

Cherry, Brigid, Charles O'Brien, and Nikolaus Pevsner. *The Buildings of England: London 5: East*. New Haven: Yale University Press, 2005.

Chibnall, Steve and Julian Petley (eds). *British Horror Cinema*. London: Routledge, 2001.

Coleman, Alice and the Design Disadvantagement Team of the Land Research Unit, King's College London. *Utopia on Trial: Vision and Reality in Planned Housing*. London: Shipman, 1985.

Conrich, Ian. 'The *Friday the 13th* Films and the Cultural Function of a Modern Grand Guignol.' *Horror Zone: The Cultural Experience of Contemporary Horror* Cinema. Ed. Ian Conrich. London: IB Tauris, 2010, pp. 173–88.

Coyle, William. 'Introduction: The Nature of Fantasy.' *Aspects of Fantasy: Selected Essays From the Second International Conference on the Fantastic in Literature and Film*. Ed. William Coyle. Westport: Greenwood, 1986, pp. 1–3.

Daumann, Christian. *Wonderlands in Flesh and Blood: Gender, the Body, Its Boundaries and Their Transgression in Clive Barker's* Imajica. München, Germany: AVM, 2009.

De Quincey, Thomas. 'On the Knocking at the Gate in *Macbeth*.' *On Murder*. Ed. Robert Morrison. Oxford: Oxford University Press, 2006, pp. 3–7.

Deleuze, Gilles. *Cinema 1: The Movement-Image*. [1983]. Trans. Hugh Tomlinson and Barbara Habberjam. London and New York: Continuum International Publishing Group, 2005.

Denton, Eric Hadley. 'Johann Wolfgang von Goethe.' *The Handbook to Gothic Literature*. Ed. Marie Mulvey Roberts. New York: New York University Press, 1998, pp. 70–2.

Doty, Alexander. *Flaming Classics: Queering the Horror Canon*. London: Routledge, 2000.

Dufour, Éric. *Le Cinéma d'horreur et ses figures*. Paris: Presses universitaires de France, 2006.

Dunnett, James. 'A Terrible Beauty … .' *Ernö Goldfinger: Works I*. Eds. James Dunnett and Gavin Stamp. London: Architectural Association, 1983, p. 7.

Dunnet, James and Gavin Stamp (eds). *Ernö Goldfinger: Works I*. London: Architectural Association, 1983.

Dyer, Richard. *Culture of Queers*. London: Routledge, 2001.

Elwall, Robert. *Building a Better Tomorrow: Architecture in Britain in the 1950s*. Chichester: Wiley-Academy, 2000.

Fiske, John. *Television Culture*. London: Routledge, 1987.

Foucault, Michel. 'What is An Author?' [1969.] *Essential Works of Foucault 1954–1984* Vol. 2: Aesthetics. Ed. J.D. Faubion. London: Penguin Books, 1994.

Fowles, John. *The Magus*. Suffolk: Triad Granada, 1966.

Fox, Robert Elliot. *Master of the Drum: Black Lit/oratures Across the Continuum*. Westport: Greenwood, 1995.

Freeland, Cynthia. 'Feminist Frameworks for Horror Films.' *Film Theory and Criticism*. Eds. Leo Braudy and Marshall Cohen. Oxford: Oxford University Press, 2004.

Freeland, Cynthia. *The Naked and the Undead: Evil and the Appeal of Horror*. Boulder: Westview Press, 2000.

Gates, Henry Louis, Jr. *The Signifying Monkey: A Theory of African-American Literary Criticism*. New York: Oxford University Press, 1988.

Gilroy, Paul. *The Black Atlantic: Modernity and Double Consciousness*. Cambridge, Mass: Harvard University Press, 1993.

Gochros, Jean S. 'Homosexuality and Heterosexual Marriage.' *Homophobia: How We All Pay the Price*. Ed. Warren J. Blumenfeld. Boston: Beacon Press, 1992.

Grainge, Paul. *Brand Hollywood: Selling Entertainment in a Global Media Age*. London: Routledge, 2007.

Grant, Barry Keith (ed.). *The Dread of Difference: Gender and the Horror Film*. Austin: University of Texas Press, 1996.

Grant, Catherine. 'Auteur machines? Auteurism and the DVD.' *Film and Television After DVD*. Eds. James Bennett and Tom Brown. London: Routledge, 2008, pp. 101–15.

Halberstam, Judith. *Skin Shows: Gothic Horror and the Technology of Monsters*. Durham and London: Duke University Press, 1995.

Halley, Janet and Andrew Parker. *After Sex? On Writing since Queer Theory*. London: Duke University Press, 2011.

Hanley, Lynsey. *Estates: An Intimate History*. London: Granta, 2007.

Hansom, Dick. 'To Hell and Back.' *Speakeasy*. Issue: 102 (September 1989). Quoted in *Clive Barker's Shadows in Eden*. Ed. Stephen Jones. Lancaster, PA: Underwood-Miller, 1991, p. 359.

Hendershot, Heather. 'Masters of Horror: TV Auteurism and the Progressive Potential of a Disreputable Genre.' *Flow TV: Television in the Age of Media Convergence*. Eds. Michael Kackman, Marie Binfield, Matthew Thomas Payne, Allison Perlman, and Bryan Sebok. New York: Routledge, 2011, pp. 144–63.

Higson, Andrew. *Film England: Culturally English Filmmaking Since the 1990s*. London: IB Tauris, 2011.

Hogle, Jerrold E. 'Introduction: The Gothic in Western Culture.' *The Cambridge Companion to Gothic Fiction*. Ed. Jerold E. Hogle. Cambridge: Cambridge University Press, 2002, pp. 1–20.

Hogle, Jerrold E. (ed.) *The Cambridge Companion to Gothic Fiction*. Cambridge: Cambridge University Press, 2002.

Holmberg, Carl B. *Sexualities and Popular Culture*. Ohio: Bowling Green State University, 1998.

Hoppenstand, Gary. *Clive Barker's Short Stories: Imagination as Metaphor in the Books of Blood and Other Works*. Jefferson, NC and London: McFarland, 1994.

Horkheimer, Max and Theodor W. Adorno. *Dialectic of Enlightenment: Philosophical Fragments*. Ed. Gunzelin Schmid Noerr. Trans. Edmund Jephcott. Stanford, CA: Stanford University Press, 2002.

Hill, Annette. *Paranormal Media: Audiences, Spirits and Magic in Popular Culture*. London and New York: Routledge, 2011.

Hills, Matt. 'An Event-Based Definition of Art-Horror.' *Dark Thoughts: Philosophic Reflections on Cinematic Horror*. Eds. Steven Jay Schneider and Daniel Shaw. Lanham, MD: Scarecrow Press, 2003, pp. 138–57.

Hollows, Joanna. 'The Masculinity of Cult.' *Defining Cult Movies: The Cultural Politics of Oppositional Taste*. Ed. Mark Jancovich. Manchester: Manchester University Press, 2003, pp. 35–53.

Hume, Kathryn. *Fantasy and Mimesis: Responses to Reality in Western Literature*. New York: Methuen, 1984.

Irwin, William. R. *The Game of the Impossible: A Rhetoric of Fantasy*. Urbana: University of Illinois Press, 1976.

Jackson, Rosemary. *Fantasy: The Literature of Subversion*. London: Methuen, 1981.

Jackson, Stevi. 'Women and Heterosexual Love: Complicity, Resistance and Change.' *Sex, Self and Society: The Social Context of Sexuality*. Ed. Tracey L. Steele. Belmont, CA: Wadsworth, 2005.

Jaggose, Annamarie. *Queer Theory: An Introduction*. Melbourne: Melbourne University Press, 1996.

Jenkins, Henry. *Convergence Culture: Where Old and New Media Collide*. New York: New York University Press, 2008.

Jones, Stephen. 'Clive Barker: Anarchic Prince of Horror.' *Knave*. Vol. 15:5 (1987).

Joshi, S.T. *The Modern Weird Tale*. Jefferson, NC: McFarland, 1994.

Kane, Paul. *The Hellraiser Films and Their Legacy*. Jefferson, NC: McFarland, 2006.

Kaveney, Roz. 'Dark Fantasy and Paranormal Romance.' *The Cambridge Companion to Fantasy Literature*. Eds. Edward James and Farah Mendlesohn. Cambridge: Cambridge University Press, 2012, pp. 214–23.

Kilday, Gregg. 'Out in America. Film: Clive Barker Raises Hell.' *Out* (March 1995) p. 14. Quoted in Harry M. Benshoff. *Monsters in the Closet: Homosexuality and the Horror Film*. Manchester: Manchester University Press, 1997.

King, Geoff. *Spectacular Narratives: Hollywood in the Age of the Blockbuster*. London: IB Tauris, 2000.

King, Stephen. *Danse Macabre*. [1982]. London: Warner, 1993.

Kynaston, David. *Austerity Britain, 1945–51*. London: Bloomsbury, 2007.

Kynaston, David. *Family Britain, 1951–57*. London: Bloomsbury, 2009.

Kynaston, David. *Modernity Britain: A Shake of the Dice, 1959–62*. London: Bloomsbury, 2014.

Kynaston, David. *Modernity Britain: Opening the Box, 1957–59*. London: Bloomsbury, 2013.

Laity, K.A. 'Imagineer: Clive Barker's Queering of the Conservative Bent of Horror Literature.' *Horrifying Sex: Essays on Sexual Difference in Gothic Litearture*. Ed. Ruth Bienstock Anolik. Jefferson, NC: McFarland, 2007, pp. 248–58.

Landon, Brooks. *The Aesthetics of Ambivalence: Rethinking Science Fiction Film in the Age of Electronic (Re)Production*, Westport, Connecticut, and London: Greenwood Press, 1992.

Latham, Rob. 'Phallic Mothers and Monster Queers.' *Science Fiction Studies*. Vol. 25:1 (1998), pp. 87–101.

Leese, Peter. *Britain Since 1945*. Hampshire: Palgrave Macmillan, 2006.

Letwin, Shirley Robin. *The Anatomy of Thatcherism*. New Brunswick and London: Transaction Publishers, 1993.

Levi, Jeffrey. 'Homophobia and the AIDS Public Policy.' *Homophobia: How We All Pay the Price*. Ed. Warren J. Blumenfeld. Boston: Beacon Press, 1992.

Lovecraft, H.P. 'Supernatural Horror in Literature.' *H.P. Lovecraft, Tales: A Miscellany of the Macabre*. Ed. Stephen Jones. London: Gollancz, 2011, pp. 423–92.

Lury, Celia. *Brands: The Logos of the Global Economy*. London: Routledge, 2004.

MacCormack, Patricia. *Cinesexuality*, Aldershot and Burlington: Ashgate Publishing, 2008.

Mains, Johnny. *Lest You Should Suffer Nightmares: A Biography of Herbert Van Thal*. Bargoed: Screaming Dreams, 2011.

Manlove, Colin N. 'On the Nature of Fantasy.' *The Aesthetics of Fantasy Literature and Art*. Ed. Roger C. Schlobin. Indiana: University of Notre Dame Press, 1982, pp. 16–35.

Marlowe, Christopher. *Doctor Faustus and Other Plays*. [1592]. Eds. David Bevington and Eric Rasmussen. Oxford: Oxford University Press, 1995.

Marquand, David. 'Moralists and Hedonists.' *The Ideas that Shaped Post-War Britain*. Eds. David Marquand and Anthony Seldon. London: Fontana Press, 1996, pp. 5–28.

McCauley, Kirby (ed.) *Dark Forces: New Stories of Suspense and the Supernatural*. New York: Viking, 1980.

McDonagh, Maitland. 'A Kind of Magic.' *The Dark Side*. No. 45. April/May 1995.

McLaren, Angus. *Twentieth-Century Sexuality*. Oxford: Blackwell Publishers, 1999.

McRoy, Jay. 'There are No Limits: Splatterpunk, Clive Barker, and the Body *In-Extremis*.' *Paradoxa*. No. 17 (2002), pp. 130–50.

McSmith, Andy. *No Such Thing as Society: A History of Britain in the 1980s*. London: Constable, 2011.

Miéville, China. *Kraken*. London: Macmillan, 2010.

Miéville, China and Joan Gordon. 'Reveling in Genre: An Interview with China Miéville.' [sic] *Science Fiction Studies*. Vol. 30:3. (November 2003), pp. 355–73.

Moten, Fred. *In the Break: The Aesthetics of the Black Radical Tradition*. Minneapolis: University of Minnesota Press, 2003.

Morgan, Kenneth O. *Britain Since 1945*. Oxford: Oxford University Press, 2001.

Nama, Adilifu. *Black Space: Imagining Race in Science Fiction Film*. Austin: University of Texas Press, 2008.

Ndalianis, Angela. 'Architectures of the Senses: Neo-Baroque Entertainment Spectacles.' *Rethinking Media Change: The Aesthetics of Transition*. Eds. David Thorburn and Henry Jenkins. Cambridge, Mass: MIT Press, 2003, pp. 355–74.

Ndalianis, Angela. 'Dark Rides, Hybrid Machines and the Horror Experience.' *Horror Zone: The Cultural Experience of Contemporary Horror Cinema*. Ed. Ian Conrich. London: IB Tauris, 2010, pp. 11–26.

Neale, Steve. 'Masculinity as Spectacle.' *The Sexual Subject: A Screen Reading in Sexuality*. London: Routledge, 1992.

Niles, Steve and Les Edwards. *Clive Barker's Dread*. London: Eclipse Books, 1993.

Penny, Laurie. *Cybersexism: Sex, Gender and Power on the Internet*. London: Bloomsbury, 2013.

Powell, Anna. *Deleuze and the Horror Film*. Edinburgh: Edinburgh University Press, 2005.

Power, Anne. *Estates on the Edge: The Social Consequences of Mass Housing in Europe*. Basingstoke: Macmillan, 1997.

Powers, Alan. *Britain*, 'Modern Architectures in History' series. London: Reaktion, 2007.

Radcliffe, Ann. 'The Supernatural in Poetry.' *Gothic Documents: A Sourcebook 1700–1820*. Eds. E.J. Clery and Robert Miles. Manchester: Manchester University Press, 2000, pp. 163–72.

Riddell, Peter. *The Thatcher Era and Its Legacy*. Oxford: Basil Blackwell, 1991.

Rodley, Chris (ed.) *Cronenberg on Cronenberg*. London: Faber and Faber, 1997.

Rosen, Andrew. *The Transformation of British Life 1950–2000*. Manchester: Manchester University Press, 2003.

Russo, Vito. *The Celluloid Closet: Homosexuality in the Movies*. Revised Edition. New York: Harper & Row, 1987.

Ryall, Chris and Gabriel Rodriguez. *Complete Clive Barker's Great and Secret Show*. San Diego: Idea & Design Works, 2007.

Sabouraud, Frédéric. *L'Adaptation: Le Cinema a tant besoin d'histoires*. Paris: Cahiers du cinéma/Scérén-CNDP. Les Petits Cahiers, 2006.

Sandbrook, Dominic. *Never Had It So Good: A History of Britain from Suez to the Beatles*. London: Abacus, 2006.

Sandbrook, Dominic. *Seasons in the Sun: The Battle for Britain, 1974–1979*. London: Allen Lane, 2012.

Sandbrook, Dominic. *State of Emergency: The Way We Were: Britain, 1970–1974*. London: Allen Lane, 2010.

Sandbrook, Dominic. *White Heat: A History of Britain in the Swinging Sixties*. London: Abacus, 2007.

Schleir, Curt. 'The Future of Horror is Here: His Name is Clive Barker.' *Inside Books*. (November 1988).

Schneider, Steven Jay. 'Toward an Aesthetics of Cinematic Horror.' *The Horror Film*. Ed. Stephen Prince. Piscataway, NJ: Rutgers University Press, 2004, pp. 131–49.

Sedgwick, Eve. *Epistemology of the Closet*. Los Angeles: University of California Press, 1990.

Sharett, Christopher. 'The Horror Film in Neoconservative Culture.' *The Dread of Difference: Gender and the Horror Film*. Ed. Barry Keith Grant, Austin: University of Texas Press, 1996, pp. 253–78.

Stewart, Graham. *Bang! A History of Britain in the 1980s*. London: Atlantic, 2013.

Stregnell, Heidi. *Dissecting Stephen King: From the Gothic to Literary Naturalism*. Madison: University of Wisconsin Press, 2006.

Swinfen, Ann. *In Defense of Fantasy: A Study of the Genre in English and American Literature Since 1945*. London: Routledge, 1984.

Todorov, Tzvetan. *The Fantastic: A Structural Approach to a Literary Genre*. Trans. Richard Howard. London: Case Western Reserve University Press, 1973.

Turner, Alwyn W. *Rejoice! Rejoice! Britain in the 1980s*. London: Aurum, 2010.

Van Thal, Herbert (ed.) *The Pan Book of Horror Stories*, 30 vols. London: Pan, 1959–1989.

Vandermeer, Ann and Jeff Vandermeer (eds). *The New Weird*. Tachyon: San Francisco, 2008.

Waddington, Mark. 'Leroy Cooper: The Toxteth Riots Were a Wake-Up Call and Did Some Good.' *Liverpool Echo*, 4 July 2011.

Wagner, Chuck and Fred Burke, Denys Cowan and Michael Davis. 'Clive Barker's *The Midnight Meat Train*.' *Tapping the Vein*. Vol. 3. London: Eclipse Books, 1990.

Warburton, Nigel. *Ernö Goldfinger: The Life of an Architect*. London: Routledge, 2005.

Wells, Paul. 'On the Side of the Demons: Clive Barker's Pleasures and Pains. Interviews with Clive Barker and Doug Bradley.' *British Horror Cinema*. Eds. Steve Chibnall and Julian Petley. London: Routledge, 2002, pp. 172–82.

Wells, Paul. *The Horror Genre: From Beelzebub to Blair Witch*. London: Wallflower, 2000.

Wexman, Virginia Wright. *Creating the Couple: Love, Marriage, and Hollywood Performance*. Princeton: Princeton University Press, 1993.

Wiater, Stanley. 'Horror in Print: Clive Barker.' *Clive Barker's Shadows in Eden*. Ed. Stephen Jones, Lancaster, PA: Underwood-Miller, 1991, pp. 191–8.

Williams, Linda. 'When the Woman Looks.' *Horror: The Film Reader*. Ed. Mark Jancovich. London: Routledge, 2002.

Winter, Douglas, E. *Clive Barker: The Dark Fantastic*. London: HarperCollins, 2001.

Wood, Robin. 'An Introduction to the American Horror Film.' *Planks of Reason: Essays on the Horror Film*. Ed. Barry Keith Grant. Metuchen, NJ: Scarecrow Press, 2004, pp. 164–200.

Zipes, Jack. 'Why Fantasy Matters Too Much.' *The Journal of Aesthetic Education*. Vol. 43:2 (2009), pp. 79–91.

Žižek, Slavoj. 'The Specter of Ideology.' *The Žižek Reader*. Eds. Elizabeth Wright and Edmund Wright. Oxford: Blackwell, 1999, pp. 53–86.

Film and television references

Bill and Ted's Excellent Adventure. Dir. Stephen Herek, 1989.

Book of Blood. Dir. John Harrison, 2009.

Candyman. Dir. Bernard Rose, 1992.

Child's Play. Dir. Todd Holland, 1988.

Clive Barker.' *The South Bank Show*. BBC, 1994.

Clive Barker: The Man Behind the Myth. Dir. Sam Hurwitz, 2007.

Clive Barker's A-Z of Horror. BBC. Six part series, 1997–98.

Dread. Dir. Anthony DiBlasi, 2009.

F for Fake. Dir. Orson Welles, 1975.

Forbidden, The. Dir. Clive Barker, 1978.

Frankenstein. Dir. James Whale, 1931.

Gods and Monsters. Dir. Bill Condon, 1998.

Halloween. Dir. John Carpenter, 1978.

Hellbound: Hellraiser II. Dir. Tony Randel, 1988.

Hellraiser. Dir. Clive Barker, 1987.

Hellraiser: Bloodline. Dir. Kevin Yagher (as Alan Smithee), 1996.

Hellraiser: Deader. Dir. Rick Bota, 2005.

Hellraiser III: Hell on Earth. Dir. Anthony Hickox, 1992.

House of 1000 Corpses. Dir. Rob Zombie, 2003.

Is Spiritualism a Fraud? Dir. Robert Paul, 1906.

Jurassic Park. Dir. Steven Spielberg, 1993.

Leviathan: The Story of Hellraiser and Hellbound: Hellraiser II. Dir. Kevin McDonagh, 2015.

Lord of Illusions. Dir. Clive Barker, 1995.

The Magnificent Ambersons. Dir. Orson Welles, 1942.

Man With A Movie Camera. Dir. Dziga Vertov, 1929.

Masters of Horror. Showtime. 2005–7.

The Midnight Meat Train. Dir. Ryuhei Kitamura, 2008.

Nightbreed. Dir. Clive Barker, 1990.

Open to Question. BBC, 1984–94.

Philadelphia. Dir. Jonathan Demme, 1993.

Pinocchio. Dirs. Ben Sharpsteen, Hamilton Luske et al. 1940.

The Plague. Dir. Hal Masonberg, 2006.

Rawhead Rex. Dir. George Pavlou, 1986.

The Rocky Horror Picture Show. Dir. Jim Sharman, 1975.

Saint Sinner. Dir. Joshua Butler, 2002.

Salomé. Dir. Clive Barker, 1973.

Saw. Dir. James Wan, 2004.

Saw III. Dir. Darren Lynn Bousman, 2006.

The Silence of the Lambs. Dir. Jonathan Demme, 1991.

Sleepy Hollow. Dir. Tim Burton, 1999.

Spitting Image, ITV, 1984–86.

Tales from the Crypt. HBO, 1989–96.

Tales from the Darkside. CBS, 1983–88.

Underworld. Dir. George Pavlou, 1985.

Videodrome. Dir. David Cronenberg, 1983.

The X-Files. 20th Century Fox Television, 1993–2004.

Internet sources

Anonymous. 'Clive Barker: AOL Appearance.' Transcript. AOL. 16 July 1996. *Revelations: The Official Clive Barker Website*. www.clivebarker.com/html/visions/confess/nonls/cb71696.html. Date accessed: 30 May 2012.

Anonymous. 'Clive Barker: Banking on Blood.' *Locus*. Vol. 19:7. Issue 306 (July 1986), reproduced in www.clivebarker.info/ints86.html. Date accessed: 12 April 2015.

Anonymous. 'Clive Barker's *Freakz*.' Press Release. Universal Studios, October 1998. *Revelations: The Official Clive Barker Website*. www.clivebarker.info/halloweenhorror.html. Date accessed: 2 June 2012.

Anonymous. 'Clive on the Midnight Meat Train.' Reprinted on *Revelations: The Official Clive Barker Website*. www.clivebarker.info/mmt.html. Date accessed: 10 June 2011.

Anonymous. 'Halloween Horror Nights III.' Universal Studios Press Release, 1999. Reprinted on *Revelations: The Official Clive Barker Website*. www.clivebarker.info/halloweenhorror.html. Date accessed: 2 June 2012.

Barker, Clive. 'Edgar Allan Poe.' *Independent* magazine. 30 November 1991. *Revelations: The Official Clive Barker Website*. www.clivebarker.info/essaysb.html. Date accessed: 30 July 2012.

Barker, Clive. 'News – Clive Wants To Save Midnight Meat Train!' *Revelations: The Official Clive Barker Website*. www.clivebarker.info/newssavemmt.html. Date accessed: 2 June 2012.

Barker, Clive. 'Interview with Larry King. *Larry King Live*.' CNN. 6 May 1987. Transcript rpt. on *Revelations: The Official Clive Barker Website*. www.clivebarker.info/ints87.html. Date accessed: 2 June 2012.

Barker, Clive. Interview. 'Clive from New York.' *Spawn.Com*, 13 February 2001, www.spawn.com/news/news.aspx?id=5174. Date accessed: 7 June 2014.

Barker, Clive. Interviewed by Madeline Puckett at *Fangoria* Weekend of Horrors, 20 May 2007. *Revelations: The Official Clive Barker Website*. www.clivebarker.info/mbgbarker.html. Date accessed: 7 June 2014.

Barker, Clive. 'Interviews 1990: Part One.' *Revelations: The Official Clive Barker Website*. www.clivebarker.info/ints90.html. Date accessed: 25 June 2012.

Barker, Clive. Interviewed by Lucy A. Sneider. 'It's All Part of the Fun.' *Revelations: The Official Clive Barker Website*. www.clivebarker.info/mbgbarker.html. Date accessed: 7 June 2014.

Barker, Clive. Interviews on 'Lord of Illusions.' *Revelations: The Official Clive Barker Website*. www.clivebarker.info/lordofillusions.html. Date accessed: 28 June 2012.

Barker, Clive. Interviews on 'Nightbreed.' *Revelations: The Official Clive Barker Website*. www.clivebarker.info/nightbreed.html. Date accessed: 24 June 2012.

Barker, Clive. Interviewed on *Open to Question*. 8 December 1987. BBC Two. www.youtube.com/watch?v=ZOqKgrbjfQ. Date accessed: 15 December 2015.

Beeler, Michael. '*Lord of Illusions* – Filming the *Books of Blood*.' *Cinefantastique*. Vol. 26:3. 1995. *Revelations: The Official Clive Barker Website*. www.clivebarker.info/ints95b.html. Date accessed: 4 June 2012.

Bohling, James. 'Dreaming of a Nightmare.' *Frontiers*, 27 October 2000. *Revelations: The Official Clive Barker Website*. www.clivebarker.info/coldheartbarker.html. Date accessed: 10 January 2016.

Cherry, Brigid. 'Gothics and Grand Guignols: Violence and the Gendered Aesthetics of Cinematic Horror.' *Participations: International Journal of Audience Research*. Vol 5:1 (May 2008). www.participations.org/Volume%205/Issue%201%20-%20special/5_01_cherry.htm.

Cooper, Dennis. 'Fuck the Canon.' *LA Weekly*. 31 August–6 September 2001. Literary Supplement. Reprinted on *Revelations: The Official Clive Barker Website*. www.clivebarker.info/halloweenhorror.html. Date accessed: 2 June 2012.

Ebert, Roger. Rev. of *Hellbound: Hellraiser II*. 23 December 1988. *Roger Ebert Online Archive*. www.rogerebert.com/reviews/hellbound-hellraiser-ii-1988. Date accessed: 15 January 2016.

Ebert, Roger. Rev. of *Hellraiser*. 18 September 1987. *Roger Ebert Online Archive*. www.rogerebert.com/reviews/hellraiser-1987. Date accessed: 15 January 2016.

French, Philip, 'The Firm.' *Observer* (20 September 2009). https://www.theguardian.com/film/2009/sep/20/the-firm-film-review. Date accessed: 24 April 2009.

Garcia, Irene. 'The Horror!' *LA Times*. 15 October 1998. *Revelations: The Official Clive Barker Website*. www.clivebarker.info/halloweenhorror.html. Date accessed: 28 May 2012.

Hughes, David. 'High Abuse From the Left, Low Abuse From the Right.' *The Telegraph*. 16 February 2009. http://blogs.telegraph.co.uk/news/davidhughes/8594817/High_abuse_from_the_Left_low_abuse_from_the_Right_/. Date accessed: 18 September 2015.

Isaacson, Walter, 'Hunting for the Hidden Killers: AIDS Disease Detectives Face a Never Ending Quest,' *Newsweek* (122) 1, 4 July 1983. http://content.time.com/time/magazine/0,9263,7601830704,00.html. Date accessed: 18 September 2015.

Jenkins, Simon. 'This Icon of 60s New Brutalism Has its Champions. So Let Them Restore It.' *Guardian*, 20 June 2008. https://www.theguardian.com/commentisfree/2008/jun/20/architecture. Date accessed: 26 April 2015.

Jones, Anderson. 'Movie Scoop.' Yahoo Entertainment. 11 October 2002. *Revelations: The Official Clive Barker Website*. www.clivebarker.info/ints02b.html. Date accessed: 2 June 2012.

Lowman, Rob. 'Freakz Alive, Clive! His "Living Movie" an A-Maze-ing Experience.' *Daily News* (14 October 1998). *Revelations: The Official Clive Barker Website*. www.clivebarker.info/halloweenhorror.html. Date accessed: 2 June 2012.

McDonald, B. 'Knott's Berry Farm Unveils Halloween Haunt 2014 Mazes.' *LA Times*. 8 August 2014. www.latimes.com/travel/themeparks/la-trb-halloween-haunt-2014-knotts-berry-farm-20140807-story.html. Date accessed: 1 April 2015.

Miéville, China. 'Candy and Carrion.' Rev. of *Abarat* by Clive Barker. *Guardian*. 19 October 2002. www.theguardian.com/books/2002/oct/19/sciencefictionfantasyandhorror.clivebarker. Date accessed: 1 March 2016.

Moorcock, Michael. 'Epic Pooh.' Revised edition. *Revolution Science Fiction*. www.revolutionsf.com/article.php?id=953. Date accessed: 30 July 2012.

Murder, Mike. 'Clive Barker's Harvest.' *Horror Night Nightmares*. www.horrornightnightmares.com/forums/index.php/topic/2664-clive-barkers-harvest/. Date accessed: 12 April 2015.

Nelson, Andrew. 'Cinema From Attractions: Story and Synergy in Disney's Theme Park Movies.' *Cinephile: The University of British Columbia's Film Journal*, 4 (2008). www.cinephile.ca/archives/volume-4-post-genre/cinema-from-attractions-story-and-synergy-in-disney%E2%80%99s-theme-park-movies/. Date accessed: 2 April 2012.

Newman, Kim. 'Clive Barker.' *Interzone*. No 14. Winter (1985/86). www.clivebarker.info/damnatbarker.html. Date accessed: 9 January 2016.

Nutman, Philip. 'Birth of the Nightbreed.' *Fangoria*. No. 86 (1989). *Revelations: The Official Clive Barker Website*. www.clivebarker.info/nightbreed.html. Date accessed: 4 June 2012.

Peterson, Evan J. 'The Company of Monsters: An Interview with Clive Barker.' *The Southeast Review*. Vol. 26:2, 2008. *Revelations: The Official Clive Barker Website*. www.clivebarker.info/scarletbarker.html. Date accessed: 9 January 2016.

Poe, Edgar Allan. 'The Philosophy of Composition.' *'The Raven' and the Philosophy of Composition*. San Francisco and New York: Paul Elder & Company, 1907. Archive.

org. https://archive.org/details/ravenandphilosop00poeerich. Date accessed: 27 July 2012.

Pouncey, E. 'Barker Psychosis.' *New Musical Express*. 13 February 1993. *Revelations: The Official Clive Barker Website*. www.clivebarker.info/ints93.html. Date accessed: 2 June 2012.

Ruby, Smilin' Jack. 'Clive Barker's Busy, Busy, Busy Year.' *13th Street*. 13 July 2001. *Revelations: The Official Clive Barker Website*. www.clivebarker.info/ints01b.html. Date accessed: 2 June 2012.

Shaw, Daniel. 'A Humean Definition of Horror.' *Film-Philosophy*. Vol. 1:4 (1997). www.film-philosophy.com/vol1-1997/n4shaw.

Stokes, Phil and Sarah Stokes. 'A Spiritual Retreat: The Seventeenth Revelatory Interview.' *Revelations: The Official Clive Barker Website*. 26 March, 2007. www.clivebarker.info/intsrevel17.html. Date accessed: 14 January 2016.

Stokes, Phil and Sarah Stokes. 'Hellfire and the Demonation.' *Revelations: The Official Clive Barker Website*. www.clivebarker.info/intsrevel19.html. Date accessed: 2 June 2012.

Stokes, Phil and Sarah Stokes. 'Universal's Halloween Horror Nights.' *Revelations: The Official Clive Barker Website*. 7 September 2007. www.clivebarker.info/halloweenhorror.html. Date accessed: 12 April 2015.

Tucker, Ken. 'One Universe at a Time Please.' Rev. of *The Great and Secret Show* by Clive Barker. *New York Times Book Review*. 11 February 1990. www.nytimes.com/1990/02/11/books/one-universe-at-a-time-please.html. Date accessed: 14 January 2016.

Turek, Ryan. 'Facing the Beast: On the Set of Clive Barker's Dread.' October 2008. http://shocktillyoudrop.com/news/topnews.php?id=12919. Date accessed: 8 June 2011.

Twelker, Eric. 'Crossing Over.' Amazon. January 2001. *Revelations: The Official Clive Barker Website*. www.clivebarker.info/undying.html. Date accessed: 2 June 2012.

Variety Staff. Rev of *Hellbound: Hellraiser II*. *Variety*. 31 December 1987. http://variety.com/1987/film/reviews/hellbound-hellraiser-ii-1200427565/. Date accessed: 15 January 2016.

Video games

Clive Barker's Jericho. MercurySteam. 2007. Codemasters.
Clive Barker's Undying. DreamWorks Interactive. 2001. EA Games.

Index

Note: page numbers in *italic* refer to illustrations.
'n.' after a page reference indicates the number of a note on that page

Milton Keynes UK
Ingram Content Group UK Ltd.
UKHW021846080124
435668UK00032B/412